The Victorian Pulpit

The Victorian Pulpit

Spoken and Written Sermons in Nineteenth-Century Britain

Robert H. Ellison

Selinsgrove: Susquehanna University Press
London: Associated University Presses

Associated University Presses
440 Forsgate Drive
Cranbury, NJ 08512

Associated University Presses
16 Barter Street
London WC1A 2AH, England

Associated University Presses
P.O. Box 338, Port Credit
Mississauga, Ontario
Canada L5G 4L8

The paper used in this publication meets the requirements of the American National Standard for Permanence of Paper for Printed Library Materials Z39.48-1984.

Library of Congress Cataloging-in-Publication Data

Ellison, Robert H., 1967–
    The Victorian pulpit : spoken and written sermons in nineteenth
-century Britain / Robert H. Ellison.
        p.   cm.
    Based on the author's thesis (doctoral)—University of North
Texas.
    Includes bibliographical references (p.   ) and index.
    ISBN 1-57591-014-4 (alk. paper)
    1. Preaching—Great Britain—History—19th century. 2. Sermons,
English—History and criticism.   I. Title.
BV4208.G7E44   1998
251'.00941'09034—dc21
                                                          98-19025
                                                          CIP

Contents

Acknowledgments

RECOGNITION FOR ASSISTANCE WITH *THE VICTORIAN PULPIT* GOES first to my wife Lori, who endured without complaint the many sacrifices and inconveniences that are part of life with a graduate student and junior member of a university faculty.

I also wish to acknowledge the invaluable assistance of my colleagues at the two institutions at which this manuscript was prepared. The project began as a doctoral dissertation at the University of North Texas. I am indebted to Robert Stevens, who introduced me to orality-literacy theory as a vehicle for the study of Victorian preaching, and to the other members of the committee—Thomas Preston, James Linebarger, and Larry Gleeson—who encouraged me to pursue a topic outside the mainstream of English studies.

The manuscript was recast into its present form during the first two years of my tenure at East Texas Baptist University. I extend my appreciation to President Bob Riley and the rest of the administration for encouraging the faculty to be scholars as well as teachers. I am especially grateful to Marvin Harris, chair of the English Department, who modified my teaching duties to allow me time to write; Narine Brooks, whose diligence in interlibrary loan secured critical books and articles; Henry Hood and the Professional Development Committee, who provided funding for research; and Mandy Estep, who spent many hours checking quotations and reformatting the manuscript.

Most of all, I wish to thank LuAnn Herrell, who gave so much of her time and energy to offering moral support and to editing the manuscript at all stages of the project. To her, and to all who contributed to this book, I owe an immeasurable debt of gratitude.

I am grateful to the following copyright holders for permission to quote from their works:

Cicero, *De Inventione*. Reprinted by permission of the publishers and the Loeb Classical Library from *Cicero: De Inventione: De*

Introduction

"To TELL THE STORY OF VICTORIAN BRITAIN AND TO LEAVE RELI-
gion out . . . impresses us as an example of blatant disregard of
evidence."[1] This claim is the opening sentence of "Recent Studies
in Victorian Religion," a selective, annotated bibliography of 146
books and articles published between 1962 and 1989. While the
compilers of this bibliography may be correct in asserting that
"some historians in our own day" give insufficient attention to the
place religion held in Victorian Britain,[2] it is not the case that
recent nineteenth-century studies are devoid of significant scholarship in the field. Major studies of Victorian religion have been
published regularly since 1950;[3] according to the annual bibliographies in *Victorian Studies,* nearly eight hundred books and articles dealing with Victorian religion were published between 1989
and 1994.[4]

These studies address subjects ranging from social histories of
the clergy to the role of women in the church to Buddhism and
Judaism in nineteenth-century England. There is, however, a significant omission in their scope: virtually none of them takes
preaching as its primary focus. Unlike their colleagues specializ-
ing in the Renaissance and eighteenth century, who have published articles on the preaching of Jeremy Taylor, John Donne,
George Whitefield, and John Wesley, students of Victorian literature have done virtually no work on prominent nineteenth-century
pulpiteers.[5] Many of the preachers who achieved considerable literary stature during this time—Frederick W. Robertson, James
Parsons, Henry Melvill, and Thomas Guthrie, for example—do
not appear in the Modern Language Association bibliographies at
all. Those preachers who are in the canon are generally included
on the basis of their achievements outside the pulpit. Students of
John Keble, for example, focus on his aesthetic theories and the
Christian Year, a collection of ecclesiastical poems; students of
Charles Kingsley write about his novels, his role in the Muscular
Christianity movement, and his polemical relationship with John
Henry Newman; and students of Gerard Manley Hopkins focus
on his poetry rather than his prose. The only preacher included

11

in the Victorian canon *as a preacher* is John Henry Newman, and his writings for the pulpit are often eclipsed by the scholarship on his other works—*Apologia Pro Vita Sua, The Idea of a University,* and *A Grammar of Assent.*

Scholars have also paid little attention to the history of the Victorian pulpit. Several major studies of preaching in the Middle Ages, the Renaissance, and the eighteenth century have been published since 1950,[6] but only one book on the Victorian pulpit—Eric Mackerness's *The Heeded Voice: Studies in the Literary Status of the Anglican Sermon, 1830–1900* (Cambridge: W. Heffer & Sons, 1959)—has been published in the past forty years.[7] The pulpit is also underrepresented in shorter scholarly work; Victorian preaching is addressed in only one of the scores of articles and book chapters listed in the *Victorian Studies* bibliographies for 1989 through 1994.[8]

The few studies of Victorian preaching that have been published follow, as F. R. Webber has noted, "a familiar, well-beaten path": while they may include a "short account of the style of preaching" in effect during the period in question, their books consist primarily, if not entirely, of biographical essays on "representative preachers."[9] This approach first appears in Edwin Charles Dargan's *A History of Preaching,* published early in this century. Dargan moves from brief, broad overviews of Victorian society to equally brief biographical sketches of the most important preachers, paying virtually no attention either to the history of the pulpit or to the sermons of individual pulpiteers. His book is, moreover, more an appreciation than a true history. He begins with the claim that "at no time and among no people does the Christian pulpit appear to greater advantage on the whole than in Great Britain during the nineteenth century," and he ends with a grandiose statement about the significance of his subject:

> Our study has brought before us an inspiring history. It presents, when seen whole and large, a spectacle of high endeavor and noble achievement in the loftiest sphere of human effort—the region of the spirit. Here we have seen strong intellect, ample culture, strenuous toil, lofty character, self-sacrificing life again and again consecrated to the high and holy purpose of so presenting the truth of God to men as to win them out of sin and loss to righteousness and eternal life.[10]

Although Dargan's work illustrates Webber's claim that a biographical approach can often produce "an outline of the subject" rather than a true history,[11] Webber's own study, the three-volume *History of Preaching in Britain and America,* demonstrates how such a method can be used as the foundation for truly worthwhile scholarship. His biographies, while certainly not comprehensive, are substantial and informative, and he is careful to place them within the context of important religious developments such as the Oxford Movement, the rise of Higher Criticism, and the Disruption of 1843, the event that led to the formation of the Free Church of Scotland. It is somewhat ironic, in fact, that Webber has called Dargan's *History* "scholarly, careful, and fairly complete," an assessment which, to my mind, applies more accurately to Webber's own work.[12]

Finally, biography is the focus of the only recent book to deal exclusively with Victorian preachers: Eric Mackerness's *The Heeded Voice: Studies in the Literary Status of the Anglican Sermon, 1830–1900*. Mackerness discusses six representatives of the Established Church—John Henry Newman, Henry Parry Liddon, Frederick W. Robertson, Charles Kingsley, William Connor Magee, and Benjamin Jowett—and he often departs from the stated scope of his book. Instead of examining "the Literary Status of the Anglican Sermon" in depth, he often gives superficial treatment to his subjects' preaching careers, focusing instead on such aspects as Liddon's "political and social thinking," Kingsley's work as a novelist and Christian socialist, and Jowett's contributions to *Essays and Reviews*.[13]

Though widely employed, the biographical method tells only a small part of the story of Victorian preaching. True, it is important to know the lives of the great preachers; but it is at least as important to be familiar with their work and with the theories and techniques that shaped their sermons. My purpose here, therefore, is to move away from biography to a rhetorical study of the nineteenth-century pulpit.

The sources for this study come from an extensive body of primary materials. In addition to publishing many volumes of sermons, the Victorians published several books and scores of periodical articles about preaching. Most of the articles are concerned not with biography or even with theology, but with literary and rhetorical issues; as H. H. M. Herbert stated in a representative article, "This is not the place to consider the spiritual, the doctrinal, the higher and more purely religious side of a sermon. . . . our object is here rather with the form and method, the practice and the externals of preaching."[14]

The methodology I employ in the study of the "form and method" of Victorian preaching is that of orality-literacy studies, the branch of literary and rhetorical inquiry concerned with the differences between spoken and written language. Building on the groundbreaking work of Milman Parry in the 1920s, Albert B. Lord and Eric A. Havelock in the 1960s and 1970s, and especially Walter J. Ong in the 1970s and 1980s, orality-literacy studies has recently become an active, wide-ranging discipline. Over the past fifteen years, scholars have published well over seven hundred studies of the oral and written traditions of cultures around the world. Approximately 65 percent of this scholarship focuses on the literatures and oral narratives of non-English speaking countries; African nations are by far the most widely studied, with some attention also given to China, France, Germany, Greece, Hungary, India, Italy, Peru, Russia, and Spain.

The remaining scholarship is fairly evenly divided between the United States and Great Britain. Students of orality and literacy in American cultures have dealt with subjects ranging from Native American narratives to blues music to the Amish oral tradition; some work has also been done on oral characteristics in the writings of established literary figures such as Ernest Hemingway, Eudora Welty, Ezra Pound, Walt Whitman, William Faulkner, and Mark Twain. Concern with canonical authors is even more prevalent in orality-literacy studies and British literature; virtually all the published scholarship examines *Beowulf* and the work of Geoffrey Chaucer, John Milton, William Blake, Rudyard Kipling, Jane Austen, Joseph Conrad, D. H. Lawrence, James Joyce, and William Butler Yeats.

There is, however, a significant omission amid this scholarly diversity: like their counterparts in Victorian studies, orality-literacy scholars have given very little attention to the sermon. Preaching is the subject of only eleven articles; representative titles include "The Ramist Style of John Udall: Audience and Pictorial Logic in Puritan Sermon and Controversy"; "Frontier Preaching as Formulaic Poetry"; and "The Message of the American Folk Sermon."[15] None of these works, moreover, is concerned with the homiletics of nineteenth-century Britain. Few genres of British or American literature illustrate the juxtaposition of the oral and written traditions as clearly as the Victorian sermon; thus, my purpose here is not only to redraw the boundaries of Victorian studies, but to expand the scope of orality-literacy scholarship as well.

Specifically, I believe we can regard the sermon as a genre of "oral literature." Some scholars have objected to the use of this phrase. Bruce Rosenberg, for example, has protested that it is paradoxical, even oxymoronic, and has proposed that we speak instead of "Oralature," a phrase "employing both 'oral' and a suffix implying language which is ordered for an aesthetic purpose."[16] Walter J. Ong uses even stronger language, calling "oral literature" a "monstrous" term and arguing that it is "preposterous" to discuss the creative works of an oral culture in terms of a form that is, by definition, written.[17] Ong argues persuasively against using such language to describe the "oral productions of, say, the Lakota Sioux in North America or the Mande in West Africa"[18]—peoples who have had no exposure whatever to the written word. I propose, however, that there is a place for this term in orality-literacy studies, that it may properly describe genres like the sermon, which, more than any other form of nineteenth-century prose, is characterized by the often uneasy juxtaposition of oral and written traditions.

The first part of this study of the sermon as "oral literature" focuses on orality-literacy intersections in the rhetorical and social history of the Victorian pulpit. I begin with homiletic theory, examining Victorian expectations that the preacher exhibit the ethos of the classical orator while delivering sermons exemplifying the literary sophistication of the accomplished essayist. I then consider methods of delivery, analyzing the debate over whether, and to what extent, the artifacts of literacy—manuscripts of sermons and the like—should be introduced into the oral lifeworld of pulpit oratory. Finally, I discuss public reception of the sermon, focusing on how the common practice of attending preaching services on Sunday and reading sermons during the week provides yet another illustration of the intersection of the spoken and the printed word.

Having laid a historical and theoretical foundation for the sermon as a meeting point between orality and literacy, I move on to an examination of the work of three highly popular and respected pulpiteers—Charles Haddon Spurgeon, John Henry Newman, and George MacDonald. The significance of these preachers is threefold. First, they occupy different places in the literary canon. Spurgeon is all but absent from the canon; preachers and other students of religion have written extensively about his sermons, but these studies are generally not published in literary journals, nor are they usually indexed in bibliographies and other reference materials that students of literature consult in their research.[19] In contrast, Newman's place in the prose canon is well established, although students of his work have paid relatively little attention to his numerous volumes of sermons. Finally, MacDonald occupies a small but growing place in the canon. The last few years have seen renewed interest in his work, but, as is the case with Newman, the contributors to MacDonald's scholarly renaissance have focused on a small body of his works; virtually no studies of his poems, essays, or sermons have appeared in the last twenty or thirty years. Whereas Richard Reis, author of the Twayne biography of Mac-Donald, asserts that "the fiction must be the chief subject of any study," MacDonald himself believed that he was a preacher first and a writer of fiction second, and many of his contemporaries held him in high esteem as an essayist and Christian teacher.[20] John Ruskin, for example, wrote that the addresses in the first volume of MacDonald's *Unspoken Sermons* were "the best sermons—beyond all compare—I have ever read."[21] Thus, given that MacDonald's Victorian reputation was based on both his essays and his novels, I propose to take a first step toward expanding the modern MacDonald canon by examining the literary contributions he made in his printed sermons, the product of a lifelong exercise of his primary vocation.

Spurgeon, Newman, and MacDonald also belong to highly dissimilar denominational traditions—Spurgeon is an evangelical Baptist, Newman a High-Church Anglican, and MacDonald a Congregationalist with Unitarian sympathies. Most important, they represent three very different approaches to the art of preaching. Although Spurgeon well understood the power of the press—he published thousands of sermons during his forty-year career—his pulpit style was fundamentally oral. He spoke extemporaneously, guided by only a half-page of notes, and the style and structure of his sermons have more in common with the classical oration than with the Victorian prose essay.

Newman, in contrast, epitomizes the Victorian juxtaposition of orality and literacy. Throughout his tenure at St. Mary's Church in Oxford, where he served from 1828 to 1843, he wrote complete manuscripts of his sermons and read these manuscripts in the pulpit; when these discourses were published in a series entitled *Parochial and Plain Sermons,* they were widely praised as welcome—even unparalleled—contributions to the canon of English literature. Newman's literacy did not, however, detract from his effectiveness as a speaker. Despite the lack of "pulpit presence" caused by reading from a manuscript, Newman was an unusually charismatic figure, and the large and loyal congregations he drew to St. Mary's each week are evidence of his ability to combine the stylistic gifts of the literary artist with the ethos on which the success of the orator depends.

Finally, MacDonald's sermons belong primarily to the literate tradition. Unlike Spurgeon and Newman, MacDonald did not have a long and illustrious career as a pulpiteer. Only two years after taking his first post, he resigned amid charges of heresy and was never again able to secure regular employment as a minister. He did not, however, abandon his vocation as a preacher. He continued to preach, and transcripts of some of his sermons appeared in such periodicals as *The Christian World Pulpit*. He also published sermons that were never preached; his best-known homiletic work is found in a three-volume series appropriately titled *Unspoken Sermons* and in the sermons he incorporated in such novels as *Annals of a Quiet Neighbourhood* and its sequel, *The Seaboard Parish*. There is, therefore, no oral component to much of MacDonald's preaching; many sermons did not have the dual status of both oration and essay, but instead were disseminated only as written documents. In short, Spurgeon, Newman, and MacDonald belong to three different categories in orality-literacy studies, and their work illustrates some of the many ways in which the oral and written traditions intersect in the preaching of Victorian Britain.

1

Victorian Homiletic Theory

THE JUXTAPOSITION OF SPOKEN AND WRITTEN WORD IN VICTORIAN preaching first appears in the theories on the structure and style of the sermon. While homiletic theorists held that the purpose of preaching was similar to that of classical, orality-based public discourse, they maintained that the sermons themselves should be constructed in accordance with the techniques governing the written, rather than the spoken, word.

Parallels between Victorian homiletic theory and the classical oral tradition are best seen in the widespread insistence that the sermon be practical and persuasive, rather than merely abstract or informative. Both Aristotle and Cicero stipulated that rhetoric is, above all else, the art of persuasive speaking; in pre-Victorian Britain, this stipulation was echoed by such prominent secular and sacred rhetoricians as John Tillotson, John Ward, Hugh Blair, and Richard Whately.[1]

In the nineteenth century, J. H. Rigg and William Gresley explicitly acknowledged the link between classical rhetoric and Victorian preaching, and several of their contemporaries joined them in emphasizing the persuasive nature of pulpit oratory.[2] Representative comments include Islay Burns's assertion that the preacher's "main business" is "to plead and persuade"; J. G. Wenham's claim that the "best sermons are those by which men are most persuaded"; and William Thomson's insistence that "the sermon must . . . be solemn and affecting, loving and urgent, full of persuasion, warning, and rebuke."[3]

While many Victorian theorists echoed H. Rogers's stipulation that the only discourses "entitled to the name" of sermons are those "*specially adapted* to the object of instructing, convincing, or persuading the common mind," they were quick to point out that the persuasion toward which the sermon should be directed was not merely intellectual.[4] Sermons, in other words, were not to be "dissertations," "abstruse speculations," or "discussions of hard speculative points."[5] B. G. Johns, for example, argued that sermons should not address "the high and great mysteries of religion";[6] John Henry Newman declared that University sermons should not be discourses "upon theological points, polemical discussions, treatises *in extenso,* and the like"; and the author of an 1854 article in the *London Quarterly Review* maintained that "Biblical criticism, or ancient manners and customs, or natural theology . . . ought not to be the main subjects of pulpit discourses."[7]

The purpose of preaching, then, was not to bring a congregation to assent to a theological theory or set of propositions, but rather to persuade—indeed, to compel—men and women to embark upon a spiritual course of action. The sermon was to be a practical discourse, one that would not only offer "words of guidance or counsel, comfort or assistance," but also "declare and enforce common rules for the right government of life."[8]

Clear and specific didacticism, or what Islay Burns called an "intimate relation in the teaching of the pulpit with the actual facts and realities of human life," was therefore regarded as an indispensable aspect of Victorian preaching.[9] William Thomson, Lord Archbishop of York, wrote that a sermon should "teach the sinful how to love God, and those who have already repented how to love Him more"; several of his contemporaries believed that a preacher should often give specific "*directions* or *instructions*" to his congregation.[10] In Letter XXIX of *Ecclesiastes Anglicanus,* William Gresley suggested that "if you have been speaking of any sin, and have brought it home to your hearers, you should then tell them *the means* to avoid it; or, if you have filled them with love and desire of any Christian grace, you should instruct them how to attain it."[11] Similarly, R. W. Dale insisted that, in addition to demonstrating "some Christian truth" or explaining "some Christian duty," a preacher must also "project the truth into the very depths of the thought and life of [his] congregation" in such a way that will "constrain them to discharge the duty."[12] The best sermons, in short, were not those which "extend[ed] theological science" or "sound[ed] the foundations of speculative truth," but rather those which offered "honest manly advice" about how to live a "noble, pure, and earnest life."[13]

The Victorian sermon's links to the oral tradition are evident not only in the insistence that sermons be persuasive, but also in the expectations set forth concerning the character, or ethos, of the clergymen who delivered them. Aristotle called the orator's character "the most effective means of persuasion he possesses," and he listed "three things"—"good sense, good moral character, and goodwill"—that could help an orator win the trust and confidence of his audience.[14] Aristotle's list appears almost verbatim in William Gresley's discussion of the preacher's ethos in *Ecclesiastes Anglicanus*—he wrote that a preacher's parishioners must know that he has *"good principle, good will towards them, and good sense"*—and his emphasis on character appeared throughout Victorian works on preaching.[15] The author of an essay published in *The Congregationalist* asserted that "many of the greatest preachers are great not by virtue of great sermons, but by reason of great souls," and the popular Birmingham preacher R. W. Dale told ministerial students, "One of your first objects should be to secure the confidence of your people. They will get very little good from your preaching unless they trust you."[16] William Thomson offered what may be the most succinct Victorian insistence on the character of the preacher: "I have ventured to think," he wrote, "that good men sometimes preach bad sermons, but I do not forget that bad men will never preach good ones."[17]

While Victorian homileticians followed classical rhetoricians in their emphasis on persuasion and the ethos of the preacher, they departed from their predecessors in stipulating that preachers should compose their sermons not in accordance with the practices of the oral tradition, but rather in accordance with the conventions that governed other forms of nineteenth-century literary prose. This departure is first evident in the Victorians' rejection of the model Cicero set forth for the structure of an oration. In *De Inventione*, Cicero stated that the art of public speaking can be divided into five major components:

> Invention, Arrangement, Expression, Memory, Delivery. Invention is the discovery of valid or seemingly valid arguments to render one's cause plausible. Arrangement is the distribution of arguments thus discovered in the proper order. Expression is the fitting of the proper language to the invented matter. Memory is the firm mental grasp of matter and words. Delivery is the control of voice and body in a manner suitable to the dignity of the subject matter and the style.[18]

Cicero further asserted that invention "is the most important of all the divisions,"[19] and his book focused on the six categories into which invention itself can be divided. He stipulated that an oration should consist of six major elements—"exordium, narrative, partition, confirmation, refutation, [and] peroration"—and his paradigm was a prominent feature of pre-Victorian rhetorical theory.[20] The "first systematic attempt to acquaint English readers with . . .

the Ciceronian doctrine of invention" appeared in 1530, when Leonard Cox published *The Arte or Crafte of Rhethoryke*. [21] Like Cicero, Cox believed invention to be the most important of the rhetorical arts, and his *Rhethoryke* is concerned primarily with setting forth the "parts of an oration prescribed of Rhetoricians," which he enumerated as "The Preamble or exorden," the "Tale or narration," the "proving of the matter or contention" and "The conclusion."[22]

The application of Ciceronian invention to British oratory that Cox began continued throughout the seventeenth and eighteenth centuries. Some of the more prominent seventeenth-century rhetoricians were the "Neo-Ciceronians," who objected to the Ramists' attempts to restrict rhetoric to the study of style and delivery.[23] Important Neo-Ciceronian treatises include Thomas Vicars' *Manuduction to the Rhetorical Art* (1621), Thomas Farnaby's *Index Rhetoricus* (1625), and William Pemble's *Enchiridion Oratorium* (1633), all of which sought to return invention—and, with it, the six-part structure of the classical oration—to the study of British rhetoric.[24]

The influence of the Neo-Ciceronians, whom Wilbur Samuel Howell has identified as the "dominant" faction in British rhetoric from 1621 to 1700, was reflected in a number of important eighteenth-century rhetorical treatises.[25] In 1739, John Holmes, a schoolmaster known for his "zealous enthusiasm for the educational value of . . . Ciceronian rhetoric," published *The Art of Rhetoric Made Easy*.[26] His treatise reduced "the whole doctrine of Ciceronian rhetoric to twenty-four principles," and, although invention is not the primary focus of the work, Holmes made it clear that students' orations "should be arranged into the exordium, narration, proposition, confirmation, refutation, and peroration."[27]

Twenty years after Holmes published *The Art of Rhetoric*, John Ward published *A System of Oratory*, which has been called "the most extensive restatement of ancient rhetorical theory in the English language."[28] Although he drew on such classical authorities as Aristotle, Horace, Plutarch, and Quintilian, Ward's greatest debt was to Cicero. His treatment of invention closely resembles Cicero's discussion in *De Inventione:* he asserted that "oratory consists of these four parts: *Invention, Disposition, Elocution*, and *Pronunciation*," and he further divided invention according to Cicero's sixfold structure, which he regarded as the "most full and explicit" of the ancient rhetorical models.[29]

Perhaps the most popular and influential eighteenth-century classical rhetorician was Hugh Blair, a renowned preacher and professor of rhetoric at the University of Edinburgh. In 1793, Blair published *Lectures on Rhetoric and Belles Lettres*, which "had a phenomenal sale in Europe and the United States during the first century after publication."[30] In Lecture XXXI, entitled "Conduct of a Discourse in all its Parts," Blair followed Cicero's structure exactly, maintaining that "the parts that compose a regular formal oration, are these six; first, the exordium or introduction; secondly, the state, and the division of the subject; thirdly, narration or explication; fourthly, the reasoning or arguments; fifthly, the pathetic part; and lastly, the conclusion."[31]

Cicero's six-part oratorical structure was a prominent aspect of pre-Victorian sacred oratory as well. W. Fraser Mitchell has shown that "the devices of classical rhetoric . . . were employed to a greater or less extent in the mediaeval sermon,"[32] and references to preaching appear in the Ciceronian systems of such early works as Lorenzo Guglielmo Traversagni's *Nova Rhetorica* (Cambridge, 1479), and Thomas Wilson's *The Arte of Rhetorique* (London, 1553).[33]

One of the first Ciceronian rhetorics devoted exclusively to homiletics was Andreas Gerardus Hyperius' Latin treatise *De Formandis Concionibus Sacris*, which first appeared in Germany in 1555 and was published in an English translation entitled *The Practise of Preaching* in 1577. In *De Formandis*, Hyperius explicitly aligned himself with the Ciceronian tradition, writing that "the parts of an Orator, which are accounted of some to be, *Invention, Disposition, Elocution, Memory,* and *Pronunciation,* may rightly be called also the parts of a Preacher."[34] While he appears to depart from Cicero in matters of invention—he writes that "the Preacher hath many points, chiefly in Invention, wherein he differeth from the Orator"—he nonetheless followed Cicero's paradigm in his discussion of sermon structure.[35] This discussion, which occupies nine chapters of Book I, assigned seven parts to a sermon: a *"reading of the sacred scripture"* followed by *"Invocatio, Exordiu, propositio or divisio, Confirmation, Confutation, coclusio"*—categories that conform closely to the six-part structure Cicero prescribes in *De Inventione*.[36]

Strict application of the Ciceronian paradigm to British pulpit oratory appeared as late as the early nineteenth century. In 1772 and 1773, George Campbell delivered a series of homiletic lectures to his divinity students at Marischal College in Aberdeen, Scotland. He repeated these lectures annually until his retirement in 1795, and in 1807 they were published posthumously under the title *Lectures on Systematic Theology and Pulpit Eloquence.* The last six of these lectures set forth a distinctly Ciceronian approach to the composition of a sermon: Campbell held that a pulpit address should have "a text, and introduction of subject, an explanation of the connection between subject and text, a partition, a discussion of parts, and a conclusion."[37]

While some pre-Victorian homiletic theorists adopted Cicero's sixfold paradigm in its entirety, others modified his model to fit what they believed to be the special requirements of pulpit oratory. One of the best-known preachers to depart from a strictly Ciceronian approach was John Donne, dean of St. Paul's cathedral in London from 1621 to 1631. Donne divided his sermons into a "*praecognitio textus*," which took "the place of the old exordium"; the "*partitio et propositio*—division and enunciation of theme"; the "*Explicatio verborum*"; and finally the "*Amplification*" and the "*Application*."[38]

A number of prominent seventeenth-and eighteenth-century preachers modified Cicero's model even further. Many neoclassical sermons did not make a strict distinction between the exordium and the explication or between the proposition and the partition. Between 1646 and 1796, theorists such as John Wilkins, William Chappell, William Leechman, and Jean Claude published treatises requiring that a sermon consist of only three major divisions.[39] By the end of the eighteenth century, five of Cicero's six categories—the "exordium, explication, proposition, partition, and conclusion"—had come to be regarded as optional, rather than required, components of pulpit discourse; as Rolf Lessenich has noted, "The argumentative part and the application may, then, be considered as the central parts or main body of a sermon to which everything else was either preparation or aftermath."[40]

Although the sermon structure stipulated by Wilkins, Chappell, Claude, and others was not directly modeled on the sixfold paradigm introduced in *De Inventione*, it does indicate the indirect influence of Cicero and therefore a degree of association with the classical oral tradition. Their work, in other words, is evidence of what Walter Ong has called "oral residue"; their emphasis on the formal divisions of a discourse is grounded in "habits of thought and expression tracing back to preliterate situations or practice."[41] By the nineteenth century, however, even this "residue" had virtually vanished from homiletic theory, and the structural elements of a sermon were ignored or rejected far more than they were emphasized. The exordium, for example, was a prominent feature of many important earlier rhetorics. It is discussed at length in such works as Cox's *Arte or Crafte of Rhethoryke*, Ward's *System of Oratory,* and Campbell's *Lectures on Systematic Theology,* but it is mentioned in only five of the scores of homiletic books and articles written during Victoria's reign.[42]

The only structural component Victorian homileticians insisted on was the application, the portion that would accomplish the persuasive ends toward which all true sermons were directed. In the 1840s, for example, H. Rogers wrote that the preacher's main concern should be "the ample circle of [Christian] doctrines and precepts, in all their applications to the endless diversities of life," and William Gresley devoted Letter XXVIII of his *Ecclesiastes Anglicanus* to a detailed discussion of the application, which he regarded as an "essential part of every good sermon."[43] Twenty years later, B. G. Johns argued that sermons should consist of "clear, concise, well-applied argument, of the plainest and most practical kind," and E. T. Vaughan declared that sermons must finally be judged for "their worth as attempts to utter Christ's gospel and apply it to use."[44] The most explicit acknowledgment that the application was the most important—perhaps the only important—structural component of the Victorian sermon was offered by James Davies in 1868. He wrote that, instead of constructing their sermons in accordance with "stiff" structural formulas, which "would either drive away a congregation or else send it to sleep," preachers should simply follow "some such general mapping of the subject as is suggested by the Scriptural interpretation and personal application of the text."[45]

After the application, the structural component that received the most attention was the partition, which was rejected rather than affirmed as a desirable or necessary aspect of a sermon. In *De Inventione,* Cicero listed the partition as the fourth of the six essential components of the classical oration, and he defined it as the setting forth of "the matter which we intend to discuss . . . in a methodical way," a practice that can help make "the whole speech clear and perspicuous."[46]

Like his stipulations regarding the structure of a discourse, Cicero's suggestions that orators explicitly outline the contents of their speeches influenced British preaching for several hundred years. Intricate divisions of sermons began in twelfth- and thirteenth-century Scholasticism; many homiletic manuals of the time "reproduce the invariable pattern of the elaborately 'divided' sermon, with the chief heads . . . set forth in the opening paragraph."[47] Throughout the sixteenth, seventeenth, and eighteenth centuries, many prominent preachers—including John Wycliffe, Richard Bernard, John Wilkins, James Arderne, and Hugh Blair—

also advocated the use and early introduction of the various heads of a discourse.[48]

Theorists in the Victorian period largely rejected this method. William Gresley, the only nineteenth-century homiletician to discuss the exordium in detail, was also one of the few clergymen to advocate the division of a sermon into heads. In Letter XXIII of *Ecclesiastes Anglicanus,* he suggested that preachers first "consider into what principal heads [their] subject should be divided," and then dissect these heads into "subdivisions and separate paragraphs," a practice he called "the filling up of the canvas."[49] Perhaps the most prominent preacher to employ multiple divisions was Charles Haddon Spurgeon, who traced his advocacy of this technique to a childhood trip to the market:

> Ever since the day I was sent to shop with a basket, and purchased a pound of tea, a quarter-of-a-pound of mustard, and three pounds of rice, and on my way home saw a pack of hounds, and felt it necessary to follow them over hedge and ditch . . . and found, when I reached home, that all the goods were amalgamated . . . into one awful mess, I have understood the necessity of packing up my subjects in good stout parcels, bound round with the thread of my discourse; and this makes me keep to firstly, secondly, and thirdly, however unfashionable that method may now be.[50]

The use of multiple divisions was indeed "unfashionable" in nineteenth-century preaching. Some argued that, while a sermon could be divided into heads, these heads should not be announced to the congregation in advance. Anthony Wilson Thorold, Lord Bishop of Rochester, cautioned "that it is usually inexpedient to alarm the congregation by a too extensive and fatiguing prospect of the road in front of them," and in his *Nine Lectures on Preaching,* R. W. Dale suggested that ministerial students avoid the practice, asserting that "If the thoughts of the sermon are well massed . . . the sermon will be effective at the time, and the main points of it will be remembered afterwards, whether the divisions are announced or not."[51]

While Thorold and Dale permitted the subtle division of a sermon into heads, most nineteenth-century theorists rejected the practice altogether. Opponents of this technique included H. Rogers, who spoke out against "those complicated divisions and subdivisions into which our forefathers thought proper to chop up their discourses"; William Davies, who argued that "Too much division and subdivision" was "decidedly undesirable"; and S. Leslie Breakey, who captured the Victorian arguments against the division of sermons when he wrote that "the thing which forms the lowest of characters in a man is the highest of merits in a sermon—that it has not two ideas in its head."[52]

The lack of emphasis on the structural elements of Victorian sermons represents a shift away from the practices of the oral tradition, but it does not signify a corresponding shift toward literacy-based methods of sermon construction. That shift is seen instead in nineteenth-century discussions of the style of the sermon. It is style, not structure, that is the overriding concern of many Victorian homileticians. In his 1840 review of Augustus William Hare's *Sermons to a Country Congregation*, H. Rogers set aside "doctrinal questions" and considered "only the general conditions on which all religious instruction . . . should be conveyed; and especially the *style* and the *manner* peculiarly appropriated to this department of public speaking."[53] Forty years after Rogers's review appeared, H. H. M. Herbert published "The Art of Preaching." The focus of his article is not "the spiritual, the doctrinal, the higher and more purely religious side of a sermon," but "rather . . . the form and method, the practice and the externals of preaching."[54] The next year, a discussion of prominent clergymen appeared in *Living Age* magazine, and its author again noted that "sectarian doctrines of these various clergymen must be left out of account in such a review," that the purpose of the article was only "to describe the preachers as they appear to the chance occupant of a pew, who has entered their respective churches . . . with some purpose of weighing what he hears and of observing the manner in which it was delivered."[55]

The style Victorian theorists valued in a sermon was not the style that had dominated classical oratory and characterized many of the sermons preached in Britain prior to the nineteenth century. In the same way that Cicero's *De Inventione* introduced the six-part structure of the classical oration, his *De Oratore* established an ornate, elaborate style as the normative method of public speaking. Using the eminent orator Lucius Licinius Crassus as his mouthpiece, Cicero asserted that "nobody ever admired an orator for merely speaking good Latin" and stipulated that a truly eloquent orator will adorn his language in such a way that will impart a "certain splendour" to his expression.[56]

The ornamented style which Cicero advocated in *De Oratore* was employed by British pulpiteers of the eighth through the eighteenth centuries. The use of the elaborate rhetorical devices that Cicero discusses in Book III of *De Oratore* was introduced into

England by the Venerable Bede. In *Liber de Schematibus et Tropis*, which appeared in 701 or 702, Bede wrote that it is often

> customary for the sake of elegance that the order of words as they are formulated should be contrived in some other way than that adhered to by the people in their speech. These contrivances the Greek grammarians call schemes, whereas we may rightly term them attire or form or figure, because through them as a distinct method speech may be dressed up and adorned. On other occasions, it is customary for a locution called the trope to be devised. This is done by changing a word from its proper signification to an unaccustomed but similar case on account of necessity or adornment.[57]

Bede's treatise is a discussion of a number of these schemes and tropes, and similar discussions appear in many British rhetorics.[58] Theorists such as Richard Sherry, Henry Peacham, and George Puttenham in the sixteenth century; John Prideaux in the seventeenth; and John Ward and John Lawson in the eighteenth all included systems of tropes and figures in their works.[59]

Like their counterparts in secular rhetoric, many British homileticians employed an elaborate, ornamented style. In the Middle Ages, the sermon "shared the tendency of other contemporary art forms to become ever more complex and decorated"; as W. Fraser Mitchell has noted, medieval preachers were often more concerned with "the pursuit of allegories and analogies, and the cultivation of schematic patterns . . . than the body of their addresses."[60] Common rhetorical "affectations" in medieval sermons included "forced etymologies," "fatuous metaphors . . . stilted Latin verses, and a plentiful use of superlatives."[61]

Many pulpiteers of the sixteenth and seventeenth centuries followed their medieval predecessors in cultivating an elaborate, ornamented method of sacred speaking. Sermons of the Elizabethan age were often "marred by an affected display of learning . . . by coarse wit and unworthy word-play, and still oftener by extreme prolixity."[62] Similarly, as J. E. Spingarn has noted, the "witty" or "metaphysical" preaching of the Jacobean era was characterized by the "far-fetched simile, the conceit, the pun, the absurd antithesis"; examples of this style can be found in the sermons of Lancelot Andrewes, whose discourses were full of "wit and word-play," and John Donne, who delighted in "allegory and cabalistic speculation."[63]

One of the rhetorical ornaments most often employed during this period was the use—or, more precisely, the overuse—of quotations from classical and patristic authorities. The sermons of

John Williams, Archbishop of York, were "intricate mosaics of patristic quotation," and classical references appeared throughout the sermons of Thomas Adams, Joseph Hall, and Nathanael Culverwell.[64] One of the preachers most given to the use of quotations was John Smith, whose sermons contained so many citations from ancient authorities that it was "almost impossible to find a straightforward piece of English" in his sermons.[65]

The preference for the learned, elaborate style we see in the preaching of Adams, Smith, Culverwell, and others is not reflected in the homiletic theory of the nineteenth century. Instead, the stylistic guidelines set forth by the Victorians represent the culmination of a shift from an ornamented oral rhetoric to a plainer, more natural, more literary approach to sacred speaking.

The first stage in this shift occurred in the latter part of the seventeenth century, when, according to W. Fraser Mitchell, the sermon "passed from a period in which its form and content were governed by certain rhetorical and homiletical ideals to a period when it became almost a province of literature."[66] Beginning in the 1640s, a number of preachers—including John Eachard, John Wilkins, Richard Baxter, and Robert South—published treatises echoing Joseph Glanvill's charge that "affectations of wit and finery, flourishes, metaphors, and cadences" were nothing more than "a bastard kind of eloquence that is crept into the Pulpit."[67] By 1688, "the sermon as a whole" was expected to conform to "genuinely literary considerations." Preachers who satisfied the new stylistic criteria included Anthony Tuckney, the only Westminster divine whose sermons "can lay claim to literary finish"; John Tillotson, in whose hands "the sermon became an essay"; and John Fisher, who, according to Mitchell, "deserves to be styled the father of the English literary sermon."[68]

The expectation that "a sermon should be a work of literary art" was also reflected in the homiletic theory of the eighteenth century.[69] In order to satisfy the "rules of neoclassic art," which stipulated that the "ideal sermon had to be plain and simple," eighteenth-century pulpiteers were expected to find a middle ground between two stylistic extremes.[70] First, in keeping with the requirement that a sermon not be "uncouth," James Fordyce admonished preachers not to "disgrace" their sermons "with vulgarity and cant"; Thomas Secker cautioned ministers to "Avoid rusticity and grossness in [their] style"; and J. Barecroft wrote that a sermon "ought not to be flat and dull, like to two Country People talking one to the other."[71] The style of a sermon, then, could not be mean or "vulgar," but neither could it be ornate or "affected."[72] Several neoclassical theorists joined Wilkins, South, and Glanvill in rejecting the elaborate rhetoric previously in vogue. J. Barecroft admonished preachers to "STUDY more *Clearness*, than *Quaintness* of Expression"; Charles Rollin criticized preachers who indulged in "childish affectation" or "trifling ornaments"; and William Leechman insisted that preachers "avoid with a particular care all affectation of fine language, and a glittering kind of eloquence."[73] In the *via media* between "ostentation and rusticity" lay the neoclassic ideal of a simple yet elegant prose style, and the sermons of preachers who achieved this ideal—men such as Samuel Clarke, Thomas Secker, Benjamin Fawcett, and Thomas Sherlock—were praised as worthy contributions to an "important branch of literature."[74]

Victorian homileticians followed their neoclassic predecessors in insisting that simplicity, not ornamentation, was the basis of true pulpit eloquence. Whereas earlier, orality-oriented theorists such as Bede believed that the language of a sermon "should be contrived in some other way than that adhered to by the people in their speech,"[75] the Victorians believed that such a style created an unnecessary and undesirable distance between the preacher and his congregation. As S. Leslie Breakey lamented in an 1861 edition of the *Cornhill Magazine*,

> As soon as the preacher ascends the pulpit steps he seems to ascend into a new social atmosphere. From being natural and spontaneous, he becomes "ceremonious and traditional." He goes on without remorse serving up for the hundredth time the same stereotyped phrases, the same conventional idioms which, by right of immemorial possession, have somehow come to be thought necessary to the very existence of a sermon.[76]

A primary concern of many Victorians, then, was suggesting ways in which preachers could set aside rhetoric which "savours too much of the pulpit" and cultivate instead "a clear, vigorous, and thoroughly English style."[77] According to J. G. Wenham, the "most useful thing" preachers could do to accomplish this goal was "to adapt the language and ideas used, to the character of the audience."[78] Wenham does not elaborate on how this adaptation might be carried out, but the writings of his contemporaries show that it involved the cultivation of a simple, straightforward approach to both the content and the style of the sermon. Theorists such as William Gresley and R. W. Dale believed that clergymen should be well educated, but, in contrast to their seventeenth-century counterparts, they insisted that sermons must not be used as a vehicle for the display of the preacher's knowledge.[79] One reviewer went so far as to suggest that "Copious quotations of poetry" were not a sign of the preacher's intellectual sophistication, but were instead merely a device employed "to supply the place of freshness of thought."[80]

The exclusion of ostentatious displays of learning was just one aspect of the insistence on "Simplicity of style and manner" in Victorian preaching.[81] To fully achieve that "plain, outright" style which James Davies believed was "best adapted to [his] matter-of-fact generation," preachers were expected to set aside all appearances of "rhetorical effect and display"—devices such as "turgid language," "florid declamation," "imaginative finery," and "tawdry ornament"—in favor of "a highly idiomatic and homely diction" and illustrations "marked more by their homely propriety than by their grace and elegance."[82] In short, Victorian pulpiteers were expected to adhere to a new definition of "eloquence," one that avoided all extravagant, self-conscious expression. As H. Rogers wrote in his 1840 review of the sermons of Augustus William Hare,

> True eloquence is not like some painted window, which not only transmits the light of day variegated and tinged with a thousand hues, but calls away the attention from its proper use to the pomp and splendour of the artist's doings. It is a perfectly transparent medium; transmitting light, without suggesting a thought about the medium itself.[83]

As was the case in the neoclassical period, the stylistic criteria to which Victorian preaching was expected to conform were the same as those used to judge other forms of literary prose. Although some theorists were reluctant to specify absolute standards—one stated that "There are no settled canons, and no accepted arbiter of the elegances of prose"[84]—they did set forth plainness, simplicity, and clarity as basic "principles of style."[85] Frederic Harrison, for example, advised Victorian writers to "Be natural, be simple, be yourself; shun artifices, tricks, fashions. Gain the tone of ease, plainness, self-respect."[86] The author of an unsigned article in the *Edinburgh Review* also objected to artificial, unduly elaborate language when he identified the "most perfect prose style" as "the one which calls least attention to itself."[87]

Finally, another unidentified critic used an analogy between essays and machinery to illustrate the importance of simplicity in writing. He described language as "an apparatus of symbols for the conveyance of thought," arguing that, just as with any other mechanical device, "the more simple and the better arranged its parts, the greater will be the effect produced." He went on to state that "there seems reason to think that in all cases the friction and inertia of the vehicle deduct from its efficiency; and that in composition the chief if not the sole thing to be done, is to reduce this friction and inertia to the smallest possible amount." The best way to achieve this goal, he believed, was to use "Saxon English, or rather non-Latin English" whenever possible, to "express an idea" not only in "the smallest number of words," but in "the smallest number of syllables" as well.[88]

The similarities between the criteria for sacred and secular prose style are illustrated not only in essays by anonymous and lesser-known contributors to Victorian periodicals, but also in the extent to which the homileticians' arguments resemble those advanced by the foremost essayists of the time. Thomas Babington Macaulay, for example, believed that obscurity was an essay's greatest flaw—he held that "To write what is not understood in its whole force [is] absurd"—and Augustus William Hare and Thomas Guthrie were praised for their ability to preach "in terms that are incapable of ambiguity."[89] Similarly, in "Preface to Poems" and "The Literary Influence of Academies," Matthew Arnold echoed James Davies' insistence on a "plain, outright" approach to the art of composition.[90] He identified "simplicity of style" as one of the qualities that can "be learned best from the ancients," rejecting what he called the "extravagant" style of "provincial" prose in favor of "classical English," which he regarded as "perfect in lucidity, measure, and propriety."[91] Finally, Walter Pater believed that "the true artist may best be recognized" not by his inclination toward rhetorical extravagance, but rather "by his tact of omission."[92] Just as the best preachers were men like R. W. Church, who omitted any "parade of learning" from his sermons, and E. C. Wickham, noted for delivering "the best scholarly preaching without mannerism," the best writers, according to Pater, were those who avoided "really obsolete or really worn-out words" and who showed "no favour" to any "affectation of learning designed for the unlearned."[93]

Thus, by the end of the nineteenth century, reforms in the style of the sermon initiated by John Eachard and his colleagues in the 1640s were virtually complete. Sermons were no longer regarded primarily as orations, but rather as "written pieces"; consequently, they were expected to "follow the rule of all other writings."[94] Rather than eliminating the practices of orality from Victorian homiletics, however, these reforms, instead, led to a conflation of the oral and written traditions, as preachers were expected to employ literary means—a simple, conversational rhetorical style—to accomplish an orality-based end—persuading the members of a congregation to embark on a specific, spiritually beneficial course of action. This conflation is one of the most prominent elements of the theory of Victorian preaching. It is also, I propose, the theoretical concern that first identifies the sermon as an important contribution to the "oral literature" of the British Isles.

2

Methods of Delivery

IN ADDITION TO PUBLISHING NUMEROUS BOOKS AND ARTICLES ON how sermons should be constructed, the Victorians spent a good deal of time discussing how they should be delivered. Issues of orality and literacy are a prominent part of this aspect of homiletic theory as well; one of the topics most frequently debated was whether, and to what extent, the oral act of preaching should be guided by written materials—notes, outlines, even complete manuscripts—taken into the pulpit.

Throughout British history, preachers employed three basic oratorical techniques. Some wrote out their sermons in full and read their manuscripts in the pulpit; others spoke extemporaneously, guided by notes rather than a manuscript; and still others sought a middle ground between reading and improvisation, memorizing their written sermons and delivering them "as if they were extemporaneous."[1] Victorian theorists were divided as to which of these approaches was best suited to the nineteenth-century pulpit. J. H. Rigg framed the terms of the debate when he asked

> What ought to be the aim or scope of sermons? Ought they to be read from the manuscript or to be spoken? If the sermon ought to be spoken, what is the best method of preparing for its delivery? Should the sermon be written and learnt, or should it be premeditated and afterwards delivered as the thoughts rise and the words are freshly suggested; or may a sermon be delivered in part from memory, in part only from premeditation? or may different persons use either of these plans, or the same person use either, according to the circumstances? These are the questions which, with the utmost brevity, we will now try to answer.[2]

Contrary to Rigg's expectation, Victorian discussions of this matter were anything but brief. The only part of his inquiry to receive a definitive answer was the question of whether a sermon should be "written and learnt." The few Victorian theorists who addressed this question unanimously rejected the practice. Charles Haddon Spurgeon admonished his ministerial students not to recite their sermons from memory, and Dinah Mulock noted with pleasure that "the practice of first writing sermons, and then committing them to memory, is being gradually discontinued."[3] Rigg himself objected to "reading from the page of memory," asserting that a "public speaker who can only recite . . . is like the man who has only lernt to swim with bladders or floats."[4]

The other issues Rigg raised generated considerably more discussion. While a few theorists argued, as Islay Burns did in 1863, that it would be "hopeless to reach any absolute rule applicable to every case alike,"[5] many others engaged in a lively debate over whether a sermon ought "to be read from the manuscript or to be spoken."[6] Some suggested that preachers who lacked experience or a natural gift of eloquence should read their sermons. Charles Abel Heurtley, Canon of Christ Church, Oxford, recommended that young preachers begin their ministries "with written sermons, whatever they may think right to do after two or three years' experience." Edward Garbett believed that "men not naturally gifted with utterance may . . . become more moving and effective preachers, with the written sermon than without it."[7]

Others recommended that manuscripts be used only when a preacher was delivering an intellectually intricate discourse to a learned congregation. In 1863, for example, Islay Burns suggested that "the read discourse may be not only the most natural, but the most effective instrument" in cases "where the sermon approaches the character of a theological lecture or didactic essay."[8] Four years later, J. H. Rigg presented a similar claim, writing that "an elaborate and minute exposition of Scripture, addressed to a select audience—an audience trained closely to follow a sustained argument or discussion—may not improperly be read."[9]

Conversely, several theorists emphasized that written sermons had little place among the less affluent or less educated. In an essay entitled "What Constitutes a Plain Sermon?" Harvey Goodwin, Lord Bishop of Carlisle, contended that "sermons preached *extempore* . . . are more easily understood by poor folks than written sermons."[10] R. W. Dale echoed Goodwin's claim in his *Nine Lectures on Preaching,* suggesting that the "thought of an extemporaneous preacher is more likely to be of a kind to interest and impress an ordinary congregation than the thought of a preacher who reads."[11] Finally, J. H. Rigg balanced his approval of reading sermons to "select" audiences with the insistence that "read discourses are altogether unfit" in churches whose congregations include "persons of common-place intelligence and character."[12]

While some participants in the Victorian discussion about manuscript versus extempore preaching dealt with what might be considered extrinsic concerns—the experience of the preacher or the economic or intellectual status of the congregation—most of the debate focused on which mode of preaching was intrinsically more likely to achieve a greater rhetorical effect. Several theorists believed that sermons written in advance were, as a general rule, better organized and more logically sound than discourses composed extemporaneously. B. G. Johns acknowledged that "a written sermon has the better chance of being accurate, correct, and clearly arranged." John Henry Newman believed that written sermons were superior to extempore discourses in "accuracy of wording, completeness of statement, or succession of ideas." The author of an article in *Fraser's Magazine* held that preachers who read their sermons could ensure "that accuracy of statement and citation, that precision of argument which are so often wanting in the discourses of extempore preachers."[13]

One of the most extensive arguments in favor of preaching from manuscript was offered by William Gresley, curate of St. Chad's in Lichfield and author of the 1835 treatise *Ecclesiastes Anglicanus*. Gresley contended that extemporaneous preaching should be restricted to "remote villages, where two or three only are gathered together" and offered several arguments in support of written sermons. He argued, first, that a preacher who used a manuscript would be more confident in his delivery than one who composed his discourse in the pulpit. Whereas "the extemporaneous preacher is often evidently embarrassed at the close of his sentences, in gathering what he is to say next," a preacher who reads his sermon "continues confidently to the end of each paragraph." This confidence, Gresley maintained, was beneficial to the congregation as well, for when parishioners know that their minister has a manuscript before him, they will not be "distracted by anxiety lest [he] should come to a stand."[14]

In Gresley's view, preachers who read their sermons would not only be more confident than their extempore counterparts, they would also be better able to adjust their delivery in accordance with the reactions of the congregation. The extemporaneous preacher, he maintained, could not be attentive to his congregants' responses because he "is obliged to turn his whole mind to his subject; he can spare no portion of his attention elsewhere; every faculty is absorbed in composing as he goes along." In contrast, a preacher who reads is "at liberty to give a part of his attention to the feelings of those whom he addresses. If he finds them inattentive, he is not abashed and confused, as the extemporary preacher is apt to be, but goes straight forward, striving to regain their attention; if, on the other hand, he marks excited interest, his own feelings are sympathetically moved, and fresh force is given to his delivery."[15]

The third advantage of manuscript preaching, according to Gresley, lay in the preacher's ability to improve his craft by continually revising his sermons. In *Ecclesiastes,* Gresley suggested that soon after the service had ended, preachers should "mark with a pencil any parts" of the sermon which "should be cancelled or improved," and he instructed them to "Note when [the] congregation seemed interested, and where their attention began to flag, with a view to correct [the] sermon for another occasion." As they encountered "any fresh arguments or illustrations" in the course of their later "reading or meditation," they should also "note them down carefully in their proper place in the sermon." By so doing, Gresley asserted, preachers would be able to "write [their] sermons over again with much additional matter," and, presumably, deliver much better versions in the future.[16]

Gresley's endorsement of the use of written sermons placed him in the minority among Victorian homiletic theorists. In 1887, A. Eubule Evans noted that "written sermons seem gradually to be falling into something like disrepute," and preachers throughout the second half of the nineteenth century published statements declaring the "unwritten address" to be "the proper and normal kind of preaching."[17] A representative list of such statements includes an anonymous reviewer's claim that "extempore preaching . . . is by far the more effective style"; J. H. Rigg's argument that "the basis of all pulpit power is the power of extempore speech"; and John Henry Newman's claim, made after his conversion to Catholicism, that "preaching is not reading, and reading is not preaching."[18] In short, it was not just the "vulgar," as Evans claimed, but well-educated reviewers and clergymen as well, who believed that "to read is human, to extemporise divine."[19]

Opponents of reading from a manuscript offered several grounds for their contention that the extemporaneous address was "the highest style of preaching."[20] While some theorists believed that a written sermon was generally superior in its accuracy and logical development, R. W. Dale and J. H. Rigg suggested that it was extempore preachers who were likely to be more successful in constructing their arguments. Dale believed that a preacher who did not use a manuscript would have a better idea of the detail with which he needed to develop his claims. In *Nine Lectures on Preaching,* he argued that, whereas preachers who wrote their sermons could not "be sure whether [they] ought to be satisfied with saying a thing once, or whether [they] ought to say it over again," those who preached extemporaneously could "watch the faces of the people" and thereby "discover that statements which seemed . . . perfectly clear, require to be repeated, illustrated, and expanded."[21] Rigg contended, moreover, that the experienced extemporaneous preacher could execute such repetition, illustration, or expansion with the same "accuracy of wording, completeness of statement, or succession of ideas" found in the best manuscript sermons.[22] In his 1867 essay "On Preaching," he asked, "Why . . . when a man has been trained to speak, should not the speaker's ideas flow more freely, find expression for themselves in words more apt and powerful, and be not materially less correct, than as they are indited in the study?"[23]

Dale and Rigg touched on the intellectual advantages of the extempore sermon over the written address, but most Victorian arguments in support of extemporaneous preaching proceeded from the conviction that a sermon's success depended not on the precision with which it was developed, but on the passion with which it was delivered. Some theorists who believed that "The principal object of preaching without reading is, of course, to convey . . . the strong sense of the preacher's earnestness" focused on the ways in which the use of a manuscript hindered the ethical or emotional impact of the sermon.[24] Islay Burns, for example, contended that "oratory in the full sense cannot consist with the interposition of a written manuscript between the speaker and his audience," and J. H. Rigg maintained that "Reading is incompatible with the full play of passion and appeal," that even the most "impassioned reader is but an orator in chains."[25] B. G. Johns and William Davies, moreover, published comments echoing Canon Robinson's claim that, for "Whatever of clearness, accuracy, and order is secured by the written discourse, there is a counterbalancing loss of warmth and reality."[26] In an 1868 essay entitled "The Manufacture of Sermons," Johns argued that reading from a manuscript was more likely to produce "slumber or empty benches" than to stir a congregation to action because, in most cases, the preacher "clings to his velvet cushion with either hand, keeps his eye riveted on his book, speaks of the ecstasies of joy and fear with a voice and with a face which indicate neither, and pinions his body and soul into one attitude of limb and thought, for fear of being called theatrical and affected."[27]

Five years later, in an article published in the *Quarterly Review,* Davies argued that the reading of a sermon was almost always devoid of the "lively energy of speech and manner" on which an earnest delivery depends. Use of manuscript, he contended, was generally "lamentably defective and unsatisfactory" because the preacher's

> action in the pulpit (if he has any) is a merely artificial thing, not dictated by the inward power, but assumed as a mere matter of propri-ety—perhaps, even learnt from someone else. His intonation and mode of utterance are purely artificial. His preaching and reading tone is altogether different from his natural one, which at once re-moves what he has to say out of the close sympathy of his hearers. . . . Even the facial muscles of the preacher seem to be paralysed, as if by the aridity of his own discourse.[28]

Other theorists chose to emphasize the advantages of the ex-temporaneous address rather than the disadvantages of manu-script preaching. R. W. Dale offered a corollary to Canon Robinson's claim that manuscript preachers' emphasis on "clear-ness, accuracy, and order" often deprived their sermons of the "warmth and reality" essential to effective preaching.[29] He argued that the extemporaneous preacher ought not place too much con-cern on delivering a logically precise discourse, for "what [he] loses in accuracy, he may more than gain in ease, directness, and vigour. He will escape the formality and the 'bookishness' of manner which are the snare of most writers, and which are intolerable to all listeners; and in the generous heat which comes from direct contact with his audience, he may achieve a boldness both of thought and expression which are rarely achieved at the desk."[30]

Several of Dale's contemporaries echoed his claim that a sermon delivered extemporaneously would be more direct and vigorous than one read from a manuscript. Some focused on the extempore preacher's ability to avoid "formality and 'bookishness'." Several reviewers asserted that "direct oral preaching" is much more "natural" than reading.[31] A. Eubule Evans maintained that "the spoken sermon sounds fresher than the written"; and William Davies acknowledged that "the extempore method" is often "desir-able as more spontaneous, vivacious, and flexible" than reading.[32]

Others agreed that extemporaneous preachers were more likely to preach with "generous heat" and "boldness." Two reviewers maintained that extempore discourses were "fresher, brighter," and had "more life and vigour and power" than sermons that had been written in advance, and Islay Burns suggested that the extempore sermon was the "most effective instrument" when the "great point" is "to awake interest, sustain attention, and hold the listening multitude under the spell of the speaker's eye, and voice, and soul."[33] In short, although we do find some support for manuscript preaching in the homiletic theory of Victorian Britain, the evidence suggests that most theorists agreed with the statement, published in *Methodist Magazine* in 1815, that "The advantages supposed to proceed from the habit of hearing written discourses, in point of affecting the heart and determining the will, are abundantly better secured by hearing extemporary sermons."[34]

While there were clear—and occasionally strongly stated—differences of opinion over whether sermons should be written in advance or preached extempore, there was some common ground in the debate as well: advocates of both approaches encouraged ministers to cultivate a style that combined the advantages of reading and extemporaneous speech. Those who encouraged, or at least permitted, the use of written sermons frequently suggested that preachers should not merely read, but should instead invest their delivery with the force and passion found in the best extemporaneous addresses; as B. G. Johns put it, "there is no reason why, if well written, and well delivered," a sermon read from manuscript "should not have all the vigour and freshness of an extempore discourse."[35] William Gresley suggested that the first step in achieving this "vigour and freshness" was to adopt a method of composition that might be described as extemporaneous writing:

> when you once begin to write your sermon, you should *write it off with as little interruption as possible*. . . . Do not now pause to inquire and investigate; do not think of correcting, amending, or polishing; care not for your rules of rhetoric; but go on without rest or pause . . . until either you have finished your course, or are fairly out of breath. I should even advise you to leave blanks, rather than stop to seek for words. By this mode your sermon will have all the freshness and animation of the extemporaneous style—probably more; for you will not, when you preach it, be embarrassed for words, or nervous from fear of failure.[36]

Although Gresley was "in favour of written discourses in a parish pulpit," he believed that "no clergyman, on any account," should "*read* his sermon," but that he should "*preach* it" instead.[37]

Several of his contemporaries suggested ways in which this ideal could be achieved. Charles Abel Heurtley and H. H. M. Herbert believed that ministers who used manuscripts could move from mere reading to true preaching by mastering the art of reading "with effect."[38] In "The Preparation of Sermons for Village Congregations," Heurtley reminded his readers that if they were to "be real, natural, [and] unaffected," they must not "read a sermon as if [they] were reading an essay or a dissertation." He wrote, "We must speak to them as we should do if our sermon were merely spoken, and not written, varying our tone and manner . . . according to our matter, whether as stating certain truths, or reasoning and conducting an argument, or pressing home some weighty duty, or remonstrating or pleading with sinners."[39]

Herbert emphasized the importance of effective reading in "The Art of Preaching," an article published in 1883. He wrote that the "occasional change of key, the skilful inflexion of the voice, the varied intonations, are quite as necessary to the preacher as they are grateful to the audience," and he maintained that the "presence" of "eloquence and good reading" in the pulpit "doubles the merit of an ordinary composition."[40]

Two other theorists suggested that manuscript preachers could capture the vigor of the extemporaneous style not by reading "with effect," but by making it appear that they were not reading at all. The author of an 1887 article in the *Church Quarterly Review* maintained that if a minister "preaches a written sermon, he ought surely to take pains to know it well, and not to keep his eyes upon the manuscript, but look his people in the face."[41] Similarly, Harvey Goodwin argued that manuscript preachers should deliver their sermons in such a way as to make it "very difficult for any one in the congregation to say whether the preacher has a book before him or not."[42] In "What Constitutes a Plain Sermon?" Goodwin insisted that "a preacher ought never, in the ordinary sense of the word, to *read* his sermon; he may have, if necessary, a manuscript before him, but he ought to have so far mastered his own composition . . . that his manuscript is rather an aid to memory than a book out of which he is to read his sermon."[43] In short, many proponents of the use of written sermons believed that the coldness and artificiality of which B. G. Johns and William Davies complained was not an inevitable aspect of manuscript preaching; that it was possible and desirable to deliver "a written sermon . . . as if it were unwritten"; and that a minister "who is master of this art need not fear a comparison with the best of extemporary preachers."[44]

Just as several theorists argued that the best manuscript preachers were those whose delivery captured the liveliness and energy of extempore speech, many others believed that extemporaneous preachers could benefit from the study, preparation, and intellectual discipline practiced by their colleagues who wrote their sermons. Although proponents of the extempore method believed that preachers should not read their manuscripts in the pulpit, they did not condone the practice of preaching impromptu. C. H. Spurgeon, for example, maintained that preaching without previous study was as unacceptable as reading, and the author of an 1872 article in the *London Quarterly Review* condemned "the utterance, on the spur of the moment, of the thoughts which then and there arise" as an "abuse of the extemporising practice."[45]

Some homileticians attempted to end this "abuse" by stipulating new definitions of extemporaneous preaching that emphasized the importance of advance study and preparation. One reviewer asserted that "Perfect extemporisation is the art of clothing in acceptable words the thoughts which have been studied in their order and connection"; H. Rogers advocated extemporaneous preaching "with regard to the *expression*," insisting that "the bulk of the thoughts ought never to be extemporaneous"; and C. H. Spurgeon defined the practice as "the preparation of the sermon so far as thoughts go, and leaving the words to be found during delivery."[46]

A number of theorists, moreover, believed that writing sermons was one of the ways preachers could best frame and organize their thoughts; as one reviewer wrote in 1872, "The study of improvisation ought not . . . to be carried on in such a manner as to wean the preacher from the habit of carefully writing his sermons."[47] C. H. Spurgeon "Very strongly" warned his ministerial students "against reading," but he also believed that writing could be a "healthful exercise."[48] John Henry Newman made a similar claim in "University Preaching," one of the lectures that comprise *The Idea of a University.* He maintained that writing was a safeguard against "venturing upon really *extempore* matter." The "more ardent a man is," he wrote, "so much the more will he need self-control and sustained recollection. . . . His very gifts may need the counterpoise of more ordinary and homely accessories, such as the drudgery of composition."[49] In his *Nine Lectures on Preaching,* R.W. Dale suggested that writing could help produce not only greater intellectual discipline, but a more refined pulpit style as well, arguing that an extemporaneous preacher could achieve "the perfect beauty which comes from perfect simplicity" if he "writes carefully, though without any intention of recalling, when he is in the pulpit, the precise language in his manuscript."[50] Finally, one of the most extensive arguments that good extemporaneous preaching was often the result of extensive writing was offered by J. H. Rigg, one of the Victorian period's most outspoken advocates of the extemporaneous address. In "On Preaching," Rigg wrote,

> We assume that the speaker is also a writer; that in the study he is habitually careful and exact, if not fastidious, in the style of all that the writes; that he is also inured to habits of reflection, to the logical arrangement of his subject in his mind before speaking; to the provision and use of illustrations, to all that belongs to complete premeditation. Such a speaker will often far excel in his extemporaneous utterances anything that he could have prepared on the subject at his desk.[51]

The juxtaposition of orality and literacy in Victorian preaching did not end when preachers completed their manuscripts or notes, or even when they finished their sermons and stepped down from their pulpits. The intertwining of the spoken and the written appears not only in the ways in which preachers were expected to plan and deliver their addresses, but also in the roles that preaching, and conversations about preaching, played in Victorian society. Sermons were an important part of both the oral and print cultures of nineteenth-century Britain; they were published as well as preached, and both spoken and written discourses were frequently discussed in the press. This public status of the sermon is the focus of the next chapter.

3

Preaching and Sermon Publishing

ALTHOUGH FEW SCHOLARS HAVE PUBLISHED EXTENSIVE STUDIES of the Victorian sermon, several have offered brief assessments of the subject. Some touch on the importance the Victorians placed on preaching. Eric Mackerness, for example, writes of the "seriousness" with which "cultured people of the Victorian age" regarded sermons, while Horton Davies and Lewis Drummond have characterized the Victorians as a "nation of 'sermon tasters',", people for whom church attendance was an intellectual and aesthetic "delight" as well as a religious "duty."[1]

Others argue that the sermon should have a prominent place in present-day scholarship. Just as Walter Arnstein faults "some historians" for neglecting the religious aspects of Victorian Britain, Desmond Bowen has argued that it "would be unwise for any historian to underestimate the power and influence of the Victorian pulpit."[2] Finally, still others use sweeping statements and a language of superlatives to place the pulpit in what they believe to be its proper historical context. Amy Cruse and Edwin Dargan, for example, maintain that the Victorian age was "the age of the preacher" and that "the nineteenth century English pulpit occupies an exalted rank in the annals of Christian preaching."[3] One of the strongest accolades was offered by George Kitson Clark in 1962. "It might not be too extravagant," he writes, "to say of the nineteenth century that probably in no other century, except the seventeenth and perhaps the twelfth, did the claims of religion occupy so large a part in the nation's life, or did men speaking in the name of religion contrive to exercise so much power."[4]

The rhetoric is different, but the idea is the same: Davies, Drummond, Cruse, and Dargan all believe that sermons—whether oratorical or literary, whether read from manuscripts or preached extempore—made significant contributions to nineteenth-century intellectual and religious life. These contributions were made, moreover, not only by sermons delivered from

43

the pulpit, but also by those distributed through the press. It is in this dual public function—the sermon as oration and the sermon as essay—that we find the third major confluence of oral and written traditions in Victorian preaching.

Victorian sermon-tasting began on Sunday mornings; weekly services were the most prominent aspect of Anglican and Dissenting religious observance, and the sermon was in turn the focal point of these services. In the Established Church, the sermon was regarded as the most effective method of religious instruction; as J. G. Wenham wrote in 1854, the Anglican communion "enjoins on its members that, as the necessary part of a Christian education, 'they shall chiefly be called upon to hear sermons'."[5] Preaching consequently became the "most conspicuous feature in the priest's work," and the sermon "assumed a significance slightly out of proportion to the rest of the full service."[6] At times, the emphasis on preaching became so strong that many candidates for Anglican ordination had to be reminded that "prayer is an equally important item of religious observance, and must not be neglected in favour of the sermon itself."[7]

The central place of the sermon in Anglican worship was reflected in Dissenting observances as well. "Dissenters go to chapel chiefly to hear sermons," Charles Kingsley wrote; and Nonconformists' insistence on preaching was such that a sermon came to be "regarded as *de rigueur* in all Evangelical services—even a prayer-meeting being considered a somewhat flat affair without an address."[8] It does not seem excessive, therefore, to suggest that the sermon was the raison d'etre of many Dissenting churches; as J. Baldwin Brown wrote in 1877, "it is distinctly by the power of the preacher that [Evangelical] congregations are gathered and sustained."[9]

Preaching, then, was the duty of every minister, but, for many, it was also an art form. Those who excelled at their craft attracted large and loyal congregations. In 1884, the editors of *Contemporary Pulpit* asked readers to send in lists of the "greatest living English-speaking Protestant preachers." Three hundred and fifty ballots were returned, and the results were printed in *Contemporary Pulpit* and the October 4 issue of *The Spectator*. Henry Parry Liddon, Canon of St. Paul's, London, received the most votes, followed by C. H. Spurgeon; Joseph Parker of London's City Temple; Alexander Maclaren of Manchester's Union Chapel; and Frederic William Farrar, Canon of Westminster and rector of St. Margaret's Church. Henry Ward Beecher, the only American clergyman recognized, took sixth place. The list of the ten best preachers was rounded out by William Magee, Bishop of Peterborough; William J. Knox-Little, who succeeded Liddon at St. Paul's; William Boyd Carpenter, Canon of Windsor; and R. W. Dale, pastor of the Dissenting Carr's Lane church of Birmingham.[10]

Many clergymen who did not appear in the *Contemporary Pulpit's* "Top Ten" list were recognized in other Victorian articles and in twentieth-century histories of preaching. Noteworthy preachers of the Scottish Establishment included Norman Macleod, the "enormously popular" pastor of Glasgow's Barony Church; Andrew W. Williamson, who earned renown as the pastor of North Leith and St. Cuthbert's, two of the "most important pulpits" in the Edinburgh vicinity; and Thomas Guthrie, whose pulpit ministry "surpassed that of any man in Scotland."[11]

Pulpits of many Free churches in Scotland were occupied by prominent pulpiteers. Among the distinguished names in Scottish Dissenting preaching were Thomas Chalmers, who preached "remarkable sermons to congregations that filled his church to overflowing three times a week"; Gustavus Aird, who drew audiences "from throughout the Highlands"; John Kennedy, the "Spurgeon of the Highlands" and longtime pastor of the Free church at Dingwall; and Alexander Whyte, whose church in Edinburgh was always crowded "to the very pulpit steps."[12]

Many Anglican and Dissenting preachers throughout England shared the popularity enjoyed by their Scottish counterparts. "Multitudes flocked to hear" E. B. Pusey at Oxford's Christ Church, and the parish church at Leeds, Yorkshire, grew from 50 to 4,000 members under the powerful oratory of Walter F. Hook.[13] Two of the most eminent nonconforming preachers were James Parsons, "a man of rare powers in the pulpit," and Hugh S. Brown, a Baptist preacher who "attracted large numbers of working people" to the Myrtle Street Baptist Church in Liverpool.[14]

Many of the greatest preachers occupied pulpits in London; as one observer wrote, "There is no city in the world which offers such a large choice of good preachers."[15] At various times throughout the nineteenth century, Anglican churches in London featured such pulpiteers as Frederick Denison Maurice, who drew "a host of earnest and thoughtful young men" to his services at Lincoln's Inn, and Henry Melvill, the "Demosthenes of the London pulpit," who was admired by William Gladstone, John Ruskin, and Robert Browning.[16] London's Nonconforming churchgoers could sit under the preaching of equally accomplished and popular men such as Thomas Binney, "the greatest Congregational preacher of the period"; John Cumming, the "popular" and "sensational" pastor of the National Scottish Church in Covent Garden; and F. B. Meyer, the Baptist pastor of Christ Church, "one of the most noted Nonconformist chapels" in south London.[17]

Many Victorians' interest in preaching was not confined to the one, two, or even three services they attended each Sunday;[18] their "sermon-tasting" also involved purchasing printed discourses and reading them during the week. Pulpiteers throughout the British Isles routinely published their addresses in religious magazines, in periodicals devoted exclusively to sermons, and in book-length collections; one Victorian observer noted that "Some of the most distinguished preachers of the day appear again through the press almost before they have left the pulpit."[19] This practice produced an enormous body of work. In 1866, Louisa Merivale noted that "library shelves and our publishers' circulars" were teeming with collections of sermons; at the end of the century, Sir Edward Fry estimated that English Anglicans alone were publishing over a million sermons each year.[20]

Richard Reis, a recent biographer of George MacDonald, argues that this widespread publishing took place despite the lack of a reading audience, that few Victorians wanted to "read sermons or to concentrate on their philosophical content."[21] The contemporaneous evidence suggests otherwise.[22] One observer alluded to the popularity of printed sermons when he wrote, "Independently of elementary works, the two most remarkable departments of modern literature . . . are novels and sermons."[23] A statement in Islay Burns's 1863 article in the *North British Review*, moreover, directly contradicts Reis's claim. Burns wrote that sermons did not "remain a drug in the market," but were "greedily bought up and read," and he gave a good illustration of the popularity of the printed sermon in Scotland:

> Of the popular productions of the day, among the most popular have been the published sermons of our chief divines. Guthrie's sermons have sold as fast, and run through as many thousands, as Macaulay's history; a single sermon of Caird's, in the course of a few weeks, became known and read in every corner of the kingdom; the sermons of Dr Hanna have passed through five editions in the course of as many months; Arnot's "Lectures on the Proverbs" are already in their 17th thousand; and the "Graver Thoughts of a Country Parson" are winning their way with equal rapidity, not because they are sermons disguised, but because they are sermons of a high class. So much for Scotland alone, hitherto deemed by many . . . the very Sahara of theological and homiletic literature.[24]

The popularity Burns describes was apparent throughout Victorian England as well. Alexander Maclaren, pastor of Union Temple in Manchester from 1858 to 1910, published his sermons each week in *The Freeman,* which "doubled its subscription list" as a result, and his series entitled *Sermons Preached in Manchester* was "a boon and a blessing to ever widening circles of readers."[25] While Maclaren's work in Manchester was prospering, J. B. Mozley, canon of Christ Church, Oxford, "reached and influenced a wide circle of readers" with *Sermons Preached Before the University of Oxford* (1876) and *Sermons Parochial and Occasional* (1879).[26]

Two of the most notable figures in Victorian sermon publishing were John Henry Newman and Charles Haddon Spurgeon. In 1868, twenty-five years after he resigned his position at St. Mary's Church, Newman set a precedent in sermon publishing with a new edition of his *Parochial and Plain Sermons:* never before had continued popular demand led to republication of a series of pulpit addresses thirty years after they had first appeared in print.[27]

Spurgeon's achievements in the press were even more remarkable. Regular weekly publication of his sermons began in January 1855;[28] by the time of his death in 1892, Spurgeon had become the center of a sermon-publishing empire. A total of 2,241 sermons was published and, if Lewis Drummond is correct in fixing the average weekly circulation at 25,000 copies, Spurgeon sold approximately 56,025,000 copies of his sermons during his forty-year preaching career.[29] Charles Ray, one of his early biographers, summed up the impact of Spurgeon's published sermons when he wrote, "There has never been anything like it in the history of printing. The Scriptures have circulated enormously, but nothing to compare with Spurgeon's sermons, and it is pretty safe to say there never will be another publication that can be called a rival."[30]

The significance of the sermon in Victorian society is illustrated not only in churchgoing and sermon-reading habits, but also in the large number of articles about the pulpit published in religious and secular periodicals. In addition to discussing whether sermons should be read from manuscripts or preached extempore, many theorists engaged in a vigorous debate over the "efficiency" of the spoken sermon. Indictments of preaching appeared as early as 1840, when H. Rogers published an article in the *Edinburgh Review* criticizing the "inefficiency" and "mediocrity" that "so generally distinguishes pulpit discourses."[31] Statements such as these appeared throughout the century; representative commentary includes David Masson's 1844 assertion that "the Pulpit is out of gear with the age"; William Hanna's 1856 claim that the sermon "has sunk from a first into a second-rate power in the State"; and a lament, published in the *Saturday Review* in 1895, that it would be "idle to pretend that in any large percentage of cases our sermons are good, or are even up to such a standard of goodness as we have a reasonable right to expect."[32]

This "chronic recalcitration against the sermon" was often accompanied by analyses of the reasons behind the apparent "collapse" of British preaching.[33] Many attributed the decline to the monotony of pulpit discourses; as the author of an 1869 article in *Fraser's Magazine* put it, "The first and most natural charge against sermons is their dulness."[34] This "charge" was echoed in a number of late-nineteenth-century articles: in 1863, Canon Robinson maintained that "the vague, discursive, unsystematic character" of many sermons is the primary reason why they "do not produce the effect they should."[35] B. G. Johns indicted dull preaching even more strongly in his 1892 article in *Nineteenth Century:* "the preaching of the English clergy," he wrote, "is not efficient. It may be loud, fluent, unctuous, learned, and larded with scriptural texts; but, too often, it is wearisome and soporific, and therefore a failure."[36] The monotony of preaching had apparently become so severe that the word *sermon* had become synonymous with "dull." The anonymous author of an 1857 *Fraser's Magazine* article wrote that "The very word *sermon* . . . has become a byword for long, dull conversation of any kind. When a man wishes to imply in any piece of writing the absence of what is agreeable and inviting, he calls it a sermon."[37]

Victorian critics argued that the monotony that plagued a good deal of pulpit oratory could be traced to two primary factors. The first of these was the clergy's lack of education and preparation for their task. In 1840, H. Rogers argued that "the inefficiency that so generally distinguishes pulpit discourses, is in a great degree owing to the two following causes: first, that preachers do not sufficiently cultivate . . . a systematic acquaintance with the principles upon which all effective eloquence must be founded . . . and secondly, that they do not . . . give sufficient time or labour to the preparation of their discourses."[38] This claim was made somewhat more concisely in 1874 by William Davies, who contended that the inefficiency of preaching was due to "the inadequacy of the education preparatory for the pulpit" and "an imperfect recognition of the requirements of the pastoral office."[39] It was echoed again in 1892 by B. G. Johns, who stated that the "one main cause of failure" in English preaching was that the clergy "have had, before taking Orders, little training in the choice of fit topics, and none at all in the writing of sermons."[40]

The second factor was that, in addition to being poorly trained in the art of sermon preparation, many Victorian preachers were hampered in their efforts by an excessively heavy workload. Each minister was expected to produce an "unintermittent stream" of sermons—at least two per week for every week of the year; the "severe tax" that this expectation placed on most of the clergy was expressed well in an 1869 article in *Fraser's Magazine:* "what can be more absurd or unreasonable than to expect each and every of 18,000 men of average ability and education and with no special training either in oratory or composition, to write year after year two sermons a week and a few over, even if they had nothing else to do, or to preach them decently when written?"[41]

Finally, dull preaching was often a consequence of the means many preachers employed of overcoming their own lack of time and lack of skill. Some clergymen attempted to remedy their shortcomings in the pulpit by participating in the "traffic in sermons"— reading discourses written by someone else. A "regular and well-organised trade in sermons" was in place by the middle of the nineteenth century.[42] The price of individually purchased sermons ranged from sixpence for an everyday sermon to "two guineas for the rarest vintages;" a minister who wanted to build a library of prepared discourses could "be supplied with a whole year's sermons at the cost of 26s. per quarter, or £5 4s. per annum."[43]

Many preachers and critics believed that this practice exacerbated the problem of poor preaching rather than ameliorating it. The author of an 1857 article in *Fraser's Magazine* argued that, because "No words can ever flow from a man's lips so aptly, so wisely, so effectively, as *his own*," the preaching of prepared sermons inevitably led to "dryness and dulness in the preacher, and, as matter of course, drowsy indifference and listlessness on the part of the hearer."[44] B. G. Johns echoed this conviction thirty-five years later when he wrote that the majority of ready-made sermons were little more than "'dull, dry, dreary, commonplace' platitudes of seeming wisdom" and asked, "Who can smite heartily with a sword that he has never proved? or ever rise to a noble passion when wrapped in the stolen mantle of another?"[45] H. Rogers offered the strongest indictment of the traffic in sermons when he wrote, "we deny *in toto* that a borrowed discourse, whatever its merit, can be so impressive as one, even though intrinsically inferior, which has been made [a preacher's] own by conscientious study."[46]

Although they believed that the office of preaching in Victorian Britain was severely flawed, none of these critics suggested that the problems were so severe as to justify the elimination of the spoken sermon. They were "anxious, not that the sermon should be abolished, but that it should become more popular," and they devoted their articles to making "such remarks and suggestions as may lead to its greater efficiency."[47]

The most radical solution proposed involved separating worship and preaching into two separate activities. The author of an 1886 article in *Eclectic Magazine* saw "no obvious reason why all worshippers should be compelled . . . to hear a sermon," and Louisa Merivale suggested that more churches adopt the practice "of interposing a pause between the prayers and sermon, so as to permit the withdrawal of those whose attention to the service is already fatigued, or who flinch from the possible dreariness or objectionable doctrine of the next half hour."[48]

Other critics suggested ways of making the sermon more palatable to those who regarded "an hour or half an hour's tedious listening" as "the necessary penalty which they must pay for the privilege of worshipping God with their fellows, and remaining devout members of their mother-church."[49] Several argued that higher standards should be enforced for those desiring to enter the preaching ministry; the author of a *Fraser's Magazine* article, for example, asked, "A man with one leg cannot enter the navy;— why send one who can neither write nor speak into a profession for which writing and speaking are essential qualifications?"[50]

Others suggested that sermons would be much more effective if they were shorter and employed a wider variety of homiletical techniques. Although the sermons of earlier divines were often more than an hour in length, many Victorian congregations grew impatient if their ministers spoke for more than thirty minutes;[51] many critics maintained that "A short exposition, strongly felt and well studied . . . might have all the usefulness and efficacy of a longer treatment and more elaborately constructed discourse."[52] William Hanna argued that, in addition to being more concise, the clergy should be permitted to exercise a "larger 'liberty of prophesying'." Instead of being restricted to working "within that one model of orderly and well-nigh exclusively doctrinal discourse," preachers should deliver a variety of sermons: doctrinal, historical, biographical, allegorical. By addressing their congregations in the same variety of voices God used to address men and women, Hanna maintained, the clergy could once again "turn the pulpit into a many-sided instrument of power."[53]

Finally, it is interesting (and somewhat ironic) to note that the traffic in sermons, the enterprise many condemned as a leading cause of dull preaching, was also the very activity several critics recommended as a solution to the problem. The use of other preachers' texts had historical precedent—St. Augustine "advised those who were unable to compose their own sermons, to take those of others, to commit them to memory, and so to rehearse them to the congregation"—and several critics advocated a return to the "re-preaching of old and approved discourses."[54]

B. G. Johns held that this "re-preaching" should consist only of the borrowing of ideas, not the verbatim reproduction of form. He suggested that a preacher who lacked either the time or the ability to write his own sermons should base his work on existing models: "Let him take some short, pointed, practical sermon by a well-known standard writer, read it carefully, digest, and rewrite it in his own words."[55] Others, such as Canon Robinson, argued that a preacher could be justified in reading a sermon just as it had been printed: "if preachers will eschew all surreptitiousness in the matter," Robinson wrote, "and do the thing openly and avowedly, it is perhaps . . . the very best thing that some of them can do."[56]

While some critics sought to determine the causes of the decline of preaching and offered ways in which the pulpit might be redeemed, others challenged the notion that British preaching was even in a state of crisis. Islay Burns, for example, contended that there was "a manifest haste and recklessness of assertion" in many of the published claims that the institution of preaching was on the decline. He cited such factors as "crowded churches, doors besieged long before the time of service, open air preachings . . . and thronging audiences in theatres and cathedral naves" as evidence that the power of the spoken sermon had not vanished.[57]

Burns was far from alone in affirming the power of the Victorian pulpit. A number of observers believed that the pulpit was in a state of improvement rather than a condition of decay, and they were quick to come to the defense of what they believed to be a noble and important institution. Some of the positive commentary took the form of praise for individual preachers. The author of an 1869 article in *Fraser's Magazine,* for example, cited the sermons of such men as Robert Hall, Henry Melvill, and John Henry Newman as evidence that "the preaching of the present day is in no way inferior . . . to that of any former age."[58] Margaret Oliphant added a name to this list when she contended that F. W. Robertson's ability to "[keep] the popular ear and [secure] the general attention" was "unquestionable proof that the office of the preacher has in no way lost its hold upon the mind of the people."[59]

Other "allies of the pulpit" expressed their confidence about the institution of preaching in general.[60] In 1857, J. H. Rigg suggested that "perhaps a larger amount of knowledge, intellectual enjoyment, and other elements of sound education, are imparted to a vast proportion of the community by [preaching] than by all the other means put together."[61] John Dowden echoed Rigg's opinion twenty-five years later, contending that the pulpit "is still . . . a moral and religious power of an efficiency much more considerable in degree than is commonly supposed."[62]

In addition to insisting on the vitality of the preaching of their own day, critics writing throughout the nineteenth century predicted that the pulpit would continue to be an important force in British society. In 1844, before most of the indictments of preaching appeared in the press, David Masson maintained that, "as a mechanism for producing social effects . . . the Pulpit must last for ever."[63] Thirty years later, when skepticism about pulpit efficiency was in full force, William Davies argued, "It does not follow from the imperfect fulfilment of the office of preaching that it is a vain or useless one. We believe the time will come when the pulpit will be again the means of disseminating truth."[64] Finally, two articles published in 1883 showed that faith in the future of preaching was present even in late-Victorian Britain. H. H. M. Herbert wrote, "there is no sign that the modern world, any more than earlier and ruder ages, can dispense with the art of the preacher," and an article in the *Saturday Review* asserted that the "preaching of Christianity has not lost its power on society, and we see no signs that it is about to lose it."[65]

Discussions of the power, influence, and relevance of weekly public preaching were often complemented by reviews of sermon collections. In many cases, sectarian periodicals reviewed volumes published by members of their own parties. The High Anglican *Church Quarterly Review* reviewed sermons by Edward Bouverie Pusey, John Keble, Richard W. Church, and John Henry Newman; and the Catholic *Dublin Review* reviewed Newman's Catholic addresses and Henry Edward Manning's *The Grounds of Faith.*

In other cases, religious periodicals reviewed sermons published by preachers from other traditions. The Broad Church *Contemporary Review* reviewed Newman's *Parochial and Plain Sermons;* the Methodist *London Quarterly Review* examined *Unspoken Sermons,* a volume by the Universalist preacher George MacDonald;

the *Church Quarterly Review* considered sermons by Broad Churchmen Frederic William Farrar and Frederick William Robertson; and the Methodist *London Quarterly* reviewed *Sermons, Doctrinal and Practical,* a volume by the Anglican pulpiteer William Archer Butler.

Finally, volumes of sermons were frequently reviewed in independent religious journals and in the secular press. The *North British Review,* a nonsectarian religious periodical, reviewed the sermons of the Scots Presbyterian minister Thomas Guthrie, and of Anglican clergymen Arthur Penrhyn Stanley and William Archer Butler. Reviews in the secular press include assessments of T. Waite in *Monthly Review,* Spurgeon in *Fraser's Magazine,* Augustus William Hare in the *Edinburgh Review,* John Henry Newman in *Saturday Review,* and George MacDonald in *The Spectator.*

Unlike many of the articles concerned with spoken sermons, the reviews of published discourses were almost universally favorable.[66] In 1827, for example, an anonymous critic hailed T. Waite's *Sermons, Explanatory and Practical* as "an admirable example of the mode in which theology may be written, so as to interest and instruct the educated, without puzzling or fatiguing the ignorant."[67] Representative assessments of the 1840s include H. Rogers' assertion that Hare's *Sermons to a Country Congregation* were "in point of *diction,* perfect models of what discourses ought to be," and the judgment that Newman's *Sermons, Bearing on Subjects of the Day* were great literature as well as sound theology because they were "Brief and pointed, without studied sententiousness; pathetic, without whining; close, without obscurity; varied, without vagueness; suggestive, but never obscure."[68]

Publication of positive reviews continued throughout Victoria's reign. In 1855 and 1857, Spurgeon published the first volume of *The New Park Street Pulpit* and a second series of *Sermons of the Rev. C. H. Spurgeon,* collections which G. N. Hervey praised for their frankness, clarity, poetry, and pathos.[69] A few years later, R. W. Church ranked Newman's *Parochial and Plain Sermons* among "the very finest examples of what the English language of our day had done in the hands of a master."[70] William Hanna praised the work of three giants of the Scottish pulpit. He placed Guthrie's *The Gospel in Ezekiel* "among the enduring monuments of Scottish genius and piety"; asserted that Stanley's *Sermons and Essays on the Apostolic Age* gave "greater instruction and delight" than the work of any other preacher; and wrote that the scholarly and poetic addresses in Butler's *Sermons, Doctrinal and Practical* exhibited a "rare combination of excellencies; imagery almost as rich as Taylor's; oratory as vigorous often as South's; judgment as sound as Barrow's; a style as attractive but more copious, original, and forcible than Atterbury's; piety as elevated as Howe's, and a fervour as intense as times as Baxter's."[71] Finally, in 1885, a critic writing for *The Spectator* maintained that, while the second volume of MacDonald's *Unspoken Sermons* was not "quite equal to its predecessor," it was nonetheless to be commended for its "new power and freshness," its "profound and searching" exposition, and its "penetrating veracity of . . . spiritual insight."[72]

We find several significant intersections of orality and literacy in the Victorians' practice of hearing, reading, and writing about sermons. The interplay of the written and the spoken first appears in the published conversations about preaching. Whereas Margaret Oliphant, B. G. Johns, and William Davies used the press to question the status of the oral sermon, even to herald its demise, other critics, such as Islay Burns, J. H. Rigg, and H. H. M. Herbert published articles in support of pulpit oratory, thus defending the oral tradition through the medium of the printed word. In at least one instance, a critic used a review of published sermons to protest the "chronic recalcitration" against spoken homilies. In 1892, the author of an article in the *Church Quarterly Review* asserted that the quality of published sermons continued to speak against the "common complaint about the degeneracy of the pulpit." The reviewer examined eight volumes of sermons by such notable preachers as F. W. Farrar, R. W. Church, and T. G. Bonney and concluded that none of the sermons under consideration showed "any traces of degeneracy, either in intellectual power or in moral earnestness." One of these volumes, Dean Randall's *Life in the Catholic Church*, was singled out for special mention: it was, in the eyes of the reviewer, it was the collection that best "bears out the theory that good preaching is not a thing of the past."[73]

Juxtapositions of orality and literacy are evident not only in discussions of sermons, but also in the preaching and publishing of the sermons themselves. First, the sermon-publishing industry could not have existed without a well-established system of public preaching. While sermons advertised for sale to ministers were often written by laymen—"by schoolmasters out of employment, and literary gentlemen who have failed in everything else"[74]— those sold to the public had first been prepared in the studies and delivered from the pulpits of Anglican and Dissenting clergymen.

These publications, in turn, often helped sustain the spoken sermon. In some cases, a congregation's existence depended on the availability of published sermons. Ernest W. Bacon, for example, tells us that each Sunday, a layman in a pastorless church on the island of Erraid, off the western coast of Scotland, would read one of Spurgeon's sermons to his fellow worshipers.[75] More often, however, the publication of sermons increased attendance at the minister's own church. As his discourses circulated and his reputation grew, a minister not only drew large crowds from among his own townspeople, he also came to be viewed as something of a celebrity throughout Great Britain and his services regarded as essential components of any tourist's or businessman's itinerary.[76]

Although the circulation of sermons was almost always advantageous to prominent clergymen, publication worked both for and against preachers of less renown. Publication sometimes enabled less able or lesser-known preachers to gain a reputation they could not secure in the pulpit. F. R. Webber tells us that John Keble's "reputation rests upon his printed sermons rather than those delivered from the pulpit."[77] Similarly, some regarded Frederick W. Robertson as "feeble," "sad," and "embittered" throughout most of his tenure at Brighton's Trinity Chapel, but the five volumes of sermons published shortly after his death in 1853 made him "a household name in England."[78] These same preachers, however, could see their congregations shrink when other, more proficient ministers went to press. As churchgoers became better able to read the sermons of preachers whose services they could not attend, they sometimes became dissatisfied with the addresses delivered by their own pastors. A. Eubule Evans noted that, by 1887, many believed that "every one who desires it" could "get a better sermon at home than in his parish church."[79] Thus, the proliferation of print brought about an ironic development in the status of preaching—it placed the sermon in the awkward position of competing against itself as some Victorians came to prefer a printed discourse to a spoken one.

In addition to identifying theories and techniques that helped shape pulpit discourse throughout Victorian Britain, the ideas discussed thus far also provide a means of examining orality-literacy intersections in the work of individual pulpiteers. By examining homiletic theories and rhetorical strategies, methods of preparation and delivery, and popularity in the pulpit and the press, we can draw some conclusions about preachers' places on what Deborah Tannen has called the orality-literacy continuum.[80] In my introduction, I identify ministers who occupy representative positions on this spectrum: Charles Haddon Spurgeon, whose theory and practice is grounded in the oral tradition; John Henry

Newman, whose force of character and skill as a writer exhibit the best of both orality and literacy; and George MacDonald, whose practice of publishing sermons he never preached places him largely outside oral practice and almost entirely within the literate tradition. It is to the work of these three ministers that we now turn.

4

Charles Haddon Spurgeon

IN THE SUMMER OF 1844, RICHARD KNILL, A REPRESENTATIVE OF the London Missionary Society, paid a visit to James Spurgeon, pastor of the Stambourne Independent Chapel. Spurgeon's ten-year-old grandson, Charles Haddon Spurgeon, was living at the Stambourne parsonage at the time, and Knill spent many hours talking with the boy about the gospel and the missionary life. At the end of his three-day visit, Knill made an announcement during the Spurgeons' morning prayers: taking Charles on his knee, he said, "This child will one day preach the gospel, and he will preach it to great multitudes. I am persuaded that he will preach in the chapel of Rowland Hill, where . . . I am now the minister" (*Autobiography,* 1:27).[1] Knill's prophecy was fulfilled within ten years, and Charles Haddon Spurgeon quickly rose to a position of prominence among British Baptist preachers.

Spurgeon's ministerial career began in January 1852, when, at the age of seventeen, he accepted the pastorate of the Baptist chapel in Waterbeach, a small town a few miles north of Cambridge.[2] Fewer than twelve people attended his first service, but within two years, more than four hundred crowded into the small chapel each Sunday. The eloquence of the "boy preacher" quickly became known throughout southern England, and in November 1853, Spurgeon received an invitation to preach at New Park Street Baptist Church, the largest Baptist church in London. He preached there in December of that year, and was the only visiting preacher ever invited to return. After he preached three sermons in January 1854, the congregation extended a call to a six-month trial pastorate, and in April he agreed to a "permanent settlement" there.[3]

Spurgeon filled the pews of New Park Street as rapidly as he had at Waterbeach. The church, which could accommodate approximately twelve hundred worshipers, was only about one-sixth full when Spurgeon began his tenure there (*Autobiography,*

1:263), but after a few months it could not hold all the people who came to hear him preach.[4] Apparently troubled by the number of people being turned away each week, Spurgeon surprised his congregation with an announcement of a new building program: during one Sunday night service, he exclaimed, "By faith, the walls of Jericho fell down, and by faith, this wall at the back shall come down, too" (*Autobiography,* 1:271).

While New Park Street was being remodeled, Sunday services were held at Exeter Hall, a public auditorium in Strand Street. The hall had a capacity of about five thousand, and it was full "from the very first service."[5] Renovations to New Park Street were complete in May 1855, but the chapel was still too small,[6] and in June 1856, Sunday evening services were again moved to Exeter Hall.[7] This arrangement, however, could not last; it was inconvenient for the church to meet in two locations, and the owners of the Hall were unwilling to allow any one denomination to have exclusive long-term use of the facilities. A committee was therefore appointed to oversee the fund-raising and construction of the Metropolitan Tabernacle, a five thousand-seat auditorium to be built in the Newington Butts region of south London, a site where a number of Puritan preachers had been martyred.[8]

While the Tabernacle was being built, the New Park Street congregation held afternoon services in the Music Hall at Royal Surrey Gardens, a newly constructed concert hall whose splendor was surpassed only by the Crystal Palace.[9] The Music Hall could hold up to ten thousand people, and was filled to capacity from the first service in November 1856 to the last in December 1859.[10] After spending a year in a third series of meetings in Exeter Hall, Spurgeon's congregation moved to the Tabernacle, dedicating it on March 18, 1861 (*Autobiography,* 2:35, 40). For the next thirty years—he preached his last sermon in the Tabernacle on June 7, 1891[11]—Spurgeon preached to congregations numbering more than five thousand at both morning and evening services.

In a letter to his Uncle James in March 1854—just before he accepted the permanent pastorate of New Park Street—Spurgeon wrote, "You have heard that I am now a Londoner, and a little bit of a celebrity."[12] This would prove to be something of an understatement, for Spurgeon's ability to draw such crowds week after week made him one of the foremost tourist attractions in London. For many English men and women, no trip to London was "complete without a visit to the great religious theater . . . where Mr. Spurgeon so completely filled the stage," and most American tourists came to England with "two desires; one to visit Shakespeare's tomb ... and the other to listen to Spurgeon."[13] The American clergyman A. P. Peabody noted that upon their return, visitors were often asked two questions: "'Did you see the Queen?' and next, 'Did you hear Spurgeon?'"[14]

In addition to preaching to thousands of people in Exeter Hall, the Music Hall, and the Metropolitan Tabernacle, Spurgeon preached to thousands more through his published sermons. One of Spurgeon's favorite Puritans wrote that "Books may speak when the author cannot, and what is more, when he is not" (*Autobiography*, 2:416). Spurgeon himself was well aware of the power of the printed word; in a sermon delivered in the Metropolitan Tabernacle, he said, "he who writes addresses a larger audience than the man who merely uses his tongue. It is a happy thing when the tongue is aided by the pen of a ready writer, and so gets a wider sphere, and a more permanent influence than if it merely uttered certain sounds, and the words died away when the ear had heard them" (*Autobiography*, 2:142).

Spurgeon gained this "wider sphere" by publishing one of his sermons every week. A member of his congregation recorded his sermons in shorthand, and Spurgeon's first task every Monday morning was to revise the proofs for publication on Thursday.[15] Although many Victorians believed that the "style that suits the pulpit is not the style that suits the press," transcription and publication did not decrease the popularity of Spurgeon's sermons. As the author of an 1887 article in the *Country Quarterly* put it, "Mr. Spurgeon's sermons lose less of power in the process of change from the word *spoken* to the word *written* than those of any other preacher."[16]

The "larger audience" Spurgeon gained by publishing his sermons encompassed not only the British Isles, where millions of copies were sold, but many countries around the world. The United States was the second-largest market for his work: an unauthorized attempt to transmit his sermons by telegraph for publication in the Monday newspapers was soon abandoned, but the American edition of his collected discourses sold "not less than 500,000 volumes" (*Autobiography*, 2:360, 362). The sermons were also widely circulated in Australia and translated into nearly 40 languages including French, German, Dutch, Swedish, Italian, Arabic, Bengali, Gaelic, Syriac, Urdu, and Welsh.[17]

Spurgeon's published sermons received considerable critical acclaim. One reviewer wrote that his weekly publications "are remarkable additions to ecclesiastical literature."[18] W. Robertson Nicoll believed that Spurgeon's sermons "will continue to be studied with growing interest and wonder; that they will ultimately be accepted as incomparably the greatest contribution to the literature of experimental Christianity that has been made in this century, and that their message will go on transforming and quickening lives after all other sermons of the period are forgotten" (*Autobiography*, 2:350).

Spurgeon's death on January 31, 1892 had a profound effect on British Christendom. More than one hundred thousand mourners filed by his casket during the three days that his body lay in state in the Tabernacle, and twelve thousand people gathered at the entrance of Upper Norwood Cemetery on February 11 to watch his funeral procession pass by.[19] On March 4, the Tabernacle adopted a memorial resolution, which read in part:

> We feel that the decease of our dear Pastor has deprived us of a father in Israel, the like of whom has never been given to any people. . . . With bleeding hearts, we thus record the loss we have sustained, as we feel we shall hear his melodious voice no more in the ministry of the truth; but we bless God that our dearly-loved one was given to us, and honoured amongst us so long.[20]

This sentiment was echoed in numerous published eulogies. Obituaries in *The Freeman* and *The Baptist* lamented that "A Prince has fallen in Israel" and that "One of England's bravest, noblest, holiest hearts lies still in death."[21] London's leading religious figures offered their tributes as well. Archdeacon Sinclair, canon residentiary of St. Paul's, wrote that "Our country has lost its greatest living preacher,"[22] and Joseph Parker, the influential pastor of City Temple, eulogized Spurgeon in these words: "The great voice has ceased. It was the mightiest voice I ever heard— a voice that could give orders in a tempest, and find its way across a torrent as through a silent aisle. Meanwhile, the stress is greater upon those who remain. Each must further tax his strength so as to lessen the loss which has come upon the whole Church."[23] The Rev. S. Parkes Cadman summed up the impact of Spurgeon's death when he wrote that on January 31, 1892, "the mourning millions of the English-speaking race had lost their real, if not their historical, episcopos."[24]

Although much of Spurgeon's popularity and influence can be attributed to the scores of sermons he published, virtually every aspect of his ministry places him within the oral tradition. First, the context of Spurgeon's preaching—the education he had and the congregations he pastored—has more commonly been associated with orality than with literacy. Bruce Rosenberg has noted, for example, that present-day American folk preachers divide all clergy into two categories; they believe that "a minister is either a manuscript preacher or a 'spiritual' preacher." This "basic distinction" is made not only on the basis of pulpit technique—manuscript preachers write their sermons, whereas "spiritual" clergy preach extempore—but also on the extent of a preacher's education; manuscript preachers are "almost invariably . . . seminary-trained," but their "spiritual" counterparts believe that they "need not be learned, and in fact should not be educated, except in the ways of the Bible."[25]

Spurgeon lived a century before the pulpiteers Rosenberg studied, but he is an excellent example of a Victorian "spiritual" preacher. First, he shared folk preachers' view that extensive formal education was not a prerequisite to effective preaching. His background showed "no traces of academic fame and promise," and he had little formal schooling himself.[26] He made it plain, moreover, that he "disliked the title 'reverend'," and he refused to accept honorary degrees. He once said, "I had rather receive the title of S.S.T. [Sunday School Teacher] than M.A., B.A., or any other honour that ever was conferred by men."[27]

Spurgeon's success as a pulpiteer was due in large part to his decision not to pursue a formal education. The people who called him to the pastorate of New Park Street saw his lack of university credentials as an asset rather than a detriment; when Spurgeon told the deacons that he "was not a College man," they replied, "That is to us a special recommendation, for you would not have much savour or unction if you came from College" (*Autobiography*, 1:249).

In addition to holding similar attitudes toward education, Spurgeon and folk preachers shared a "mild contempt for those who use a manuscript."[28] Spurgeon once said that he did not "see why a man cannot speak extemporaneously upon a subject which he fully understands" (*Autobiography*, 1:268); his work as both a preacher and a teacher of preaching reflects his insistence that "To preach the Gospel is not to . . . mumble over some dry manuscript."[29] When he founded his Pastor's College in 1857, he looked for students who were "earnest preachers, not readers of sermons, or makers of philosophical essays";[30] once the students had been admitted, he admonished them to never read their sermons (*Lectures*, 141). His rejection of manuscript preaching is most forcefully expressed in a summary of his own approach to pulpit oratory: "If I cannot speak extemporaneously I will hold my tongue. To read I am ashamed" (*Autobiography*, 2:118).

Though opposed to the reading of sermons, Spurgeon did not share folk preachers' belief that a discourse must be delivered impromptu, as if it were a product of divine inspiration. Rubin Lacy, one of the most prominent folk preachers, believed that he "simply had to step up to the pulpit and he [would be] 'fed' directly from God,"[31] but Spurgeon argued that spur-of-the-moment preaching—what he called "*extemporis[ing]* in the emphatic sense"—was "as bad as reading, or perhaps worse" (*Lectures*, 132; Spurgeon's emphasis). Instead, he advocated a form of "extempore preaching" that involved "the preparation of the sermon so far as thoughts go, and leaving the words to be found during delivery" (*Lectures*, 153).

Spurgeon's method of preparing his sermons reflected his insistence on extemporaneous-but-premeditated address. He began preparing his thoughts the night before he preached, when he would retreat into his study, meditate on his chosen text, and write "a few catchwords on a half-sheet of notepaper" (*Autobiography*, 2:346). The ideas recorded on this half-sheet then served as a guide and catalyst for the actual words of the next day's sermon.

While the American folk preachers suggest that ministers with little or no formal education were most likely to preach extemporaneous sermons, some of Spurgeon's contemporaries contended that unschooled, working-class congregations were most likely to benefit from hearing them. As noted in chapter 2, Harvey Goodwin, R. W. Dale, and J. H. Rigg believed that extemporaneous discourses should be delivered only to "persons of common-place intelligence and character," and these were precisely the kind of people to whom Spurgeon preached.[32] Spurgeon was known as "The People's Preacher"[33] and the "poor man's cardinal,"[34] and several critics took note of the differences between his congregations and those of his more educated, literacy-dominant counterparts. John De Kewer Williams wrote that "though the noble and the mighty went to hear him out of curiosity, none of them ever joined his flock," and an unnamed critic observed that "the scholarly will drop in to hear Dr. Vaughn or Dr. Dykes; the intellectual gather about the pulpits of Liddon or Stanley; the lovers of oratory follow Punshon; but the crowd goes to the Tabernacle."[35] The author of an 1884 article in *The Critic* expressed a degree of personal satisfaction at Spurgeon's appeal to the "most commonplace of English classes," writing "It is because he is . . . so closely in sympathy with the ordinary, that his success is so gratifying."[36]

The circumstances of Spurgeon's life, then, created an atmosphere conducive to an oral style of preaching; those who attended his services noted the extent to which he invested his London pulpit with the energy and passion of the classical orator. According to Walter Ong, oral delivery "has a high somatic component," and several critics commented upon Spurgeon's effective use of gestures in his preaching.[37] The author of an article published in *Fraser's Magazine* in 1857 noted that Spurgeon possessed a number of "qualifications for success" as an orator: "careful preparation of the subject-matter, great earnestness and vehement gesticulation in its delivery, a commanding voice, and a copious vocabulary."[38] According to an article in the November 5, 1856 edition of the *Evening Star,* this "vehement gesticulation" was the result not of studied artifice, but rather of an innate awareness of its effectiveness; the author of the review wrote:

> There never yet was a popular orator who did not talk more and better with his arms than with his tongue. Mr. Spurgeon knows this instinctively. When he has read his text, he does not fasten his eyes on a manuscript, and his hands to a cushion. As soon as he begins to speak, he begins to act—and that not as if declaiming on the stage, but as if conversing with you in the street. He seems to shake hands with all around, and put everyone at his ease. (*Autobiography,* 1:454)

One critic believed that Spurgeon surpassed even the classical rhetoricians in his command of the somatic aspects of oratory. Writing in the January 1855 edition of *The Earthen Vessel,* James Wells asserted that Spurgeon had "caught the idea" of classical oratory, that while the rhetors of ancient Greece occasionally carried their discourses "to such an extent that one person had to speak the words, and another had to perform the gestures," Spurgeon was able to perform "both parts himself" (*Autobiography,* 1:306).

The most significant evidence of Spurgeon's status as an orality-dominant preacher appears, of course, in the rhetoric of the sermons themselves. Virtually all his discourses contain four of the six components set forth by secular and sacred rhetoricians from Cicero to George Campbell. He begins with a brief introduction—two to three pages of an eighteen to twenty-two page sermon—in which he employs a variety of strategies to "awaken and fix the attention of the audience."[39] In some sermons, he focuses on a key word in his text, showing, for instance, that power is the "exclusive prerogative of God" or making "one or two remarks on the different translations of the word rendered 'Comforter'" in John 14:26 (*Ser-*

mons, 1:68, 113). In others, he tells a story about a biblical character mentioned in his text, recounting David's victory over the Amalekites or presenting his own version of Jacob's "parting benediction upon his twelve sons" (19:145–47; 1:192). In still others, he draws analogies between the Scriptures and the present day, contending that "If ever there was a time when it was needful to say, 'Beware ye of the leaven of the Pharisees, which is hypocrisy,' it is now" (6:334).

Whichever approach he employs, Spurgeon always ends his introductions the same way—with a brief statement of what he will discuss in the body of the sermon. At times, as in "Esther's Exaltation," he indicates simply that he will "lay out [his] sermon in four parcels, arranging it under four words" (*Sermons,* 15:76). More often, however, he states up front what these "parcels" will be. A representative partition appears at the end of the introduction to "An Earnest Invitation": Spurgeon writes, "I . . . shall divide my text thus:—First, *the command,* 'Kiss the Son;' secondly, *the argument used,* 'lest he be angry, and ye perish from the way;' and thirdly, *the benediction with which the text closes*—'Blessed are all they that put their trust in him'" (6:110; Spurgeon's emphasis).

Having set forth his main points, or "heads," in the partition, Spurgeon closely, even self-consciously, follows his outline throughout the exposition. He uses such transitional phrases as "First, then," "Now for the second point," and "This brings me to my third and last point" (6:320; 1:123; 19:73) to help his audiences "keep pace with the progress of the Discourse."[40] These divisions are marked even more explicitly in the printed texts: main points are preceded by Roman numerals and cast in capital letters, with subpoints and other important phrases italicized for additional emphasis.

The conclusions to Spurgeon's sermons follow a pattern similar to that employed in the explications. Whether the last major head also serves as the conclusion, as is the case in "Faith" and "Christ's People—Imitators of Him," or whether the conclusion begins after the entire explication is complete, Spurgeon uses such phrases as "Lastly," "To conclude," and "Now, I must close with this point" to indicate that he is approaching the end of his address (*Sermons,* 6:332; 1:209; 15:311). The final thoughts offered are different in each sermon, but the closing sentences are very much the same; in virtually every instance, they are either admonitions— "Begin, O soldiers of Christ, to be more true to your colors," "In God's name I charge you, believe on the Lord Jesus Christ"—or prayers—"May God give you true grace and true faith," "may we all meet in heaven at last" (6:141; 15:182; 6:349; 1:320).

The application, which Victorian homileticians believed to be the most important component of a sermon, does not always exist as a distinct division in Spurgeon's discourses; emphasis on action and duty is nonetheless present throughout his preaching. Some of his sermons, such as "Christ's People—Imitators of Him," consist almost entirely of application. Spurgeon's text is Acts 4:13—"Now when they saw the boldness of Peter and John, and perceived that they were unlearned and ignorant men, they marvelled; and they took knowledge of them, that they had been with Jesus" (1:252)—but Peter and John and their interrogation before the Sanhedrin are not the subject of the sermon. Spurgeon instead devotes the entire address to speaking directly to his congregation, telling them "what a Christian should be," "when he should be so," "why he should be so," and "how he can be so" (1:253; Spurgeon's emphasis).

In other sermons, such as "The Power of the Holy Ghost," Spurgeon uses what William Gresley called a "summary application," placing the practical emphasis at the very end of the discourse.[41] Spurgeon alludes to his application at the end of the introduction: "It is concerning the power of the Holy Ghost that I shall speak this morning; and may you have a practical exemplification of that attribute in your own hearts, when you shall feel the influence of the Holy Ghost is being poured out upon me . . . and bestowed upon you when you are feeling the effects of it in your own spirits." After using passages throughout the Bible to illustrate "the outward and visible displays" of the Holy Spirit's power, the "inward and spiritual manifestations of it," and "the future and expected works thereof," Spurgeon ends the sermon by taking "a moment or two for practical inference." Because the "Spirit is very powerful," he contends, unbelievers should rely on that power "to justify [them] in Christ," while Christians should "go out and labor . . . with the conviction that the power of the Spirit is [their] great help" (Sermons, 1:113, 130, 132; Spurgeon's emphasis).

In most cases, Spurgeon's applications occupy a middle ground between these two extremes. Rather than devoting the entire sermon to application or delaying the application until the very end, he employs a "continuous" mode, blending application and explication and assigning a different practical emphasis to each of his main points.[42] One of the best examples of this technique appears in "Abram's Call; Or, Half-Way and All the Way." Spurgeon ends the introduction by indicating that he will be "gathering instruction from the call and outcoming of Abram," and he ends his sermon with a prayer that his hearers "be the children of believing Abram, for Jesus' sake" (*Sermons,* 19:60, 78). In the intervening pages, he offers three ways in which his prayer can be fulfilled. First, Spurgeon shows that, in Abram's case, the call from God was "*only half obeyed*"—Abram was told to go to Canaan, but he first settled in Haran instead—and exhorts his hearers to avoid the "perilous state" of "Half-way house godliness," to not only "be saved by the cross of Christ," but also to "take up Christ's cross, and come right out decidedly upon his side at all times" (19:60, 67; Spurgeon's emphasis).

Spurgeon's second point is that calls such as the one Abram received are "*of a very special character.*" For Abram, the call was geographical; he was to leave his "country" and his "kindred" and settle in a new land. For Spurgeon's hearers, the call is "wholly *spiritual.*" They are called, he says, "to a much more difficult position" than Abram—"namely, to stay on the old spot, among old friends, and yet to lead a wholly new life." In order to fulfill that call, they must "Avoid the appearance of evil. Separate [themselves] from all that which Christ would have disapproved. Be so decided, also, as to leave everything that is hesitating. Be out-and-out for Jesus" (19:60, 67–69; Spurgeon's emphasis).

Finally, Spurgeon tells his auditors that if they will fully obey the call and live a life "set apart for God and truth," they will be placed "*upon a special footing.*" Abram gained this "footing" when he finally arrived in Canaan; Jehovah became "his shield," blessing him in times of peace and strengthening him in times of war. Abram's experience is, once again, a model for Spurgeon's congregation: they too should "aim at perfect conformity to the will of God, for this will place [them] in quiet nearness to God" (19:60, 73, 75; Spurgeon's emphasis).

The style of Spurgeon's sermons, like their structure, exhibits many of the traits orality-literacy scholars have identified as hallmarks of spoken language. Many of his partitions, for example, are characterized by alliteration and parallelism, constructions commonly associated with oral expression.[43] The sermon entitled "The Comforter" has "three divisions: first, the *comforter;* secondly, the *comfort;* and thirdly, the *comforted*"; Spurgeon's agenda in "Hypocrisy" is to describe "*the character of a hypocrite,*" to "*cast up his accounts for him,*" and to "offer a *cure for hypocrisy*" (*Sermons* 1:72, 6:335; Spurgeon's emphasis). Sermons in which Spurgeon employs parallelism include "Christ Crucified," in which he examines "a gospel rejected," "a gospel triumphant," and "a gospel admired," and "A Psalm of Remembrance," in which he discusses 1 John 4:16 as "*an abstract of Christian experience; . . . the summary of Christian testimony;* and *. . . the groundwork of Christian encouragement*" (1:89, 6:172; Spurgeon's emphasis). A somewhat extreme example of Spurgeon's fondness for alliteration and parallelism appears in the partition to "Peter's Restoration," where he writes: "first, *let us look at the Lord who looked;* and secondly, *let us look into the look which the Lord looked;* and then, thirdly, *let us look at Peter, upon whom the Lord looked*" (19:282; Spurgeon's emphasis).

The expositions Spurgeon offers in his sermons are as characteristically oral as the heads that introduce them. His addresses are replete with personal pronouns, which generally appear far more often in spoken language than in written.[44] Spurgeon frequently refers to himself—he uses words like "I," "me," and "my" an average of fifty times per sermon—but he speaks directly to his audience even more often; first- and second-person plural constructions—"we," "us," and "you"—and other forms of direct address—"weary sinner," "dear friends," "my brother"—appear numerous times in virtually every paragraph.

In addition to drawing his hearers into his sermons by speaking directly to them, Spurgeon helps them understand his arguments by drawing frequent analogies between the Scriptures and familiar Victorian people and events. Spurgeon learned the importance of keeping his preaching "close to the human lifeworld" when a student in his Sunday school class complained that the lesson was "very dull" and asked him to "pitch us a yarn"; he emphasized this technique in his lectures to the students at his Pastor's College.[45] He writes,

In addressing my students in the College, long ago, I was urging upon them the duty and necessity of using plenty of illustrations in their preaching that they might be both interesting and instructive. I reminded them that the Saviour had many *likes* in His discourses. He said, over and over again, "The kingdom of heaven is like;" "The kingdom of heaven is like." "Without a parable spake He not unto them." The common people heard Him gladly, because He was full of emblem and simile. A sermon without illustrations is like a room without windows. (*Autobiography*, 2:138)

Spurgeon drew his "emblems" and "similes" from a broad range of everyday human experiences. In one sermon, he compares the daily self-examination all Christians should practice to an author's careful proofreading of a manuscript; in another he likens Christians who live "in communion with sinners" to fish out of water; in yet another, he suggests that the pleasure God feels in a Christian's "early attempts after holiness" is much like the joy a mother experiences watching her child's first steps (*Sermons*, 1:271, 11:22, 15:161).

Spurgeon's language becomes most concrete when he discusses the most abstract ideas—theological concepts such as salvation and grace. Instead of simply drawing an analogy, he suggests a course of action his hearers should undertake in order to understand these terms. In "Esther's Exaltation," Spurgeon suggests that the essence of salvation lies not in understanding the theological nuances of the term, but rather in fulfilling the "obligations" incumbent upon the elect—teaching others about Christ, helping the poor and hungry, and practicing one's vocation in a manner appropriate for a "steward" of God (*Sermons*, 15:84–86). Similarly, after spending the first three pages of "Distinguishing Grace" arguing that the grace a Christian has received "should be a reason for humiliation, and not for boasting," Spurgeon tells his hearers that they can best understand grace by experiencing it firsthand. He writes,

> the best way for you to feel this part of the discourse is, to go tomorrow into the hospital, and walk along the wards, and see how poor men's bodies suffer, and then go into the operating-room and see what flesh and blood may have to endure. Then when you have done, go round the neighborhood to see the sick who have lain for ten, or twelve, or fifteen years upon the same bed, and after that go and visit some of God's poverty-stricken children. ... Go and see their poor, miserable, unfurnished rooms, their cellars and their attics, and that will be a better sermon to you than any thing I can utter. (6:80, 81)

Finally, the heavily oral nature of Spurgeon's pulpit rhetoric is demonstrated by his recurring use of what Milman Parry has called "the adding style."[46] Several scholars have noted that spoken language is characterized by various forms of repetition and redundancy, techniques Spurgeon employs at every level of his sermons.[47] First, he regularly adds clauses together to create his sentences; coordinating constructions such as "and," "but," and "yet" are far more common in his sermons than subordinating constructions such as "although" and "because." Next, he combines statements or questions to make his points. One of Spurgeon's subpoints in "Plain Directions to Those Who Would Be Saved From Sin" is "Trust in the Lord, next, *that by the work of his Holy Spirit he can renew you*"; he develops this point, in part, with three consecutive "if" statements: "If you are given to anger, the Holy Spirit can make you calm and loving. If you have been defiled with impurity, he can make you pure in heart. If you have been grovelling, he can elevate you" (*Sermons*, 19:270–71; Spurgeon's emphasis). In "Abram's Call," Spurgeon employs a similar technique, asking multiple questions to drive home his point. He wants his congregation to understand that if they "obey the divine call" they will "be honored with still greater tests of [their] fidelity," and he asks, "Are you willing to accept so high an honor? Will you count the cost, and make your calling and election sure? Will you cry with Esais, 'Here am I! Send me'? As the Roman consul devoted himself to death in battle for the sake of the beloved city, will you devote yourself to God, and his cause and truth?" (19:72, 73).

The most extended example of Spurgeon's repetition is found in the sermon entitled "Faith." Spurgeon's second head is "the ARGUMENT,—why, without faith, we cannot be saved," and his first subpoint is Hebrews 11:6—"Without faith it is impossible to please God" (1:371, 372). Spurgeon devotes just over a page to this subpoint, and fully half of his discussion is a string of fourteen verses from Hebrews 11 which all begin "by faith":

> "By faith Abel offered unto God a more excellent sacrifice;" "By faith Enoch was translated;" "By faith Noah built an ark;" "By faith Abraham went out into a place that he should afterwards receive;" "By faith he sojourned in the land of promise;" "By faith Sarah bare Isaac;" "By faith Abraham offered up Isaac;" "By faith Moses gave up the wealth of Egypt;" "By faith Isaac blessed Jacob;" "By faith Jacob blessed the sons of Joseph;" "By faith Joseph, when he died, made mention of the departure of the children of Israel;" "By faith the Red Sea was dried up;" "By faith the walls of Jericho fell down;" "By faith the harlot Rahab was saved" (1:372–73).

Finally, just as Spurgeon adds clauses to form sentences and sentences to form points, he adds points together to create his sermons. He seldom gives a formal conclusion to his heads; at times, he may employ a closing phrase such as "I think I have shown this," "There has been enough said" or "Thus much, then, upon my first point" (6:152, 161; 19:67), but his usual practice is simply to stop developing one point and move on to the next. When he begins a new point, moreover, he does not refer to the previous ones; instead, he looks only ahead, saying such things as "Now we come to the second thought" or "I must now close with the fourth point" (6:326; 19:269). By using these types of closures and transitions, Spurgeon often produces the impression that his sermons are not unified expositions of a single theme, but rather a collage of three or four brief, semi–independent discussions joined together to create a full-length sermon.

In nearly every regard, then, Spurgeon's sermons were shaped by the conventions and techniques of oral expression, and Victorian critics disagreed about the rhetorical merits of this orality-dominant pulpit style. Some of those who wrote positive reviews noted the extent to which Spurgeon's preaching reflected the oral tradition's emphasis on earnestness and practical application. Spurgeon believed that "rousing appeals" were not out of place in the pulpit (*Lectures,* 71); several critics wrote about his "genuine religious fervour," his "fervid and impassioned eloquence," and his "freshness and earnestness of *feeling.*"[48] They also focused on the "instruction" that Spurgeon insisted must accompany such appeals. G. N. Hervey, for example, attributed Spurgeon's "excellence as a preacher" to "the directness of his applications," to his ability to make a hearer "feel that religion is not merely the great interest of mankind in general, but your own personal concern."[49]

Other critics commended Spurgeon for keeping his preaching "close to the human lifeworld" by addressing his working-class congregations in their own "market language."[50] Representative statements include Stanford Holmes' assertion that Spurgeon was unsurpassed in "simplicity and purity of language" and G. N. Hervey's claim that he "has the rare power of expressing grand and sublime ideas in language the most simple and unambitious."[51] Two critics noted that Spurgeon did not employ the stylized ecclesiastical language that so often characterized pulpit oratory. One wrote that Spurgeon's congregation allowed him to "talk English, instead of Pulpit," and another noted that "There is not a trace of *pulpitism* in [his preaching]. The speaker might be a chartist leader, addressing a multitude on Kennington Common, so complete is the absence of every thing from his tone and manner that might have reminded you of church or chapel."[52]

The "daring homeliness"[53] some critics admired in Spurgeon's preaching is evident not only in his choice of individual words and phrases, but also in his choice of illustrations. Because he "borrowed [them] from the customs of the retail trade, and with similes taken from the colloquialisms of the streets," his illustrations were "fresh and striking";[54] the Scottish clergyman John Anderson noted that "the richness and quaintness of his illustrations" was one of the things that "told upon his audience generally, and told powerfully" (*Autobiography*, 1:337). An article published in the *Evening Star* on November 5, 1856, gives one of the best accounts of the picturesque nature of Spurgeon's preaching:

> His colours are taken from the earth and sky of common human experience and aspiration. He dips his pencil, so to speak, in the veins of the nearest spectator, and makes his work a part of every man's nature. His images are drawn from the homes of the common people, the daily toil for daily bread, the nightly rest of tired labour, the mother's love for a wayward boy, the father's tenderness to a sick daughter. His anecdotes are not far-fetched, they have a natural pathos. . . . He does not narrate occurrences, but describes them, with a rough, graphic force and faithfulness. . . . To us, it appears . . . that the clergy of all denominations might get some frequent hints for the composition of their sermons from the young Baptist preacher who never went to College. (*Autobiography,* 1:454, 455)

While some critics focused on specific aspects of Spurgeon's preaching, others offered more general praise, portraying him as an outstanding orator, a master craftsman of the oral tradition. After hearing Spurgeon preach in May 1854, the Irish actor James Sheridan Knowles told his students at Stepney College to

> Go and hear him at once. . . . He is only a boy, but he is the most wonderful preacher in the world. He is absolutely perfect in oratory; and, beside that, a master in the art of acting. . . . he can do anything he pleases with his audience; he can make them laugh and cry and laugh again in five minutes. . . . that young man will live to be the greatest preacher of this or any other age.[55]

Knowles was by no means alone in his opinions. In his column for February 19, 1855, James Grant, editor of the *Morning Advertiser,* wrote, "There can be no doubt that he possesses superior talents, while, in some of his happier flights, he rises to a high order of pulpit oratory" (*Autobiography,* 1:347, 348). A reporter covering Spurgeon's July 1855 visit to Scotland for the *Glasgow Daily Bulletin* believed that "Spurgeon owes his celebrity to the possession of first class oratorical gifts, which seem to have attained maturity and development at a very early age."[56]

Spurgeon's reputation as an orator was not confined to the British Isles. He preached several sermons in Paris in February 1860, and the Rev. Dr. Grandpierre wrote a highly laudatory review for the French religious newspaper *L'Esperance:*

> No one will feel inclined to contradict us when we declare that this celebrated orator fully justified, or even surpassed, the high opinion

which the generality of his auditors had conceived of him. . . . As an orator, he is simple and powerful, clear and abundant. . . . Among the requisites to oratory which he possesses in a remarkable degree, three particularly struck us—a prodigious memory . . . a full and harmonious voice, . . . and, lastly, a most fruitful imagination giving colour to all his thoughts, constantly varying their expression, and painting to the eye of the mind the truths of Christ. (*Autobiography,* 1:519, 520)

Spurgeon's abilities as an orator led some critics to rank him among Britain's most gifted pulpiteers. Some members of his New Park Street congregation compared him to one of their prominent former pastors, arguing that he was John Rippon "over again";[57] this sentiment was echoed by a writer for the Exeter newspaper *Western Times,* who declared that Spurgeon "bid fair to rival, if not to eclipse, such men as Carey, Gill, Rippon, and Robert Hall."[58] The preacher to whom Spurgeon was most often likened is George Whitefield, the great eighteenth-century Methodist pulpiteer. One critic wrote that Spurgeon's preaching was "worthy of Whitefield in his best days," and a letter published in the *Essex Standard* in April 1855 under the name "Vox Populi" maintained that Spurgeon "institutes a new era, or more correctly, revives the good old style of Bunyan, Wesley, and Whitefield—men whose burning eloquence carried conviction to the hearts of their hearers."[59]

Praise for Spurgeon as an orator was widespread but not universal. Several Victorian critics maintained that he lacked oratorical talent. The author of an article published in *The Christian News* in 1855, just after Spurgeon accepted the Park Street pastorate, charged that Spurgeon's oratory was "unequal and clumsy in the extreme" and that he was "just a spoiled boy, with abilities not more than mediocre."[60] Such criticisms continued late into Spurgeon's career; the author of an article published in 1884, eight years before Spurgeon's death, believed that he had still not risen beyond the "second rank" of public speakers.[61]

Some critics explicitly rejected their colleagues' comparisons of Spurgeon and Whitefield. In describing what he regarded as Spurgeon's inadequate speaking voice, one reviewer wrote, "while it is good in some respects, it is far from being the voice we should have expected to find in so successful a public speaker. It takes a clear, sound, bell-like ring along with it, but it has no rich tones either of loftiness or tenderness. In these respects, the voice of Whitefield must have been immeasurably superior."[62] John De Kewer Williams argued that not only Spurgeon's voice, but the entirety of his oratorical art, was inferior to Whitefield's. In a reminiscence entitled "My Memories and Estimate of My Friend Spurgeon," he wrote that Spurgeon had "no artistic, no dramatic, no sacerdotal graces. His elocution was perfect, but he was not eloquent. . . . Artistically he was nowhere as compared with Whitefield, or the great French preachers, or Cardinal Wiseman."[63]

At times, criticisms of Spurgeon's oratory were little more than ad hominem attacks. A writer for the *Saturday Review* called Spurgeon "A coarse, stupid, irrational bigot" and attacked his printed sermons, calling him a "scavenger of the literary world."[64] Similar assaults came from within the religious community as well. A Baptist contemporary, the Rev. Sutton of Cottenham, once called Spurgeon the "sauciest dog that ever barked in a pulpit."[65] Perhaps the harshest criticism came from Bishop Wilberforce: when asked whether he envied Spurgeon's popularity, Wilberforce replied, "Thou shalt not covet thy neighbor's ass."[66]

Some critics questioned not only Spurgeon's abilities as a public speaker, but also his competence as a Christian minister. He publicly advertised his sermons, linking himself in the public mind with "the circus and the theater";[67] comparisons of his preaching to those forms of entertainment appear in several reviews of his preaching. He was once called "the Barnum of the pulpit,"[68] and a February 27, 1855 letter to the *Ipswich Express* charged that "All his discourses are redolent of bad taste, are vulgar and theatrical" (*Autobiography*, 1:311). Another letter, published two months later in the *Sheffield and Rotherham Independent*, echoed this assessment, comparing Spurgeon's Exeter Hall services to "some great dramatic entertainment" (*Autobiography*, 1:321). In some observer's minds, such an atmosphere ran counter to the basic purpose of preaching: striving to achieve, as Spurgeon himself put it, "the edification of saints and the salvation of sinners" (*Lectures*, 336). The author of a review in *Fraser's Magazine* wrote that people "go to hear Spurgeon—more in the hope of amusement than edification," a criticism echoed by Louisa Merivale when she noted Spurgeon's propensity for attracting "fashionable critics," who came to his services "seeking merely for a new sensation."[69]

In addition to being thought excessively dramatic and theatrical, Spurgeon was accused of defiling the pulpit with sacrilege. A representative early comment is one written in October 1856 by a reporter for the *Daily Telegraph*, who encouraged his readers to "set up a barrier to the encroachments and blasphemies of men like Spurgeon."[70] Nearly four decades later, in 1892, the charge of sacrilege appeared in the *Standard;* one of its contributors stated that Spurgeon's "endless anecdotes, apt though they were to the point to be illustrated, not infrequently savoured of irreverence."[71]

The harshest condemnation of Spurgeon's preaching appeared in a review of *The New Park Street Pulpit* published in the January 1857 edition of *Fraser's Magazine*. The first half of the article is a review of *The New Park Street Pulpit,* but accusations of Spurgeon's non-Christian conduct appear throughout the review. The reviewer begins by making note of "the sad and astounding fact" that Spurgeon achieved his popularity "mainly by volubility of style, strength of voice, and, it would seem, by the vulgarity, indecency, if not profanity, of his rhapsodies." The writer goes on to state that Spurgeon was "continually profane in preaching," that his sermons were marred by "malignant blasphemy," and even that Spurgeon was "on the most intimate and familiar terms" with Satan. In this reviewer's opinion, the irreverence of Spurgeon's preaching invalidated his claim to be a minister of the gospel; he writes, "that the utterer of such rhapsodies is to be hailed as an apostle, or that such gatherings can possibly promote the cause of true religion, is far too monstrous and absurd an assertion for any man of right feeling to tolerate for a single moment."[72]

Such criticism is both extreme and inaccurate. Spurgeon has, as he indicated in his preface to *The New Park Street Pulpit,* "most certainly departed from the usual mode of preaching,"[73] but this departure is not a shift from reverence to irreverence. It is, instead, a shift from a literate approach to preaching to an oral-aural technique, and it is this shift that is the actual basis for the reviewer's condemnation of Spurgeon's sermons. When the reviewer brands Spurgeon's statement that "To preach the Gospel is not . . . to mumble over some dry manuscript" as "vulgarity" in the extreme, he indicates his own preference for a more literate approach to sacred speaking.[74] Having thus privileged the written tradition, he denigrates as "vulgar," "profane," or "blasphemous" the ties to the oral lifeworld he finds in Spurgeon's preaching.

The first passage to which the reviewer objects is Spurgeon's description of the "plan of human redemption." In one of his sermons, Spurgeon writes, "Look here!—your soul is in pawn to the Devil; Christ has paid the Redemption money; you take faith for the ticket, and get your soul out of pawn." While it is true that Satan is not "represented as a pawnbroker in Scripture," it does not follow that Spurgeon's choice of imagery is "profane."[75] Rather, he has kept his preaching "close to the human lifeworld" by describing Christ's redemptive work in terms which his audience can readily comprehend and with which they can easily identify.[76]

A paragraph later, the reviewer accuses Spurgeon of treating the "ascent of Christ into heaven . . . with the same intolerable indecency." The offending sermon is one in which Spurgeon has written, "I think I see the Angels looking down from heaven's battlements, and crying, 'See the conquering Hero comes!'"[77] Once again, Spurgeon's portrayal of Christ as hero is in keeping with the oral tradition, a "highly polarized, agonistic . . . world of good and evil, virtue and vice, villains and heroes."[78]

Finally, the reviewer criticizes Spurgeon for his apparent preoccupation with "hell and damnation." He writes, "We think it possible to teach men the way to Heaven, without gloating over the torments of those who lose it," and he condemns Spurgeon's "gloating" by insisting that "Bigotry, profaneness, intolerance, and vulgarity, should not be the weapons of truth."[79]

The reviewer finds evidence of the "indecency, vulgarity, and profanity" of Spurgeon's obsession with hell in excerpts from two of his New Park Street sermons. In the first passage, Spurgeon tells his audience that

> The hell of hells will be to thee, poor sinner, the thought that it is to be for ever. When the damned jingle in the burning irons of their torments, they shall say "For ever!" when they howl, echo cries "For ever!"

> "For ever" is written on their racks,
>   "For ever" on their chains;
> "For ever" burneth in the fire;
>   "For ever" ever reigns.[80]

Although the reviewer has said that he will "Let one specimen suffice," he immediately reprints another excerpt emphasizing the certainty and eternity of the torment which awaits the unredeemed:

> When a thousand years have passed, you may say, "I *am* damned;" nevertheless, it is written still, "*shall be* damned;" and when a million years have passed, still written, "SHALL BE DAMNED." Be as good as you please, as moral as you can and honest as you will, walk as uprightly as you can, still written, "*shall be damned*."[81]

These excerpts, like those concerned with redemption and the heroic nature of Christ, are characteristically oral: Spurgeons's repetition of the phrases "for ever" and "shall be damned" exemplifies the redundancy, or *copia*, Walter Ong has identified as one of the fundamental "psychodynamics of orality."[82]

Virtually every aspect of Spurgeon's career—his educational background, the demographics of his congregations, the reviews of his preaching, and the rhetoric of his sermons—places him near the "spiritual" preachers on the oral end of the orality-literacy continuum. Any categorization, however, must also account for the literate component of his preaching, for, while spiritual preachers believed that using manuscripts or publishing sermons violated the spirit of their art,[83] Spurgeon used the written word throughout the preaching process, writing outlines of his sermons, referring to his outlines as he preached, and revising transcripts for publication. His preaching, then, exemplifies what might be called "secondary literacy." This phrase is a variation of Walter Ong's "secondary orality," a "deliberate and self-conscious orality" that is "based permanently on the use of writing and print." One of the best illustrations of this phenomenon is the "cultivated air of spontaneity" of modern presidential debates, in which the candidates compete in an oral arena, using previously composed statements as their weapons.[84]

Thus, secondary orality involves taking an idea that has been developed through the use of writing and using an oral medium to communicate that idea to an audience. Conversely, secondary literacy is the practice of taking an idea that has been developed through the use of extemporaneous public speaking and using the medium of print to make that idea accessible to people who were not in the church or meeting hall when the oration was first delivered. As a clergyman who first earned a reputation as the "boy preacher" of Waterbeach[85] and later gained lasting fame as the author of the multi-volume *New Park Street Pulpit* and *Metropolitan Tabernacle Pulpit*, Spurgeon is the most prominent Victorian pulpiteer whose work can be classified as belonging to the tradition of "secondary literacy." It is in this classification that we find Spurgeon's significance to literary and rhetorical studies today.

5

John Henry Newman

JOHN HENRY NEWMAN'S MOST EXTENSIVE TREATISE ON HOMILET-
ics is "University Preaching," one of the occasional lectures published in Part II of *The Idea of a University*. Although the lecture
was delivered and published after Newman's conversion to Rome,
most of the statements he makes describe his Anglican theories
as well as his Catholic views. These statements provide a starting
point for determining Newman's place on the orality-literacy
continuum.

From 1816 to 1843, Newman lived within the literacy-oriented
atmosphere of Oxford University. Just as Spurgeon's distaste for
academic degrees and focus on the working classes suggest an
affinity with extemporaneous, or "spiritual," preachers, his level
of education—the Bachelor of Arts degree from Trinity College—
and his occupations—tutor of Oriel and Vicar of St. Mary's, the
University church—are associated with the "manuscript" tradition.[1] This association is further demonstrated in "University
Preaching" and *Parochial and Plain Sermons*, documents that por-
tray Newman as one of the Victorian period's most literate—and
literary—clergymen.

Newman's status as a Victorian manuscript preacher is first
evident in his method of preparing his sermons. In "University
Preaching," Newman asserts that "one of the most effectual
means by which we are able to ascertain our understanding of a
subject . . . is to write down carefully all we have to say about it"
(*Idea*, 340–41).[2] He goes on to identify three ways in which writing sermons can help preachers improve their preaching. Sermons that are worked out on paper will be conceived well,
Newman says, because writing is the best "stimulus to . . . originality." They will be organized well because it is the best "stimulus
. . . to the arrangement of topics," and they will be preached well
because "the fuller the sketch, and the more clear and continuous
the thread of the discourse, the more the preacher will find himself at home when the time of delivery arrives" (*Idea*, 341).

Throughout his Anglican ministry, Newman practiced the habit of composing his sermons *in extenso* (*Idea*, 340). He wrote one or two sermons every week, exercising "scrupulous care in the preparation of his manuscripts."[3] In January 1838, Newman wrote a letter to his mother, describing his difficulties in completing *Lectures on Justification;* it is likely that his account illustrates not only his approach to writing books, but to his method of composing sermons as well:

> I write—I write again—I write a third time, in the course of six months . . . I literally fill the paper with corrections so that another person could not read it—I then write it out fair for the printer—I put it by—I take it up—I begin to correct again—it will not do—alterations multiply—pages are re-written—little lines sneak in and crawl about—the whole page is disfigured—I write again. I cannot count how many times this process goes on.[4]

The next step in Newman's literate approach to sacred speaking—the use of manuscripts in the pulpit—is the only point at which his Anglican practice diverges from the theories in "University Preaching." In the sixth section of the lecture, he raised the same question J. H. Rigg posed in "On Preaching"—"whether or not the preacher should preach without book" (*Idea*, 339)—and argued that sermons should be delivered without the aid of manuscript. He writes,

> While . . . a preacher will find it becoming and advisable to put into writing any important discourse beforehand, he will find it equally a point of propriety and expedience not to read it in the pulpit. I am not of course denying his right to use a manuscript, if he wishes; but he will do well to conceal it. . . . if he employs a manuscript, the more he appears to dispense with it . . . the more he will be considered to preach; and, on the other hand, the more he will be judged to come short of preaching the more sedulous he is in following his manuscript line after line. . . . What is this but a popular testimony to the fact that preaching is not reading, and reading is not preaching? (*Idea*, 342–43)

During his tenure at St. Mary's, however, Newman made no distinction between reading and preaching. He read his sermons from manuscripts which he made no attempt to conceal, "following [them] line after line" and indicating, by the "tone of his voice," that he had his text "safely before him" (*Idea*, 343).

Newman's close attention to his manuscript precluded the animated delivery practiced by Spurgeon and his orality-oriented predecessors. Newman objected to oratorical "display" in the pulpit, maintaining that it "dissipates" the preacher's energy and is often an attempt to create the appearance of earnestness where none exists;[5] his own method of preaching exhibited none of the "glory of action and passion" that characterized the orator's work.[6] The testimony of William Gladstone, who attended St. Mary's during his undergraduate days at Oxford, suggests that Newman's preaching was anything but conducive to the "mutual magnetism between speaker and hearer" which the Reverend Austin Phelps set forth as the goal of the "perfect orator."[7] Gladstone writes,

> Dr. Newman's manner in the pulpit was one about which, if you considered it in its separate parts, you would arrive at very unsatisfactory conclusions. There was not very much change in the inflexion of voice; action, there was none. His sermons were read, and his eyes were always bent on his book; and all that, you will say, is against efficiency in preaching.[8]

The rhetoric of Newman's sermons is as literacy-oriented as the techniques with which they were prepared and preached. Although Newman knew, and was influenced by, the work of Aristotle and Cicero, his Anglican discourses reflect the conventions of Victorian prose more than the practices of classical oratory.[9] Whereas Spurgeon's syntax is shaped almost entirely by the oral tradition, Newman's reflects both spoken and written practice. He uses coordinate language—"and," "but," "yet," "again"—about as frequently as Spurgeon, but subordinate constructions—clauses beginning with "which," "because," "when," and "though"— appear much more often in *Parochial and Plain Sermons* than in Spurgeon's discourses. Conversely, Newman employs references to himself and to his audience much less frequently; he uses fewer first- and second-person pronouns, and such phrases as "dear friends" and "my brethren" are virtually absent from the sermons. When he does address his hearers and readers, he uses "we" rather than "you," indicating that, although he includes his audience in his discussions, he does not speak as directly to them as Spurgeon does.

The most important difference between Spurgeon and Newman is found not in the way they construct each sentence, but rather in the patterns used to craft the entire discourse. Several scholars have suggested that while orally based thought typically is expressed through various forms of repetition, the advent of writing made it possible to convey ideas and develop arguments in a more linear and analytic fashion.[10] This distinction between speech and writing encapsulates the difference between Newman's and Spurgeon's preaching.

The linear nature of *Parochial and Plain Sermons* appears first in the way Newman moves from introduction to exposition. Following the practice of such orality-oriented theorists as John Wilkins, James Arderne, and Hugh Blair, Spurgeon divided his sermons into three or four heads, or, as he called them, "good stout parcels"[11]—ideas based on the same text but which often stood as virtually independent discourses. Newman, on the other hand, believed that "Nothing is so fatal to the effect of a sermon as the habit of preaching on three or four subjects at once" (*Idea*, 333). He recommended that preachers base their essays on a single "categorical proposition," a suggestion we see reflected in most of his Anglican sermons. Newman occasionally follows Spurgeon's pattern of announcing his heads in advance; at the end of the introduction to "Bodily Suffering," for example, he sets forth a two-part partition: "In what follows," he writes, "I shall remark briefly, first, on the natural effect of pain upon the mind; and next, upon the remedies and correctives of that effect which the knowledge of the Gospel supplies" (*PPS*, 3:143).

This is not, however, Newman's regular practice. In many sermons, Newman uses a modified version of the classical partition, announcing his topic without providing the details of his outline. At the end of the introduction to "The Crucifixion," for instance, he tells his hearers that he will "make one or two reflections by way of stirring up [their] hearts and making [them] mourn over Christ's sufferings" (*PPS*, 7:136). Similarly, he writes that the purpose of "Christian Repentance" will be to show how the parable of the Prodigal Son describes "the *nature* of all true repentance," and he introduces the exposition of "The Christian Mysteries" by stating simply, "The Feast of Trinity succeeds Pentecost; the light of the Gospel does not remove mysteries in religion. This is our subject. Let us enlarge upon it" (*PPS*, 3:91, 1:205). In many other discourses, Newman omits the partition altogether; most of the addresses in *Parochial and Plain Sermons* contain no explicit division between introduction and exposition.

The unity of Newman's homiletic thought is further illustrated in his methods of developing his claims. Unlike Spurgeon, he uses no typographical or verbal clues to call attention to the divisions of his sermons. Where Spurgeon cast his main points in capital letters and marked them with Roman numerals, Newman used less obtrusive Arabic numerals to mark the progress of some of his expositions; in many cases, his transitional phrases are not accompanied by any numbering system at all.

More significantly, the language of these transitions most often sustains a single line of thought rather than indicating a shift between two largely independent ideas. Spurgeon typically uses transitions such as "Now for the second point," "The third thing in our text is," and "Just one more argument, and then I have done with it"[12]—phrases which indicate that he has finished with one subject and is preparing to discuss another. Newman sometimes employs similar statements—the four points in "The Conversion of St. Paul" begin "Herein then, first," "In the next place," "And, in the next place," and "Lastly" (PPS, 2:97, 99, 102)—but they appear in a minority of his discourses. In most of *Parochial and Plain Sermons*, in contrast, he employs transitions that illustrate the relationships between his points. In some sermons, such as "Righteousness Not of Us, but in Us" and "Christ, the Son of God made Man," he begins one point by qualifying the previous one. He begins the expositions of these sermons with the assertions, "Whatever we have, is not of us, but of God," and "First, Christ is God," (PPS, 5:132, 6:55). These propositions then reappear in the subordinate clauses that begin the second head; Newman writes "while truth and righteousness are not of us, it is quite certain that they are also in us if we be Christ's" and "while our Lord is God He is also the Son of God, or rather, . . . He is God because He is the Son of God" (5:132, 6:56–57).

In other sermons, Newman employs a variety of phrases to integrate his arguments. His strategies include using "*anaphoric* relations" and "*cohesive ties*"[13]—words and phrases such as "the foregoing remarks," "as I have said," "however," and "moreover"; identifying the next stage of his argument—"observe what follows from this"; and exploring the implications of his claims—"All this being granted, it still may be objected" (PPS, 1:10, 105). One of the most common techniques is the use of "then" phrases—"Let us, then," "we see, then," and "such then"—to indicate that he is summarizing or drawing an inference from his previous points and using those summaries or inferences as the basis for further discussion.

One of the best examples of the linear progression of Newman's expositions is found in the sermon entitled "The Law of the Spirit." Following a page of introductory comments, Newman begins the exposition by identifying "three subjects which call for remark: the Law, Righteousness, and Faith" (PPS, 5:144), which he discusses as three related topics rather than three independent ones.

First, he devotes nearly two pages to developing his definition of the Law as God's "standard of perfection, . . . to which all creatures must conform." He then establishes a relationship between Law and Righteousness—"To be righteous," he says, "is to act up to the Law . . . and thereby to be acceptable to Him who gave it"— and argues that living in accordance with the Law is possible only if one receives the "great gift of [God's] passion, the abiding influence of the Holy Ghost, which enables us to offer to God an acceptable obedience, such as by nature we cannot offer" (5:144, 46, 49).

The third part of the exposition is Newman's response to a hypothetical objection—"How can we be said to *fulfil* the Law, and to offer an *acceptable* obedience, since we do not obey *perfectly?*" His response is twofold. First, he acknowledges the validity of the objection, conceding that "no work of ours, as far as it is ours, is perfect: and therefore by no work of ours . . . are we justified." Second, he identifies two remedies for the inevitable imperfection of human action. The first of these remedies is "the presence of the All-holy Spirit," whose "influences are infinitely pleasing to God" and who can therefore make the deeds he inspires "pleasing to God . . . though human infirmity be mixed with them." The second remedy is faith, the third point in Newman's partition. Exercising faith, Newman argues, is the only way people can attain the righteousness demanded by the Law; it "is the element of all perfection," and "he who begins with faith, will end in unspotted and entire holiness" (5:157–59; Newman's emphasis).

In the conclusion to "The Law of the Spirit," Newman emphasizes the interrelationship of his three subjects once more, arguing that the journey toward "holiness and heaven" begins with a proper understanding of law, righteousness, and faith. The "mistake of the Jews," he says, was to isolate the law from this triad and believe they could achieve "eternal life" simply by adhering to its mandates. Christians can avoid making this mistake if they return the Law to its context, recognizing that it cannot be obeyed without the help of the Holy Spirit and that the help of the Spirit is available only to those who exercise "faith in Christ." If Christians will do this, Newman maintains, they will be "justified in God's way" and, having been justified, will "reach the eternal rest of heaven" (5:160, 462).

The theories set forth in "University Preaching" and the practice illustrated in *Parochial and Plain Sermons* indicate that Newman occupies a place opposite Spurgeon on the orality-literacy continuum. His literate techniques were, moreover, the focal point of many reviews of his sermons. In a letter to John Keble, Newman wrote, "it seems to me a great object, as Sir Walter Scott beat bad novels out of the field, in like manner to beat out bad sermons by supplying a more *real* style of sermon."[14] The comments of several critics suggest that he achieved his goal.[15] Some commended him for rejecting the multi-part discourse of classical oratory in favor of a sermon that "has not two ideas in its head."[16] Early in the twentieth century, Edwin Dargan wrote that Newman's style "is informal and easy, with no clearly marked divisions or care for symmetry of that kind. He usually gets his thought from the text, and keeps that one thought prominent to the end."[17] Victorian critics also noted that Newman's addresses contain that "*definiteness of object*" which he believed to be "the one virtue of the preacher" (*Idea*, 333; Newman's emphasis). R. W. Church wrote that each discourse in *Parochial and Plain Sermons* "seized a single thought, or definite view, or real difficulty or objection, and kept closely and distinctly to it," and an unidentified reviewer of *Sermons Bearing on Subjects of the Day* noted that "a single sermon ... will rarely amount to more than a single thought."[18]

Other reviewers wrote about Newman's ability to express his single main idea in the unpretentious yet aesthetically attractive language of the essay rather than the elaborate, ornamented diction of classical speech. Newman set forth his concept of the ideal style in "Literature," another lecture published in *The Idea of a University:* "A great author," he writes, "is not one who merely has a *copia verborum*, whether in prose or verse, and can, as it were, turn on at his will any number of splendid phrases and swelling sentences; but he is one who has something to say and knows how to say it" (*Idea*, 243). E. T. Vaughan took note of the ways in which this approach to style was exemplified in Newman's Anglican sermons, crediting Newman and Thomas Arnold with breaking through "the conventionalities which fettered the preacher" in the late eighteenth and early nineteenth centuries and showing that "it was possible and right to speak from the pulpit in pure and transparent English chosen from the current language of men living in the world and dealing with the world."[19] In an 1891 article on Newman's life in the Church of England, Rowland Prothero made a similar observation about Newman's "pure" style: "his clear Saxon with austere severity advances directly towards its aim, without ornament or display.... Unceremonious, unconstrained in movement, without verbiage or circumlocution, his style combines clearness with force, richness with depth, originality with refinement."[20] Perhaps the most concise assessment of Newman's use of language in his Anglican sermons appears in an 1842 review of the *Parochial and Plain Sermons,* in which R. W. Church contended that Newman was the first to "think of writing a sermon as he would write an earnest letter."[21]

Modern scholars have also commented on Newman's unaffected pulpit style. John Hazard Wildman recalls Church's reference to letter-writing in his observation that "One gets the impression from [Newman's] sermons that he is speaking to each member personally."[22] In the chapter on Newman in *The Heeded Voice,* Eric Mackerness notes that Newman "does not waste words on inept recapitulations" or on "startling or *recherche*" illustrations; that his language is "free from trite and over-worked turns of phrase"; and that he does not "force out elaborate metaphors of his own devising."[23]

Several of Newman's contemporaries regarded his homiletic essays as examples not only of the rhetoric of literacy, but of the art of literature as well. *Sermons Bearing on Subjects of the Day,* a collection of discourses preached in 1841, was praised as an important work of both theology and literature. One reviewer wrote that the volume was "not only unequalled, but unapproached . . . in the whole stores of theology, at least since the days of St. Bernard." H. W. Wilberforce called attention to the book's stylistic merits when he wrote that it "contains some of the most striking and beautiful sermons ever published."[24] *Parochial and Plain Sermons* received even greater acclaim: praising Newman for his directness, unity of thought, and "keen and exact knowledge of the subtle and refined secrets of language," R. W. Church asserted that the sermons in the series "stand by themselves in modern English literature; it might be said, in English literature generally."[25]

Although many of Newman's contemporaries saw his sermons as works of literature, Newman himself believed that there was a fundamental difference between sermons and other forms of prose. Literature, in Newman's view, is not concerned with stimulating its readers to act in accordance with a set of propositions or a proposed standard of conduct. It is

almost in its essence unreal, for it is the exhibition of thought disjoined from practice. Its very home is supposed to be ease and retirement; and when it does more than speak or write, it is accused of transgressing its bounds. This indeed constitutes what is considered its true dignity and honour, viz. its abstraction from the actual affairs of life; its security from the world's currents and vicissitudes; its saying without doing. A man of literature is considered to preserve his dignity by doing nothing; and when he proceeds forward into action, he is thought to lose his position, as if he were degrading his calling by enthusiasm, and becoming a politician or a partisan. Hence mere literary men are able to say strong things against the opinions of their age, whether religious or political, without offence; because no one thinks they mean anything by them. They are not expected to go forward to act upon them, and mere words hurt no one. (*PPS*, 5:42)

In contrast, the necessity of Christian action is a central concern of Newman's thought. Walter Jost has written that it has become "a commonplace" to state "that Newman was drawn to the personal, practical, and concrete."[26] This "commonplace" is illustrated not only in *Discussions and Arguments,* "The Tamworth Reading Room," and the *Grammar of Assent*—works Jost cites in his study of Newman's rhetoric—but in Newman's homiletics as well.

Newman's emphasis on action begins with his belief in the persuasive power of the preacher's ethos. In "Personal Influence the Means of Propagating the Truth," Newman argues that Truth "has been upheld in the world . . . not by books, not by argument, nor by temporal power," but rather by "*the personal influence,* direct and indirect, of those who are commissioned to teach it" (*Belief,* 65, 77; Newman's emphasis). In "University Preaching," he invokes Aristotle in support of his claim that "the very presence of simple earnestness is even in itself a powerful natural instrument" of persuasion (*Idea,* 330). Newman cautions, moreover, that no degree of literary sophistication in a sermon can compensate for a preacher's lack of a compelling ethos; he writes that "any thing which interferes with this earnestness, or which argues its absence, is . . . certain to blunt the force of the most cogent argument conveyed in the most eloquent language" (*Idea,* 330).

Newman also points out that this earnestness is not something that can be consciously created; it is not brought about either by careful composition in the study or by oratorical display in the pulpit. Instead, earnestness is the natural fruit of the genuine Christian life. It is present in preachers "according to the measure of their faith and love," and it is as central to effective preaching as the content of the discourse itself. As Newman puts it, the preacher "persuades by what he is, as well as by what he delivers" (*Idea,* 332, 344).

Newman believed that, while the formation and expression of the appropriate ethos is an important, and possibly essential, component of the call to spiritual action, it is not the call itself. The preacher's earnestness can help give him a "claim of attention on the part of his hearers." Once he has captured their attention, however, he must set forth a practical application which will help them to achieve "some *definite* spiritual good" (*Idea*, 330, 332; Newman's emphasis).

In keeping with this principle, Newman's Anglican sermons do not exhibit the "unreality" of "thought disjoined from practice" that he warned against in "Unreal Words"; he often makes it clear that he expects his hearers and readers to "go forward to act upon" what he has said (*PPS*, 5:42). The theme of Newman's preaching—"it is nothing to *know* what is right unless we *do* it" (*PPS*, 1:27)—is first expressed in the titles he gave many of his sermons—"Knowledge of God's Will Without Obedience," "Faith and Obedience," "The Duty of Self-Denial," "Obedience to God the Way to Faith in Christ"—and it continues throughout the sermons themselves. Statements such as "Let us . . . learn this lesson," "Let us do our duty as it presents itself," and "knowledge is a call to action" (*PPS*, 6:311, 2:160, 8:30) appear in many of the *Parochial and Plain Sermons*, and virtually every discourse ends with a clear practical application. In "Moral Consequences of Single Sins," he exhorts his congregants to "plead for [themselves] and for each other while it is called to-day"; in "The Power of the Will," he writes, "let us gird up our loins and fearlessly obey the summons. Let us take up our cross and follow Him"; and in "Unreal Words," he exhorts his congregants to replace empty words with real Christian action:

> Let us avoid talking, of whatever kind. . . . Let us guard against frivolity, love of display, love of being talked about, love of singularity, love of seeming original. Let us aim at meaning what we say, and saying what we mean; let us aim at knowing when we understand a truth, and when we do not. When we do not, let us take it on faith, and let us profess to do so. Let us receive the truth in reverence, and pray God to give us a good will, and divine light, and spiritual strength, that it may bear fruit within us. (*PPS*, 4:51, 5:356, 5:45)

Newman's concern with "the personal and practical"[27] is evident even in sermons on the most theoretical and abstract subjects. In "The Christian Mysteries," for example, Newman states that Christians may legitimately ask such questions as "why does God permit so much evil?" and "*why is there pain in the world?*" (*PPS*, 1:206; Newman's emphasis), but he points out that they must not be surprised or disappointed if no answer is forthcoming. God does not answer such questions, Newman argues, because knowledge about such things "would do us no good, it would merely satisfy curiosity. It is not practical knowledge" (206). Similarly, in "Mysteries in Religion," Newman notes that while Christ's ascension into heaven "disclosed" some of God's "high Providence" to humans, it also raises many questions—"Whither did he go?,", "What is the meaning of His interceding for us in heaven?," why "His absence was the condition of the Holy Spirit's presence"— for which there are no answers (PPS, 2:207, 208, 210, 212). In this sermon, as elsewhere in his preaching, Newman's focus is not on what he and his congregants do not know, but rather what they do know and what they are expected to do. Near the end of the sermon, he reminds his audience that "though the prophecies of this sacred book may be still sealed from us, yet the doctrines and precepts are not; and that we lose much both in the way of comfort and instruction, if we do not use it for the purposes of faith and obedience" (207, 215).

Newman's emphasis on the preacher's ethos and the importance of practical application show that, while he employed "*literary* patterns of argument and exposition," he retained the two elements of the oral tradition upon which all Victorian homileticians insisted.[28] Students of his preaching, moreover, commented on these aspects of his ministry as well as his literary achievements. Some focused on the calls to action presented throughout his sermons. A reviewer of *Sermons Bearing on Subjects of the Day* wrote that "Mr. Newman's aim seems to build up the Christian character silently and secretly."[29] E. T. Vaughan wrote that the intention of the *Parochial and Plain Sermons* is "always practical," that Newman preached his sermons with "reality, earnestness, and simplicity of desire to instruct, direct, and animate [his hearers] for good."[30] Another reviewer believed that the *Parochial and Plain Sermons* were the most practical discourses in print; R. W. Church called the collection his age's "fullest, deepest, most comprehensive approximation . . . to representing Christianity in a practical form."[31]

Many Victorians and present-day scholars noted the unusual force of personality that accompanied Newman's insistence on practical action. In "Personal Influence, the Means of Propagating the Truth," Newman describes the effect produced by a "simple-minded, honest devotion to God":

the attraction, exerted by unconscious holiness, is of an urgent and irresistible nature; it persuades the weak, the timid, the wavering, and the inquiring; it draws forth the affection and loyalty of all who are in

a measure like-minded; and over the thoughtless or perverse multitude it exercises a sovereign compulsory sway, bidding them fear and
keep silence, on the ground of its own right Divine to rule them; its
hereditary claim on their obedience, though they understand not the
principles or counsels of that spirit, which is "born, not of blood, nor
of the will of the flesh, nor of the will of man, but of God." (*Belief*,
78, 81)

The phenomenon Newman describes is precisely the impact
his own saintly ethos had on the city and the university of Oxford.
Although Newman "hated the idea of forming a party or of gathering a following,"[32] his personal magnetism attracted a large and
loyal congregation to his Sunday services at St. Mary's.[33] David
DeLaura has described Newman's preaching as "a continuing
public 'event'"; one of Newman's contemporaries noted that the
"excitement" created by his sermons "scattered waves of feeling
far beyond the precincts of the University."[34] While Amy Cruse
has asserted that Newman "preached to a congregation that never
more than half filled the big church," statements such as these
suggest that Eric Griffiths and R. D. Middleton are correct when
they write that "the Church of St. Mary the Virgin on Sunday
afternoons was regularly full and attentively hushed," filled "usually by not less than five or six hundred graduates, besides other
members of the congregation."[35]

For some parishioners, Newman was not only a highly popular
preacher, he was also the object of "an emotion akin to supersti-
tious veneration."[36] In 1869, E. T. Vaughan recalled that Newman's disciples followed him "with an intensity of devotion which
those at a distance from Oxford scarcely understood."[37] This devotion was expressed in a variety of ways: some people crowded the
"path Newman took to the pulpit," hoping to "get a close view of
his gaunt face"; some passed the service "gazing at him as if he
were an angel"; and some, such as Wilfrid Scawen Blunt,
"had little difficulty in crediting him with supernatural powers."[38]
Newman was, in short, a virtually supernatural presence in
nineteenth-century Oxford; as David DeLaura has said, his impact
on the city and university was "a phenomenon so powerful, so
widespread and long continued, so awash with the deepest cross-
currents of thought and feeling, that it fully deserves the term
'myth'."[39]

Statements made by Newman's contemporaries indicate that
his ability to "[draw] forth the affection and loyalty" (*Belief*, 81) of
a large portion of the Oxford religious community rested in the

oral rather than the literate qualities of his preaching. Victorian
Oxford was a residually oral culture characterized by a "great preoccupation with 'voice' and personal presence;" a number of accounts of Newman's preaching recall the impact of what David
DeLaura has called Newman's "aural image."[40] Perhaps the best-
known is Matthew Arnold's tribute to Newman in *Discourses in
America:*

> Who could resist the charm of that spiritual apparition, gliding in the
> dim afternoon light through the aisles of St. Mary's, rising into the
> pulpit, and then, in the most entrancing of voices, breaking the silence
> with words and thoughts which were a religious music,—subtle,
> sweet, mournful?[41]

The "eloquence of saints" (*Idea,* 331) of which Matthew Arnold
speaks is also the focus of James Anthony Froude's reminiscence
of Newman, published in *Short Studies on Great Subjects* in 1886.
In this book, Froude recalls the impact of Newman's voice on the
day he preached a sermon entitled "The Incarnate Son, a Sufferer
and Sacrifice":

> Newman described closely some of the incidents of our Lord's Passion;
> he then paused. For a few moments there was a breathless silence.
> Then in a low, clear voice, of which the faintest vibration was audible
> in the farthest corner of St. Mary's, he said, "Now I bid you recollect
> that He to whom these things were done was Almighty God." It was
> as if an electric stroke had gone though the church, as if every person
> present understood for the first time the meaning of what he had all
> his life been saying.[42]

Two important testimonies to the power of Newman's voice were
written by John Campbell Shairp, a "nonsectarian Scottish academic" whom DeLaura credits with doing the most to shape and
preserve Newman's "aural image."[43] In 1873, Shairp published a
poetic tribute to Newman in *Macmillan's* magazine:

> The voice that from St. Mary's spake
>   As from the unseen world oracular,
> Strong as another Wesley, to re-awake
>   The sluggish heart of England, near and far,
>
> Voice so intense to win men, or repel,
>   Piercing yet tender, on these spirits fell,
> Making them other, higher than they were.[44]

Shairp also believed that the silencing of Newman's voice was the most tragic consequence of Newman's conversion to Rome. In *Studies in Poetry and Philosophy*, Shairp wrote, "How vividly comes back the remembrance of the aching blank, the awful pause, which fell on Oxford when that voice had ceased, and we knew that we should hear it no more. It was as when, to one kneeling by night, in the silence of some vast cathedral, the great bell tolling solemnly overhead has suddenly gone still."[45]

Another demonstration of the force of Newman's personality is the way in which he used the power of his voice to overcome the distance a manuscript imposes between preacher and audience and touch the souls of those who heard him preach. Froude wrote that when Newman preached, "He seemed to be addressing the most secret consciousness of each of us—as the eyes of a portrait appear to look at every person in a room."[46] William Charles Lake, dean of Durham, suggested that Newman's ability to speak to his hearers' "secret consciousness" enabled him to exert considerable influence on his congregation. In his *Memorials,* Lake tells us that Newman "seemed to enter into the very minds of his hearers, and, as it were, to reveal them to themselves, and to tell them their very innermost thoughts. . . . you were always conscious that you were in the hands of a man who was a perfect master of your heart, and was equally powerful to comfort and to warn you."[47]

It was, ironically, Charles Kingsley—one of Newman's greatest adversaries in the 1860s—who provided what may be the best account of the impact of Newman's personality on the religious life of Oxford. In an 1859 article in *Fraser's Magazine*, Kingsley bears witness to the two major components of Newman's ethos— the mysterious appeal of his voice and his ability to not only touch the mind, but also to speak directly to the spirit:

> twenty years ago, when there were giants in the earth, among Tractarians as among others, stood in that pulpit a great genius and a great orator, who knew how to use his voice. Perfectly still he stood, disdaining the slightest show of passion, trusting to eye and voice alone—to the eye, which looked through and through every soul with the fascination of a serpent; to the voice, most sweet and yet most dreadful, which was monotonous indeed; but monotonous with full intent and meaning, carrying home to the heart, with its delicate and deliberate articulation, every syllable of words which one would have too gladly escaped; words which laid bare the inmost fibres of the heart, and showed to each his basest and his weakest spot, and with their passionless and yet not untender cynicism, made the cheeks of

strong men flame, whom all the thunders of a Spurgeon would only have roused to manly scorn.[48]

In 1878, the author of an anonymous article in *The Congregationalist* suggested that there is often—perhaps always—a distinction between preachers who are oriented primarily toward literacy and those who adhere to a largely oral practice:

One thing I especially observe about preachers, that there are two classes of them; some men win people by what they *say,* and some by what they *are.* How many of the greatest preachers are great not by virtue of great sermons, but by reason of great souls. Their power dies with them; their sermons are poor reading, but men will travel miles to hear them.[49]

In the case of Newman's preaching, this reviewer's distinction is a false dichotomy. Newman's contemporaries saw him as a model of excellence as both a preacher and a writer. An article in the *Christian Remembrancer,* for example, attributed to Newman's sermons "that rarest combination of excellences, that they read well and that he preaches them well"; R. W. Church declared that the "great writers do not touch, pierce, and get hold of minds as he does, and those who are famous for the power and results of their preaching do not write as he does."[50]

Newman was able, in short, to combine the virtues of both of these categories of preachers; the sermons delivered at St. Mary's display both the literary sophistication of the accomplished stylist and the ethical force and practical concern of the classical public speaker. In Newman's preaching, the written and the spoken word are complementary rather than antithetical, and it is this complementary blending of the two diverse traditions that establishes Newman as one of the foremost practitioners of Victorian "oral literature."

6

George MacDonald

GEORGE MACDONALD IS ONE OF THE VICTORIAN PERIOD'S MOST multifaceted literary and religious figures. As one modern scholar writes, "The many MacDonalds include the fantasist, the children's writer, the realistic novelist, the Scottish regionalist, the Christian apologist, the preacher, the poet, the literary critic, and yet others, depending upon how we assign some of those works that mix or transcend genre."[1] Published studies of MacDonald, however, have not addressed the full scope of his work. In the Victorian period, critics emphasized his achievements as a poet and realistic novelist, comparing his prose to that of Sir Walter Scott and his verse to the work of such eminent poets as Shakespeare, Milton, Wordsworth, and Tennyson.[2] Most modern scholars, in contrast, believe that MacDonald's place in the canon of Victorian literature rests primarily, if not exclusively, on his pioneering work in the genre of fantasy novels.[3]

While Richard Reis may be correct in his claim that "the fiction must be the chief subject of any study of MacDonald,"[4] it does not follow that the fiction must be the *exclusive* focus of MacDonald scholarship. MacDonald was a Congregationalist clergyman before he became famous as a novelist and poet, and while his formal career as a minister lasted fewer than three years, he occupied various pulpits throughout his life.[5] He sometimes preached to informal gatherings of family and friends or addressed a church in a special preaching engagement. More important, MacDonald often preached through the printed word; he published five volumes of sermons and incorporated pulpit addresses into a number of his realistic novels. I believe that these sermons constitute an aspect of the MacDonald canon that should not be overlooked and propose that, by studying these sermons from the standpoint of orality-literacy theory, we can arrive at some conclusions about MacDonald's place in the history of Victorian preaching.

MacDonald's preaching career began in 1850, when he was twenty-five. After completing his studies in divinity at Highbury

College, a Congregational theological school in London, MacDonald became pastor of Trinity Congregational Church in Arundel, a town in West Sussex a few miles from the English Channel.[6]

MacDonald's tenure at Trinity lasted fewer than three years. During his undergraduate studies at King's College, Aberdeen, he attended Blackfriars Congregational Church, a church at the center of the "veritable storm" of Universalist revival that "rage[d] over the whole congregational body of Scotland" in the early 1840s.[7] MacDonald was one of the many students influenced by this revival, and his last two years at King's were "a period of inward ferment and outward gloom, marked by religious doubts."[8] As he worked to resolve these doubts, he became increasingly heterodox in his theology, particularly in his beliefs about the scope of the redemption made available by the crucifixion and resurrection of Christ. Ultimately, he rejected the Calvinist doctrine of predestination in favor of the Universalist belief that all humans will eventually repent and be saved.[9]

MacDonald's Universalist convictions were soon reflected in his preaching, and some members of his congregation took great offense at his declarations that "some provision was made for the heathen after death."[10] In the summer of 1852, MacDonald learned that "a small party in the church [had] for some time been exceedingly dissatisfied with [his] preaching"; he responded to this dissent by bringing the matter "before the assembled church."[11] On July 5, MacDonald announced that he would resign only if a majority, not a small group of dissatisfied members, wished it.[12] The congregation responded, "It is by no means our wish that the Revd. G. MacDonald should relinquish the office of Pastor of this Church. . . . But if on reflection he continues to hold and express such an opinion it is evident that it will cause serious difficulties in the church."[13] Such a response spoke directly to MacDonald's belief that "Chiefest of all the Christian blessings was peace, chiefest of all terrors was schism," and rather than continue to be the cause of dissension among his congregation, he resigned as pastor in May 1853.[14]

After he resigned his Trinity pastorate, MacDonald never again made a living as a minister. Instead, he embarked on a literary career: in addition to writing poems and novels, he wrote magazine and encyclopedia articles, gave popular lectures on both sides of the Atlantic, edited several volumes of poetry, and wrote a critical study of Shakespeare's *Hamlet*.[15] He did not, however, abandon his vocation as a preacher; as he told his father in a letter written a few months after his resignation, "Do not think I intend giving up preaching. . . . Preaching I think is in part my mission in this world and I shall try to fulfill it."[16]

MacDonald believed that he could no longer fulfill this mission in Arundel because the circumstances surrounding his resignation of the Trinity pastorate greatly reduced the sphere of his potential influence as a minister.[17] In the fall of 1853, he moved to Manchester, where he hoped to "find a few whom [he could] help."[18] Although some half-dozen churches were currently without pastors,[19] MacDonald's dislike of denominational ties and his reputation for unorthodoxy, if not outright heresy, kept him from finding a position with an established congregation there.[20] This difficulty did not, however, keep him out of the pulpit very long. In November 1853, MacDonald became acquainted with a "few young men in Manchester" who wanted "to meet together in some room, and have [him] for their minister";[21] eight months later, in July 1854, he fulfilled "a long cherished wish," leasing a room in which he could preach and be "unshackled in [his] teaching."[22]

In Manchester, MacDonald soon achieved the popularity as a preacher that doctrinal disputes kept him from realizing in Arundel. In August 1855, a "company of 70 seat-holders" asked him to preach to them, assuring him complete freedom in the pulpit, and he "agreed to do so for a year to see how it will do."[23] That same year, he published his first book, a dramatic poem entitled *Within and Without,* and "[f]rom this point forward, his growing literary success would attract growing audiences for his preaching."[24] Instead of serving just one congregation, MacDonald spent part of the next forty years preaching in many different houses of worship in England and America: Westminster Chapel; a Unitarian chapel in London; Congregational churches in Brixton, Sydenham, Glasgow, and Wimbledon; the Union Park Congregational Church in Chicago.

I have not been able to locate copies of the sermons MacDonald preached between 1850 and 1853, but records of his post-Arundel ministry have survived. He spoke extemporaneously, but stenographers—people whom one observer described as "reporters taking the text in shorthand to spread through the newspapers for every breakfast-table in England"[25]—were often present when he preached, and transcripts of his sermons were published in such periodicals as *The Chicago Pulpit, The Review,* and *The Christian World Pulpit.* These records of MacDonald's preaching have recently been made more accessible to scholars; in October 1996, Johannesen Publishing and Printing in Whitethorn, California, published twenty of these transcripts under the title *George Mac-Donald in the Pulpit*.

The transcripts in this volume exhibit significant ties to the oral tradition. MacDonald does not hold to the traditional structures of classical oratory; he does not provide an explicit segue between the introduction and body of his sermons; he does not repeat his main points or use transitional phrases such as "first," "next," and "finally"; and he does not use numbers, capital letters, or other typographical cues to outline the progress of his thought. In nearly every other regard, however, his sermons contain many of the same hallmarks of spoken rhetoric found in Spurgeon's preaching. First, MacDonald's syntax, like the syntax of much spoken language, employs coordinating constructions such as "and," and "but" much more often than subordinating words like "which," "because," and "who." Many of his sermons, furthermore, exhibit the oral tradition's emphasis on parallelism and other forms of repetition. In "Awakening," for example, he uses nine "We have" statements to illustrate the extent to which his contemporaries' "hearts and thoughts" have been influenced by "the cares of this world, and the deceitfulness of riches, and the first judgments of society, and the ambitions of the world":

> We have been passing judgments on our neighbors; we have been glorifying ourselves; we have been dividing and dividing from each other; we have been caring for our own dignities . . . and not for the truth. We have been denying the lowly, the weak, the simple in heart; we have been saying practically in our dealings with the world: "What He says is all very well, but it won't work in the present days." We have been drifting away from the simple, old, open life. We have been sinking deeper and deeper in evil dreams. . . . We have sank [sic] deeper and deeper, and all at once there comes a shock. The Divine Will has sent some little thing upon us, something of what we call "evil." (*Pulpit*, 13)[26]

Finally, MacDonald exhibits the orator's awareness of and interaction with his audience throughout *George MacDonald in the Pulpit*, often addressing his hearers as "friends" and using "you" and "we" dozens of times in every sermon.

The most significant link between MacDonald's spoken sermons and the oral tradition is MacDonald's continuous insistence upon the execution of Christian duty. In a letter to his father in April 1851, MacDonald complained that many preachers were "too much taken up about doctrine and far too little about practice," arguing that "The word doctrine, as used in the Bible means *teach-*

ing of duty not *theory*" and was therefore synonymous with practice.[27] In one of his spoken sermons, he told his congregation that he "[cared] to tell [them] nothing, except it be to rouse the practical in [them]"; all of the discourses in *George MacDonald in the Pulpit* contain some call to a "right order of action" (*Pulpit*, 227, 240). In some sermons, this "rousing" consists of general admonitions, of reminders that "It is he that works that is the son of God"; that "There is no liberty but in doing right"; and that "Knowledge without action, even though it may put on the lovely name of faith, is but a foreign thing in the human soul" (*Pulpit*, 87, 120, 146). In others, MacDonald offers more specific applications, exhorting his hearers not to "let [themselves] out ... to make money"; to "sweep from [their] eyes the accumulated fog of indifference"; or to be "ten-fold careful about [their] fellow-man, that [they] do him no wrong" (20, 28, 110).

Emphasis on Christian action is evident even in a sermon on faith, one of the most abstract subjects discussed in *George MacDonald in the Pulpit*. MacDonald's purpose in "Faith the Proof of the Unseen" is to explore the meaning of Hebrews 11:1—"Now faith is the substance of things hoped for, the evidence of things not seen"—and thereby to help "the man or woman who is troubled with the difficulty of believing" (*Pulpit*, 65, 69). He spends very little time, however, in doctrinal or metaphysical discussion. Although he suggests a definition early in the sermon, positing that "faith is the foundation, the root, the underlying substance of hope" (66), his emphasis throughout the discourse is on the connection between faith and practice. He makes frequent references to "duty," "work," and "obedience," concluding that the faithful person is not one who assents to a specific creed, but rather one who says, "I cannot prove that there is a God, but, O God, if Thou hearest me anywhere, help me to do Thy will" (67, 68, 72).

At the same time that he was preaching extemporaneous discourses in London, Sydenham, and Glasgow, MacDonald was also publishing manuscripts of sermons that he never delivered in a church or meeting hall. Publication began with the first series of the appropriately titled *Unspoken Sermons* (London: Strahan, 1867), which was followed by *The Miracles of Our Lord* (London: Strahan, 1870); two more volumes of *Unspoken Sermons* (London: Longmans, Green, 1885, 1889); and *The Hope of the Gospel* (London: Ward, Lock, Bowden, 1892).

When MacDonald moved from speaking in the pulpit to writing for the press, the rhetoric of his sermons changed as well, exhib-

iting more characteristics of written language and correspond-
ingly fewer similarities to the spoken word. In at least two of his
Unspoken Sermons, MacDonald acknowledges that he is writing
to an audience rather than speaking to one;[28] throughout the series, sermons exhibit some of the same characteristics of literacy—
use of both subordinating and coordinating conjunctions, for example, accompanied by less frequent alliteration, parallelism, and
other mnemonic and additive devices—that we see in Newman's
work.

The *Unspoken Sermons* also illustrate several scholars' observation that, while speakers can, and often must, interact with their
hearers, writers are almost always isolated from those who read
their work.[29] Pronouns and other forms of direct address, which
often indicate the extent of orators' interaction with their audiences,[30] appear far less often in these volumes than in Spurgeon's
and Newman's discourses. He uses indirect references—"we,"
"us," and "our"—about half as often as Newman, and direct references are even less common; phrases such as "my friends" rarely
occur, and there are even some sermons, such as "The New
Name" and "The Fear of God," in which "you" does not appear at
all. Furthermore, MacDonald refers to himself more often than
Newman does; while some may regard his references to his "own
mental processes"—"I think," "I say," "I have taken for granted"
(*US*, 1:103, 206, 225)—as evidence of orality,[31] I believe that the
prevalence of "I" over "you" in *Unspoken Sermons* instead illustrates another way in which MacDonald's rhetoric reflects the
distance of the writer rather than the close interaction of the
speaker.

MacDonald's shift away from orality and toward literacy is most
evident in the way he presents his applications. MacDonald's conviction that "obedience to Christ" is the essence of Christianity
(*Pulpit*, 170) appears throughout *George MacDonald in the Pulpit*,
but duty and practice is not consistently emphasized in *Unspoken
Sermons*. Some discourses do emphasize a specific obligation incumbent upon the Christian. In "The Hardness of the Way," Mac-
Donald declares that "It is imperative on us to get rid of the
tyranny of *things*"; in "Love Thine Enemy" he exhorts his readers
to "love the enemy now." He ends "The Voice of Job" by reminding
them that they "must make room for [God]; [they] must cleanse
[their] hearts that he may come in" (*US*, 2:37, 1:227, 2:209). In
others, MacDonald offers a more general call to action, declaring
that "Man's first business is, 'What does God want me to do?'" or

emphasizing that "the one thing [God] insists upon is the *doing* of the thing we know we ought to do" (*US*, 1:148, 2:8).

Several discourses in *Unspoken Sermons*, however, do not present a clear application. In "The Child in the Midst," for example, MacDonald sets forth what he believes to be the "highest point of [the] teaching of our Lord": the idea that "To receive a child in the name of God is to receive God himself." MacDonald derives no practical inference from this "revelation about God"; instead, he states that "the truth carries its own conviction to him who is able to receive it," evidently assuming that those who accept this "truth" will act in accordance with the "conviction" they receive (*US*, 1:2, 17, 18).

Even this implied application is absent from a number of sermons. In "Abba, Father!," "The Creation in Christ," and "The Truth," MacDonald spends more time in literary analysis—examining the nuances of Greek and English syntax or explaining the difference between "truth," "fact," and "law"—than in exhorting his readers to be more Christian in their conduct (*US*, 2:121–34, 3:2–6, 56–82). Furthermore, while MacDonald stated in one of his spoken sermons that he had "no great interest in mere instruction" (*Pulpit*, 144), two of his *Unspoken Sermons* are devoted entirely to discussions of abstract theological concepts. The subject of "The New Name" is the "mysticism" of the Book of Revelation, particularly the symbolism of the "white stone" that God will give "to him that overcometh" (*US*, 1:102, 103, 108). At no point in the sermon does MacDonald discuss the practical implications of his thoughts. Similarly, the central issue of "The God of the Living" is what the Bible means when it speaks of "the resurrection of the body" (*US*, 1:236). MacDonald spends a great deal of time describing the kinds of bodies Christians will have when they get to heaven, but he never discusses what they should do or believe in order to prepare for eternal life. In these instances, MacDonald departs from his contemporaries' stipulation that all sermons contain "well-applied argument, of the plainest and most practical kind";[32] to the extent that these addresses focus on "the high and great mysteries of religion" rather than "personal application of the text,"[33] they cease to be sermons—discourses with close ties to the oral tradition—and become essays—written documents—instead.

The Miracles of Our Lord, The Hope of the Gospel, and *Unspoken Sermons* were not the only avenues MacDonald employed to disseminate the sermons he did not preach. He regarded his work as a novelist as an extension of his vocation as a preacher; he once told his son Ronald that "having begun to do his work as a Congregational minister, and having been driven . . . into giving up that professional pulpit, he was . . . compelled to use unceasingly the new platform whence he had found that his voice could carry so far."[34]

Two novels that provided MacDonald a "new platform" for his preaching were *Annals of a Quiet Neighbourhood,* published by Hurt and Blackett in 1867, and its sequel, *The Seaboard Parish,* issued by Tinsley Brothers in 1868. Both novels are narrated in the first person by Harry Walton, pastor of a chapel in the town of Marshmallows and later in the parish of Kilkhaven. At times, MacDonald appears to be self-conscious, almost apologetic, about his tendency to use these novels as pulpits. This is first evident in Chapter 11 of *Annals,* entitled "Sermon on God and Mammon." The preaching in this chapter begins with a seventeen-page transcript of Walton's sermon on Matthew 6:24–25—"Ye cannot serve God and Mammon. Therefore I say unto you, Take no thought for your life" (*Annals,* 192)—and continues even after Walton leaves the pulpit. Back in his study, Walton meditates on the "road to contentment," and he casts his thoughts in the form of another brief sermon: "Let us acknowledge all good, all delight that the world holds, and be content without it. But this we can never be except by possessing the one thing, without which I do not merely say no man ought to be content, but no man *can* be content— the Spirit of the Father" (*Annals,* 213). Immediately afterward, MacDonald anticipates an objection some of his readers might make and promises that he will quickly turn from preaching to storytelling: "If any young people read my little chronicle, will they not be inclined to say, 'The vicar has already given us in this chapter hardly anything but a long sermon; and it is too bad of him to go on preaching in his study after we saw him safe out of the pulpit'? Ah, well! just one word, and I drop the preaching for a while" (*Annals,* 213).

MacDonald begins *The Seaboard Parish* by expressing the hope that his readers are accustomed to, and will at least tolerate, his habit of writing sermon-novels. The first chapter, entitled "Homiletic," begins,

Dear Friends,—I am beginning a book like an old sermon; but, as you know, I have been so accustomed to preach all my life, that whatever I say or write will more or less take the shape of a sermon; and if you had not by this time learned at least to bear with my oddities, you would not have wanted any more of my teaching. (*Parish,* 1)

The preaching to which MacDonald refers quickly becomes evident. Early in the novel, Constance Walton, Harry's eighteen-year-old daughter, is confined to the sickroom after being injured in a riding accident. Because she can no longer attend services at the church, Walton brings the services to her; "it became the custom" for the family "to gather in her room on Sunday evenings" and for Walton to preach to them there (*Parish*, 34).

After describing the first of these meetings, Walton indicates that such descriptions will appear throughout his book: "In the papers wherein I am about to record the chief events of the following years of my life, I shall give a short account of what passed at some of these assemblies in my child's room, in the hope that it may give my friends something, if not new, yet fresh to think about" (34). He immediately attempts to assure his readers, however, that his story will in fact be a story, and not a collection of sermons. In the very next paragraph, he writes, "I hope my readers will not be alarmed at this, and suppose that I am about to inflict long sermons upon them. I am not. I do hope, as I say, to teach them something; but those whom I succeed in so teaching will share in the delight it will give me to write about what I love most" (35).

While he does not "inflict long sermons" upon his readers, Walton does deliver shorter homilies during the family services in Constance's room. After recording one such address in the chapter entitled "Another Sunday Evening," MacDonald again feels compelled to justify, and even to apologize for, the sermonic material in his book:

> Try not to get weary, respected reader, of so much of what I am afraid most people will call tiresome preaching. But I know if you get anything practicable out of it, you will not be so soon tired of it. I promise you more story by and by. Only an old man, like an old horse, must be allowed to take very much his own way—go his own pace, I should have said. I am afraid there must be a little more of a similar sort in this chapter. (82)

Although MacDonald expressed some concern that readers would regard the tendency to "turn [his] stories into sermons" as the "great fault" of his novels, he believed that such a practice was central to his art.[35] His conviction that he had "a Master to serve first before [he could] wait upon the public"[36] therefore outweighed his fear of being thought "tiresome," and he unapologetically incorporated sermons of various lengths into *Annals of a Quiet Neighbourhood* and *The Seaboard Parish*.

The five sermons in *Annals of a Quiet Neighbourhood* fall into three categories. Only one—the "Sermon on God and Mammon," which is the focal point of Chapter 11—is a full-length discourse; it is also the only one delivered before an audience. Two others are summaries of sermons rather than complete transcripts. At the end of the chapter entitled "The Devil in the Vicar," Walton gives an overview of one of his Sunday morning sermons, and the summary reads like a sermon in itself:

> I told my people that God had created all our worships, reverences, tendernesses, loves. That they had come out of his heart, and He had made them in us because they were in Him first. . . . Therefore, we must be all God's; and all our aspirations, all our worships, all our honours, all our loves, must centre in Him, the Best. (*Annals*, 423, 24)

A few chapters later, Walton summarizes a sermon he preached on the "fortieth chapter of the prophecies of Isaiah" (*Annals*, 513). He records that, after giving a fairly lengthy "paraphrase of the chapter," he

> tried to show [the congregation] that it was in the commonest troubles of life . . . that they were to trust in God. . . . they must not be too anxious to be delivered from that which troubled them: but they ought to be anxious to have the presence of God with them to support them, and make them able in patience to possess their souls; and so the trouble would work its end—the purification of their minds, that the light and gladness of God . . . might shine in upon them. (514, 15)

Finally, two sermons in *Annals of a Quiet Neighbourhood* are not at all related to Walton's pulpit work. They are part of his private meditations, and, as such, are preached only to the readers of the novel. One of these is the mini-sermon on the "road to contentment" to which I have already alluded; the other is part of a comparison of the Gospels and Epistles which appears in Chapter 8. In an attempt to ease his "suffering" over an unspecified "disappointment," Walton takes up his Bible and discovers that while he "could not read the Epistles at all," he could find comfort in the Gospel, which "took such a hold of [him] as it had never taken before" (127, 128). Looking back at the incident, Walton realizes why this was the case, and he conveys his explanation to the reader in another mini-sermon:

> I know *now* that it was Jesus Christ and not theology that filled the hearts of the men that wrote those epistles—Jesus Christ, the living,

loving God-Man, whom I found—not in the Epistles, but in the Gospels. The Gospels contain what the apostles preached—the Epistles what they wrote after the preaching. And until we understand the Gospel, the good news of Jesus Christ our brother-king—until we understand Him, until we have His Spirit, promised so freely to them that ask it—all the Epistles . . . are to us a sealed book. Until we love the Lord so as to do what He tells us, we have no right to have an opinion about what one of those men meant; for all they wrote is about things beyond us. (127, 128)

The Seaboard Parish contains more examples of Harry Walton's preaching—both full-length discourses and mini-sermons—than *Annals of a Quiet Neighbourhood.* Here, three sermons—Walton's first sermon in Kilkhaven, a harvest sermon, and a funeral oration delivered after fifteen people died in a shipwreck—are reproduced in their entirety. While only two mini-sermons are recorded in *Annals,* at least a dozen appear in *Seaboard Parish.* Many of these shorter discourses are delivered during the Walton family's Sunday evening gatherings in Constance's sickroom. The first one appears only sixteen pages into the novel, as Walton is talking with his daughter Connie about her confusion regarding her place in the world. In response to Connie's question, "Is nobody ever to go away to find the work meant for her?," Walton says:

> What God may hereafter require of you, you must not give yourself the least trouble about. Everything he gives to you to do, you must do as well as ever you can, and that is the best possible preparation for what he may want you to do next. If people would but do what they have to do, they would always find themselves ready for what came next. And I do not believe that those who follow this rule are ever left floundering on the sea-deserted sands of inaction, unable to find water enough to swim in. (16)

Accounts of Walton's sickroom sermons appear throughout the novel; his many brief discourses address such topics as how Christians should respond to "poverty and suffering"; the importance of patience in the midst of pain; and the significance of the tears Christ shed at the grave of Lazarus (48–50, 152–53, 458–59).

Like *Annals of a Quiet Neighborhood, The Seaboard Parish* contains two mini-sermons addressed only to the reader. One is a meditation on the nature of true martyrdom, inspired by the ways in which Constance's illness had helped her develop a "more delicate and sympathetic" soul:

> But while *martyrdom* really means a bearing for the sake of the truth, yet there is a way in which any suffering, even that we have brought

upon ourselves, may become martyrdom. When it is so borne that the
sufferer therein bears witness to the presence and fatherhood of God,
in quiet hopeful submission to his will . . . [or] when it is accepted as
the just and merciful consequence of wrong-doing, and is endured
humbly, and with righteous shame, as the cleansing of the Father's
hand . . . then indeed it may be called a martyrdom. (136–37)

The second mini-sermon appears after the first of two ship-
wrecks in the novel, as Walton confronts the captain about his
choice to sail in an unsafe vessel. He is unable to convince the
captain that he is guilty of any wrongdoing, but despite their disagreement, Walton offers the captain a glass of wine before he
leaves. Walton evidently regards this as an action with some spiritual significance, for he uses the occasion to preach to the reader
about the importance of ministering to the body as well as to
the soul:

Let no man who wants to do anything for the soul of a man lose a
chance of doing something for his body. He ought to be willing, and
ready, which is more than willing, to do that whether or not; but there
are those who need this reminder. Of many a soul Jesus laid hold by
healing the suffering the body brought upon it. No one but himself
can tell how much the nucleus of the church was composed of and
by those who had received health from his hands, loving-kindness
from the word of his mouth. (238)

The sermonic passages in *Annals of a Quiet Neighbourhood* and
The Seaboard Parish, in short, demonstrate the variety of ways in
which MacDonald used his novels as vehicles for his preaching.
A study of the novels can also provide another means of assessing
his preaching from the perspective of orality-literacy studies. Mac-
Donald's biographies and letters do not provide a great deal of
evidence regarding his homiletic thought, but *Annals of a Quiet
Neighborhood* and *The Seaboard Parish* provide a fairly detailed
picture of the ways in which Harry Walton prepared and delivered
his sermons. I propose, therefore, that if we regard Walton as a
persona through whom MacDonald speaks, we can use these novels in conjunction with the statements we have from MacDonald
himself to draw additional conclusions about MacDonald's theory
and practice of preaching.[37]

First, like the sermons MacDonald himself delivered before live
audiences, Harry Walton's preaching consistently emphasizes
practical application. In Chapter 8 of *Annals of a Quiet Neighbourhood,* Walton writes, "I always made use of the knowledge I had

of my individual hearers, to say what I thought would do them good. Not that I ever preached *at* anybody; I only sought to explain the principles of things in which I knew action of some sort was demanded from them" (131–32).

Walton believed, in fact, that acting in accordance with one's duty was the best way to arrive at a true understanding of the Scriptures, and he made exhortations to action a central focus of his preaching. He tells us that when he stepped into the pulpit of his chapel in Marshmallows,

> I tried to show [my congregation] what His sayings meant, as far as I understood them myself, and where I could not understand them, I just told them so, and said I hoped for more light by and by to enable me to understand them; telling them that that hope was a sharp goad to my resolution, driving me on to do my duty, because I knew that only as I did my duty would light go up in my heart, making me wise to understand the precious words of my Lord. And I told them that if they would try to do their duty, they would find more understanding from that than from any explanation I could give them. (*Annals*, 130)

Walton presents this theory again in *The Seaboard Parish*, this time in the form of a critique of Methodist pulpit oratory. In Chapter 23, Walton and the village blacksmith, who is a Methodist, get into a discussion about "the efficacy of preaching." In Walton's view, the shortcoming of the Methodists is not that they place doctrine over practice, but that they emphasize emotional fervor during the service over practical action outside the church walls:

> You try to work upon people's feelings without reference to their judgment. Any one who can preach what you call rousing sermons, is considered a grand preacher amongst you, and there is a great danger of his being led thereby to talk more nonsense than sense. And then when the excitement goes off, there is no seed left in the soil to grow in peace, and they are always craving after more excitement. . . . And the consequence is, that they continue like children—the good ones, I mean—and have hardly a chance of making a calm, deliberate choice of that which is good; while those who have been only excited and nothing more, are hardened and seared by the recurrence of such feeling as is neither aroused by truth nor followed by action. (*Parish*, 307)

Examples of Walton's application of his theory appear throughout *Annals of a Quiet Neighbourhood* and *The Seaboard Parish*. The closing paragraph of Walton's "Sermon on God and Mammon" contains a clear summons to action on the part of the congregation:

Now you see that He took no thought for the morrow. And, in the name of the holy child Jesus, I call upon you . . . to cast care to the winds, and trust in God; to receive the message of peace and good-will to men; to yield yourselves to the Spirit of God, that you may be taught what He wants you to know. (*Annals*, 208)

Walton's first sermon in Kilkhaven contains an equally clear exhortation. Tailoring his application to the large number of sailors in the chapel that day, Walton uses maritime imagery to call his audience to a pure life:

O sailors with me on the ocean of life, will you, knowing that he is watching you from his mountaintop, do and say the things that hurt, and wrong, and disappoint him? . . . Will you say evil things, lie, and delight in vile stories and reports, with his eye on you, watching your ship on its watery ways, ever ready to come over the waves to help you? It is a fine thing, sailors, to fear nothing; but it would be far finer to fear nothing *because* he is above all, and over all, and in you all. For his sake and for his love, give up everything bad, and take him for your captain. He will be both captain and pilot to you, and steer you safe into the port of glory. (*Parish*, 221, 22)

Finally, Walton reminds his audiences of their Christian duty in each of his mini-sermons. Whether he is telling his congregation that they "must be all God's," admonishing Constance to do everything God "gives to [her] to do . . . as well as ever [she] can," or suggesting to the reader that enduring hardship in a way that "bears witness to the presence and fatherhood of God" can be considered a form of martyrdom, there can be little doubt about the specific attitude or course of action that Walton wants his audience to adopt (*Annals*, 424; *Parish*, 16, 137). In short, Harry Walton is a preacher who, as his parishioner Miss Jemima observed, "was constantly preaching works," and her reactions to his sermons—"I know I always come out of the church with something on my mind; and I've got to work it off somehow before I'm comfortable"—are what he hoped to elicit from all who heard him preach (*Annals*, 439).

While the concern with "practical decision-making" that we find throughout *George MacDonald in the Pulpit*, *Annals of a Quiet Neighbourhood* and *The Seaboard Parish* links MacDonald's and Walton's preaching to the oral tradition,[38] the circumstances under which their sermons were prepared and preached suggests that their work is best viewed as an often uneasy juxtaposition of spoken and written practice. This juxtaposition is first evident in the different places that the preachers and their congregations occupy on the orality-literacy continuum. As we have seen, Spurgeon and Newman occupied approximately the same position on this continuum as their congregations; Spurgeon's success at New Park Street and the Metropolitan Tabernacle was largely attributed to his extemporaneous, nonscholarly technique, whereas Newman's practice of reading his sermons was well suited to his academic, and therefore literacy-oriented, parishioners.

MacDonald and Walton, in contrast, are well-educated, highly literate ministers serving people with little formal schooling. MacDonald earned degrees from King's and Highbury—his schooling, like Newman's, recalls Bruce Rosenberg's link between seminary training and manuscript preaching[39]—but his parishioners were "a simple people—not particularly well-informed."[40] Walton is similarly well acquainted with books. He reads Plato, the Anglo-Saxon Gospels, and the Greek New Testament and quotes writers ranging from Thomas à Kempis to Milton to Melville, but few members of his churches are people of letters. Mr. Stoddart, the organist, has a large library and Jemima Crowther knows Shakespeare, Bacon, Pope, and Milton, but most of the residents of Marshmallows and Kilkhaven are, in Walton's words, "a company of rustics, of thought yet slower than of speech, unaccustomed in fact to *think* at all" (*Annals,* 7).

These differences sometimes hindered MacDonald's and Walton's success as ministers. As Glenn Sadler has noted, MacDonald "often had the problem of being 'too intellectual' for some congregations."[41] This "problem" first arose during MacDonald's seminary studies: John Godwin, professor of preaching at Highbury, found fault with "his tendency to be intellectual and poetical in his expositions."[42] This tendency kept him from being offered a temporary position at Stebbing, where he was viewed as overly intellectual in his preaching and therefore "not acceptable to many of the people."[43] It affected his ministry at Trinity as well; he was told on at least one occasion that "they can't understand [him] at Arundel."[44]

Several passages in MacDonald's letters and *Annals of a Quiet Neighbourhood* cast the differences between preacher and congregation in terms directly related to orality-literacy studies. It is unlikely that the citizens of Arundel were a primarily oral people— that is, people "totally unfamiliar with writing"[45]—but they evidently placed little significance on the printed word. MacDonald, in fact, believed himself to be the only reading person in the town; in a November 1850 letter to his father, he wrote, "All my spare money I laid out on books—very necessary to do when going to a country place like Arundel, where I can have no society, and no books of any kind, except what I have of my own."[46]

Tension between the preacher's orientation toward literacy and his congregation's orientation toward orality appears in *Annals of a Quiet Neighbourhood* as well. Walton's visit to Mrs. Oldcastle and Miss Gladwyn in Chapter 5 is rather tense at times. Mrs. Oldcastle denigrates formal education and the written word when she says, "I don't know that it is necessary to read any good books but *the* good book" and tells Miss Gladwyn that "Mr Walton is not so old as [she is] and has much to learn yet" (*Annals*, 57). Later in the novel, Hester Crowther criticizes Walton's preaching, telling him that he is "too anxious to explain everything," asking, "Where can be the use of trying to make uneducated people see the grounds of everything? It is enough that this or that is in the Bible" (442).

Miss Hester's complaints identify her as preferring an orality-based mode of preaching to a literacy-based one. By asking Walton to simply "tell them what is in the Bible" without engaging in extensive explanation or adding "argument to convince them of what is incorrect" (*Annals*, 442), she is asking him to abandon the literate tradition's "feel for precision and analytic exactitude" in favor of "Orally managed language and thought," which "is not noted for analytic precision."[47] Her request also reflects the perspective of some orality-oriented churchgoers in twentieth-century America, who believe that their ministers—called "spiritual" preachers to distinguish them from their "manuscript" counterparts—"need not be learned, and in fact should not be educated, except in the ways of the Bible."[48]

MacDonald and Walton, then, are literacy-oriented preachers ministering to largely oral congregations, and their methods of preparing and delivering their sermons reflect an ongoing attempt to negotiate the inherent tensions between the two traditions. MacDonald's son Greville noted that his father was a proponent of "extempore speaking," an observation supported by MacDonald's own assertion that "there are no such things as *written sermons*. It is a contradiction in terms—a sermon ought never to be printed—or read."[49] MacDonald's practice, however, did not always correspond to his theory. Several of his published letters tell us that he did in fact write at least some of his "spoken" sermons.

In 1849, for example, MacDonald was having difficulty keeping up with both his studies at Highbury and his supply-preaching duties at Youghal. In a letter to his father he expressed doubts about whether he "ever shall [be] able to write more than one sermon a week."[50] Another letter written approximately a year later indicates that MacDonald's sermon-writing involved not just jotting down outlines, as was Spurgeon's practice, but rather composing an entire manuscript: "I send you a sermon such as it is. It will require some ingenuity in you to follow it. There are little figures to tell you how to follow the pages—but as I told you, I have no time to dress up my sermons yet. When I find I can write with perfect comfort, then I shall gradually be more great."[51]

Although MacDonald prepared his sermons like Newman, he wanted to deliver them like Spurgeon. In two letters MacDonald wrote to his father in October 1850, he stated, "I don't wish to preach at all as I write" and "I have not time to spend on the composition of sermons, which I preach in a very different style from that in which I write them."[52] In short, MacDonald's homiletic style appears to have been intended to satisfy the somewhat contradictory preferences of those Victorian churchgoers who preferred "a written sermon delivered as if it were unwritten."[53]

The tensions between oral and literate expression that MacDonald faced in his own preaching reappear, in somewhat greater detail, in the experiences of Harry Walton, MacDonald's spokesman in *Annals of a Quiet Neighbourhood* and *The Seaboard Parish*. When Walton first arrives at Marshmallows, he plans to read his sermons in the pulpit but is soon forced to abandon his plans in favor of a more orally based approach. His first morning service goes well, but "as [he] had feared, it was different in the afternoon. The people had dined, and the usual somnolence had followed; nor could [he] find in [his] heart to blame men and women who had worked hard all the week, for being drowsy on the day of rest" (*Annals*, 18).

Walton accommodates his weary parishioners by deviating from the sermon he had written: "I curtailed my sermon as much as I could, omitting page after page of my manuscript." His congregation is grateful for the change: "when [he] came to a close, [he] was rewarded by perceiving an agreeable surprise upon many of the faces round [him]." This reaction then leads Walton to permanently alter his preaching style so that "in the afternoons at least, [his] sermons should be as short as heart could wish" (*Annals*, 18, 19).

As the novel progresses, Walton holds to his resolution and moves toward an extemporaneous style of preaching. He does not abandon sermon preparation altogether, as some American folk preachers do,[54] but comes to point where he claims to "always [preach] *extempore*, which phrase I beg my reader will not misinterpret as meaning *on the spur of the moment*, or *without the due preparation of much thought*" (*Annals*, 209; MacDonald's emphasis). Walton still prepares his sermons, but he does so not in his study, where he would be surrounded by the implements of literacy, but out in the woods, where his preparation can take place only in his mind. When he went out into the woods early in the week, he usually had a book in his hand, but he rarely consulted it; in fact, he tells us that "[he] seemed somehow to come back with most upon those days in which [he] did not read" (*Annals*, 245). As Sunday drew near, Walton still did not turn to writing to help him finalize his preparation to preach. Instead, he "had another custom, which may perhaps appear strange to some": "to spend the Saturday evening, not in [his] study, but in the church," meditating on the sermon he would deliver the next day (245).

Although *The Seaboard Parish* contains more sermons than *Annals of a Quiet Neighbourhood*, it contains fewer statements about Walton's method of preparing and delivering them. Only two descriptions of Walton's preaching appear in the novel; both indicate that he is continuing to follow the extemporaneous method he adopted at Marshmallows. In describing his inaugural service at Kilkhaven, Walton first speaks of the separation between preacher and congregation that is often imposed by the use of a manuscript. When he is reading the prayers, he "could see little of [his] congregation, partly from [his] being on a level with them, partly from the necessity for keeping [his] eyes and thoughts upon that which [he] read" (*Parish*, 211). Because he did not preach from a manuscript, no such isolation was present during the sermon itself; Walton notes that when he "rose from prayer in the pulpit, then [he] felt, as usual with [him], that [he] was personally present for personal influence with [his] people" (*Parish*, 211).

Several chapters later, Walton emphasizes the importance of such a personal presence in the pulpit. Shortly before returning to Marshmallows, Walton has a seaside conversation with Mr. Percivale, a member of his Kilkhaven congregation. During their talk, Walton bores holes in the sand with his stick instead of looking at his guest because "[he] could talk better when [he] did not look [his] familiar faces in the face" (*Parish*, 463). Walton quickly adds that this is not the practice to which he adheres in church: rather than keeping his eyes fixed on his book, as manuscript preachers like Newman did, Walton cultivated eye contact with the members of his congregation, seeking "the faces of [his] flock to assist [him] in speaking to their needs" (*Parish*, 463). In short, by the end of this second novel, Walton has successfully resolved the tensions between oral and literate modes of preaching, moving from a preacher who reads from his manuscript at the detriment of his orally based audience to one who shares his parishioners' conviction that "the extemporaneous ideal is the true one of public speech."[55]

The sermons MacDonald preached before various congregations and published in the three volumes of *Unspoken Sermons* were much more positively received than the discourses he incorporated in his novels. Some praise of his spoken sermons was very brief; a notice published in *The Chicago Pulpit* in 1873 called "Awakening" a "most eloquent sermon"; a Mr. Dexter, editor of the *Boston Congregationalist,* wrote that a sermon MacDonald preached in Canonbury in 1871 was "streaked everywhere with fine touches of poetic expression, which no report can convey"; and Archbishop Tait "called him 'the very best preacher' he had ever heard."[56]

Other commendations were more extensive. One positive account of MacDonald's preaching appeared in an article published in the March 16, 1901 edition of *The Spectator.* The unidentified author wrote,

> Who that has ever heard him will forget George MacDonald the preacher? Who does not recall that finely chiselled face, almost unearthly in its wonderful spiritual refinement? . . . How unlike the conventional sermon was his discourse! He told his hearers of what he knew. It was no piece of brocaded oratory, no set theological essay, it was a simple yet most profound message from a human soul to his brother souls. Here was one, you felt, who had been on the Mount of Vision and who had seen and heard things beyond mortal ken. You forgot mere logic, you were rapt into an "ampler ether, a sublimer air" than you were wont to breathe every day.[57]

A similar review was written by Phillips Brooks, a respected American Episcopal preacher, who heard MacDonald preach during his 1872 lecture tour. Recalling MacDonald's sermon in a lecture to the Yale Divinity School in 1877, Brooks wrote,

> Among the many sermons I have heard, I always remember one by Mr. George MacDonald, the English author. . . . It had his brave and

manly honesty. But over and through it all it had this quality: it was a message from God to these people by him. . . . As I listened, I seemed to see how weak in contrast was the way in which other preachers had amused me and challenged my admiration for the working of their minds. Here was a gospel. Here were real tidings. And you listened and forgot the preacher.[58]

Unspoken Sermons, which appears to be the only collection reviewed during the nineteenth century, received positive responses as well. A reviewer writing in the March 16, 1901 edition of *The Spectator* asserted that, while the discourses "cannot impart the striking personality of the preacher," they "will convey to those who never heard him somewhat of his searching spiritual power."[59] A more extensive commentary appeared in the same magazine some fifteen years earlier, in the edition of June 27, 1885. In this article, the first series of *Unspoken Sermons* was described as "a really remarkable book," the work of a man "whose spiritual instincts are naturally healthy, and who relies upon them with an unshaken and apparently unshakeable confidence."[60] The reviewer believed that, while the second series was somewhat less inspired than the previous volume, some individual discourses showed an "arresting and illuminating" inspiration. He wrote, for example, that MacDonald's sermon on Matthew 19:16–22, in which Christ tells a rich man to "go and sell that thou hast, and give to the poor" (Matthew 19:21 KJV), is "a singularly profound and searching piece of exposition" and that the two sermons on prayer "rank with the most valuable and illuminating of Mr. MacDonald's utterances" because they treat a familiar subject "with a new power and freshness."[61] Perhaps the highest praise of MacDonald's preaching came from John Ruskin, who asserted that the first series of *Unspoken Sermons* are "the best sermons—beyond all compare—I have ever read."[62]

MacDonald's use of characters such as Harry Walton as outlets for his preaching, in contrast, elicited little praise and a good deal of scorn from nineteenth- and twentieth-century readers. The only positive reaction in the Victorian period I have found appeared in the June 27, 1885, edition of *The Spectator.* The reviewer wrote, "it may fairly be said that his novels, his poems, and his criticisms owe a great deal of their permanent value, as they certainly owe not a little of their immediate popularity, to the quantity of homiletic matter which they hold in solution."[63]

Most other critics found little to praise in MacDonald's "sermon-novels."[64] A reviewer of *The Seaboard Parish,* for example, complained that Harry Walton "is always preaching, and that is scarcely generally a happy mode for a father to adopt, nor would it seem to be consistent with the typical *role* of the character."[65] Other novels came under attack for their homiletic content as well: the critic who reviewed *Robert Falconer* for the July 1868 edition of the *Fortnightly Review* found fault with MacDonald's didactic approach to novel-writing and asserted that MacDonald's "preaching was suicidal to his art."[66] Ten years later, a similar review of *Paul Faber, Surgeon* appeared in the *Athenaeum;* the reviewer dismissed the novel as little more than a "lay sermon" and found "little to criticize from a literary point of view."[67]

Positive assessments of the preaching in MacDonald's novels are outnumbered by negative ones in more recent criticism as well. The lone praise came from C. S. Lewis, who regarded Mac-Donald primarily as a religious teacher rather than a writer of fiction. Accordingly, he maintains that, while few of MacDonald's realistic novels are good and "none is very good," the preaching in the novels is excellent and the homiletic "diversions" are "welcome" aspects of his art.[68] William Raeper and Richard Reis, in contrast, view the interpolated sermons as fatal flaws in MacDonald's writing: Raeper criticizes MacDonald's prose as "like syrup, affected and latinate, full of pulpit oratory," while Reis argues that MacDonald's preaching "is inappropriate to the genre" of realistic novels, that "His insistence upon didacticism prompted him to spoil many novels by interpolating into them long sermons—good preaching, perhaps, but bad storytelling."[69]

Although these scholars and critics differ in their conclusions, their critical presupposition is the same: they regard MacDonald's novels as the primary focus of their scholarship, and their study of the sermons is limited to commentary on whether MacDonald's interpolations are an asset or a hindrance to his fiction. As I have attempted to demonstrate in this chapter, however, MacDonald's sermons, both those published separately and those incorporated into his novels, are worthy of study in their own right, and the discipline of orality-literacy studies provides a scholarly perspective from which we can conduct such a study.

How, then, can we assess the significance of MacDonald's preaching in terms of the intersection of the oral and written traditions? Spurgeon and Newman are significant because they approached the basic orality of the sermon in two very different ways. Spurgeon held to a more extemporaneous approach, preparing his "sermon so far as thoughts go, and leaving the words to be found during delivery," while Newman read manuscripts in the pulpit, allowing the implements of literacy a prominent place in his preaching.[70] In both instances, however, the pulpit was the place from which their messages were first set before the public; Spurgeon and Newman then employed publication as a means of enlarging the audience for the messages that had already been presented through the spoken word.

In contrast, the publication of most of MacDonald's sermons was not an extension of previous oral delivery. Although *George MacDonald in the Pulpit* provides a small sampling of the "more than a thousand" sermons delivered before live audiences, most of his homiletic canon consists of discourses he never preached.[71] The oral component of Harry Walton's preaching, moreover, is an orality that exists only within the context of literacy. Walton preaches to his parishioners at Marshmallows and Kilkhaven, but his "speaking" exists only in the words that MacDonald has recorded in his books.

Because much of MacDonald's preaching took place only through the printed word, his sermons cannot be described in terms of the orality-based "secondary literacy" that characterizes Spurgeon's discourses, nor can they be classified as "oral literature," the term I employed in my discussion of Newman's preaching. His place on the orality-literacy spectrum must, instead, be described using a third category, which I propose to call "primary literacy." Walter Ong has used "primary orality" to describe people who are "totally unfamiliar with writing" and therefore have the spoken word as the only available means of communication.[72] Conversely, "primary literacy" is a phrase that can describe a mode of discourse such as preaching in which the oral element has been circumvented or otherwise excluded, leaving the written word as the only avenue of communication. As a widely respected minister who preached many sermons only through the press, George MacDonald is one of the foremost illustrations of primary literacy in the preaching of the Victorian age.

7

A Rhetorical Comparison of Spurgeon, Newman, and MacDonald

At some point in their careers, Charles Haddon Spurgeon, John Henry Newman, and George MacDonald all published sermons based on John 11:1–44, the account of the death and resurrection of Lazarus. Spurgeon's "A Mystery! Saints Sorrowing and Jesus Glad!" was preached August 7, 1864, and published in volume 10 of his *Metropolitan Tabernacle Pulpit*. Newman's "Tears of Christ at the Grave of Lazarus" was "written and preached . . . between the years 1825 and 1843" and published in volume 3 of *Parochial and Plain Sermons*.[1] And the fortieth chapter of Mac-Donald's 1868 novel *The Seaboard Parish* is a funeral address entitled simply "The Sermon." We find in these sermons three very different methods of interpreting the same passage of scripture and communicating that interpretation to an audience, methods which can in large part be ascribed to the different positions these preachers occupy on the orality-literacy continuum. These sermons, in other words, provide specific illustrations of the categories I created in the previous three chapters: "A Mystery!" demonstrates how Spurgeon's oratory is dominated by the conventions of orality. "Tears of Christ" shows the prevalence of literacy over orality in Newman's homiletics, while "The Sermon" is indicative of the way in which MacDonald moved away from orality and practiced a largely literate approach to the art of preaching.

Although Spurgeon's sermon is grounded in the conventions of orality while Newman's and MacDonald's are informed by the practices of literate expression, all three discourses reflect an important tie to the oral tradition: an emphasis on "practical decision making."[2] The text on which "A Mystery!" is based is John 11:14–15—"Then said Jesus unto them plainly, Lazarus is dead. And I am glad for your sakes that I was not there, to the intent ye may believe; nevertheless, let us go unto him" ("A Mystery!," 453).[3]

114

Spurgeon's application is accordingly an appeal for his hearers to profess the belief of which Jesus speaks:

> Before God's throne to-day, if thou believest, thou art as clear as the angels in heaven. Thou art a saved soul if thou art resting upon the atonement of Christ, and thou mayst go thy way and sing—
>
> > "Now, freed from sin, I walk at large,
> > The Saviour's blood's my full discharge;
> > At his dear feet my soul I lay,
> > A sinner saved, and homage pay."
>
> If this be the result of your affliction, Christ may well say, "I am glad for your sakes that I was not there to stop the trouble, to the intent that ye may believe." May God bring you to faith for Jesus' sake. Amen. (464)

Newman finds his preaching text somewhat later in John's gospel, in verses 34–36: "Jesus said, Where have ye laid him? They said unto Him, Lord, come and see. Jesus wept. Then said the Jews, Behold how He loved him" ("Tears," 128). In his application, he exhorts his congregants to remember that Jesus has the same love for them that he had for Lazarus:

> Let us take to ourselves these comfortable thoughts, both in the contemplation of our own death, or upon the death of our friends. Wherever faith in Christ is, there is Christ Himself. . . . We will not, after our experience of Lazarus's history, doubt an instant that He is thoughtful about us. . . . We all have experience of this in the narrative before us, and henceforth, so be it! will never complain at the course of His providence. Only, we will beg of Him an increase of faith . . . a more confident persuasion that He will never put upon us more than we can bear, never afflict His brethren with any woe except for their own highest benefit. (138)

No preaching text is indicated at the beginning of MacDonald's sermon; Harry Walton, MacDonald's spokesman in the novel, points out that he "gave [his congregation] no text" when he "stood up to preach" ("The Sermon," 578). Like "A Mystery!" and "Tears of Christ," however, "The Sermon" ends with a clear application, a call to believe that Christ is able to resurrect all humans just as he raised Lazarus:

> What is it to you and me that he raised Lazarus? We are not called upon to believe that he will raise from the tomb that joy of our hearts

which lies buried there beyond our sight. Stop! Are we not? We *are* called upon to believe this. Else the whole story were for us a poor mockery. . . . That he called forth Lazarus showed that he was in his keeping, that he is Lord of the living, and that all live to him—that he has a hold of them, and can draw them forth when he will. If this is not true, then the raising of Lazarus is false—I do not mean merely false in fact, but false in meaning. If we believe in him, then in his name, both for ourselves and for our friends, we must deny death and believe in life. Lord Christ, fill our hearts with thy life! (591)

The use of a closing appeal or exhortation is the only element of oral expression we find in all three sermons. The ways in which Spurgeon, Newman, and MacDonald bring their audiences to these final applications reflect the degrees to which the conventions of orality and the techniques of literacy are present in their sermons.

Although he took a few notes into the pulpit, Spurgeon composed his discourses as he stood before his audience; virtually every aspect of "A Mystery! Saints Sorrowing and Jesus Glad!" illustrates the extemporaneous, orality-dominant nature of his preaching. The sermon is divided into introduction, exposition, and application, a sequence derived from classical rhetoric's six-fold paradigm of "introduction, narration, division, proof, refutation, and conclusion."[4] Each division of the sermon, moreover, contains elements characteristic of oral thought and expression. Spurgeon begins his sermon by telling a story, a practice that is an integral part of the oral tradition:[5]

There lived in the little village of Bethany a very happy family. There was neither father nor mother in it: the household consisted of the unmarried brother Eleazar, or Lazarus, and his sisters, Martha and Mary, who dwelt together in unity so good and pleasant that there the Lord commanded the blessing, even life for evermore. ("A Mystery!," 453)

The complete story comprises nearly two pages of Spurgeon's twelve-page discourse; in it Spurgeon freely embellishes John's account of the death of Lazarus. For example, John does not describe the type of hospitality Mary and Martha extended to Jesus during his visits to Bethany, but Spurgeon tells us that Jesus had a room of his own in their house, a room furnished with "a table, a bed, and a candlestick" (453). Similarly, John records only that Mary and Martha "sent a message to Jesus" telling him of Lazarus' illness (11:3), but Spurgeon asserts that they did so "With glowing hopes and moderated anxieties" (453). Finally, Spurgeon embellishes his source by praising Mary's and Martha's devotion to Lazarus. He tells us that Martha "has been sitting up every night watching her poor brother," and he places words in Mary's mouth: "He will come. . . . Brother, he will come and quicken thee, and we shall have many happy hours yet" (454). The result is that by the time he begins his exposition, Spurgeon has constructed an entirely new narrative version of John 11:1–44.

The core of Spurgeon's sermon is a nine-page exposition based on the story he tells in the introduction. Like the introduction, it reflects Spurgeon's extensive ties to the oral tradition. Because oral communication is "essentially evanescent"—there are no permanent records, no way to look things up—the only ideas an oral culture can preserve are those that have been committed to memory in a mnemonic, easy-to-recall way.[6] Since medieval times, one of the mnemonic devices most widely employed in the pulpit was the division of a sermon into "heads," major units of thought that serve as "great assistances to the memory, and recollection of a hearer."[7] Spurgeon divides the exposition in "A Mystery!" into three heads and begins the exposition by announcing what these divisions will be. He first states the central "principle" of his sermon: "that our Lord . . . sets so high a value upon his people's faith, that he will not screen them from those trials by which faith is strengthened" (455). He then outlines the divisions under which he will discuss this principle, the way in which he will "press the wine of consolation from the cluster of the text":

> In three cups we will preserve the goodly juice as it flows forth from the winepress of meditation. First of all, brethren, Jesus Christ was glad that the trial had come, *for the strengthening of the faith of the apostles;* secondly, *for strengthening the faith of the family;* and thirdly, *for giving faith to others.* (455; Spurgeon's emphasis)

As he moves from one "cup" to another, Spurgeon repeats these key phrases verbatim, enabling his congregants to keep track of the progression of the discourse and helping them to commit his points to memory (455, 460, 462). This repetition, moreover, receives special emphasis in the printed text: when he prepared the transcript of this sermon for publication, Spurgeon cast the three major heads in capital letters and the points and subpoints in italics. The nine pages of Spurgeon's exposition can therefore be distilled into an outline in which the mnemonic characteristics of oral expression are readily apparent:

I.   Jesus Christ designed the death of Lazarus and his after resurrection FOR THE STRENGTHENING OF THE FAITH OF THE APOSTLES.

   A. Let us once observe that *the trial itself would certainly tend to increase the apostles' faith.*

      1. *Trial takes away many of the impediments of faith.*

      2. Nor is *afflection of small service to faith, when it exposes the weakness of the creature.*

      3. Furthermore, trial is of special service to faith when *it drives her to her God.*

      4. And then *trial has a hardening effect upon faith.*

   B. But not to tarry here, let us notice that *the deliverance which Christ wrought by the resurrection of Lazarus, was calculated also to strengthen the faith of the apostles.*

      1. Here *divine sympathy became most manifest.*

      2. What an exhibition these disciples had of *the divine power* as well as the divine sympathy.

II.   Jesus Christ had an eye also to THE GOOD OF THE FAMILY.

   A. Mary and Martha had faith, but it was not very strong, for they suspected Christ's *love* . . . [and] They certainly *doubted* his power.

   B. They were three *special favourites* upon whom very distinguishing regard was set, and therefore it was that he sent them a *special trial.*

      1. Special trial was attended with a *special visit.*

      2. This special visit was attended with *special fellowship.*

      3. And soon you shall have *special deliverance.*

III. Now I come to the third point. . . . This trouble was permitted for GIVING FAITH TO OTHERS.

   A. Afflictions often lead men to faith in Christ because *they give space for thought.*

   B. Afflictions lead men to faith full often *by preventing sin.*

   C. Troubles, again, often bring men to believe in Jesus because they compel them *to stand face to face with stern realities.*

   D. Trials *tend to make men believe in Christ when they are followed by deliverances.* (455–63; Spurgeon's emphasis)

The outline is not the only place we find mnemonic repetition in Spurgeon's preaching; throughout the exposition, Spurgeon employs the rhetorical device of *copia*, the "repetition of the just-said," to keep "both speaker and hearer surely on the track."[8] Several times, for example, Spurgeon asks the same question or makes the same assertion in a number of different ways. The best illustration of the copious use of questions appears in the third point of the third head of the exposition. Spurgeon asserts that trials bring people "*to stand face to face with stern realities*," and the first half of the paragraph devoted to this point consists of five related questions:

> Did you ever lie upon the edge of death for a week? Did you ever lie with your body racked with pains, listening for the physician's whispers, and knowing that they amounted to this, that there were ninety-nine chances to one that you could not possibly recover? Did you ever feel that death was near? Did you ever peer into eternity with anxious eyes? Did you ever picture hell and think yourself there? Did you ever lie awake, and think of heaven and yourself shut out of it? Ah! it is in such times as these that God's Holy Spirit works great things for the sons of men. (463)

A page later, in the final paragraph of the discourse, Spurgeon exhorts his hearers to "Remember that the one thing needful for eternal life is trusting in the Lord Jesus Christ," and he emphasizes the certainty of this salvation with a string of five virtually identical statements:

> if Christ suffered for you, you cannot suffer. If God punished Christ he will never punish you. If Jesus Christ paid your debts, you are free. Before God's throne to-day, if thou believest, thou art as clear as the angels in heaven. Thou art a saved soul if thou art resting upon the atonement of Christ, and thou mayst go thy way and sing. (464)

The most significant repetitions in "A Mystery! Saints Sorrowing and Jesus Glad!" are Spurgeon's frequent restatements of his preaching text and the application, or central "principle" (455), he derives from that text. Spurgeon first mentions his text near the end of the storylike introduction to his sermon. After remarking on the strangeness of Jesus' claim that he was glad he was not in Bethany when Lazarus became ill and died, Spurgeon says, "we may rest assured that Jesus knoweth better than we do, and our faith may therefore sit still and try to spell out his meaning, where our reason cannot find it at the first glance. 'I am glad,' saith he, '*for your sakes* that I was not there, to the intent ye may believe'" (455; Spurgeon's emphasis). The application follows a few sentences later: Spurgeon declares, "We have thus plainly before us the principle, that our Lord in his infinite wisdom and superabundant love, sets so high a value upon his people's faith, that he will not screen them from those trials by which faith is strengthened" (455).

Spurgeon returns to these ideas throughout the explication and conclusion. The application itself is repeated only once: just before he introduces the second major point of the sermon, Spurgeon admonishes his audience not to "forget the principle we are trying to bring out, that in the case of the apostles, Christ considered that for them to have strong faith was worth any cost" (460). The preaching text, however, appears a total of eight times; the most innovative repetition occurs when Spurgeon attempts to place Jesus' words within the mouths of his congregants:

> I beseech you, rather take my text, and read it the other way say— God help thee to say it—"I am glad that my God did not deliver me, because the trial has strengthened my faith. I thank his name that he has done me the great favour to permit me to carry the heavy end of his cross. I thank my Father that he hath not left me unchastised, for 'Before I was afflicted I went astray: but now have I kept thy word.' 'It is good for me that I have been afflicted.'" (462)

The dominance of orality in "A Mystery! Saints Sorrowing and Jesus Glad!" is evident not only in Spurgeon's recurring use of *copia*, but also in his emphasis on keeping the sermon "close to the human lifeworld."[9] Throughout the discourse Spurgeon illustrates and supports his assertions by suggesting analogies between his text and his congregation's experiences. To help his hearers understand that God often sends adversity as a sign of his favor rather than his wrath, Spurgeon likens the actions of God to the work of jewellers and gardeners, occupations with which his congregation would surely be familiar:

> The lapidary, if he takes up a stone and finds that it is not very precious, will not spend much care in cutting it; but when he gets a rare diamond of the first water, then he will be sure to cut, and cut, and cut again. When the Lord finds a saint whom he loves—loves much— he may spare other men trials and troubles, but he certainly will not this well-beloved one. The more beloved you are the more of the rod you shall have. . . . The gardener gets a tree, and if it is but of a poor sort he will let it grow as it wills, and take what fruit comes from it

naturally; but if it be of a very rare sort, he likes to have every bough in its proper place, so that it may bear well; and he often takes out his knife and cuts here and cuts there. . . . You who are God's favourites must not marvel at trials, but rather keep your door wide open for them. (460, 61)

A few paragraphs later, Spurgeon moves his comparisons from the workplace to the home, comparing the compassion of Christ to the tenderness a mother shows her children:

You know when a mother is most kind to her child, she lets it run about, and scarcely notices it when it is well; but when it cries, "My head, my head!" and when they take it to the mother and tell her it is ill, how tender she is over it! How all the blandishments of love and the caresses of affection are lavished upon the little sick one! It shall be so with you, and in receiving these special visits, you shall know yourself to be highly favoured above the rest. (461)

Finally, Spurgeon assimilates the "alien, objective world" of John's gospel to the "more immediate, familiar interaction" of his congregants' own lives by directly addressing his hearers throughout his sermon.[10] Spurgeon occasionally addresses his audience through first-person plural constructions—"Thus afflictions fetch us to our God," "we may rest assured that Jesus knoweth better than we do" (455, 58)—but he employs the second person much more often. The words *you, your, thee,* and *thou* appear more than 100 times in the sermon, often in the form of questions or commands such as "If [God] spared your life, why will he not spare your soul?" and "You who are God's favourites must not marvel at trials, but rather keep your door wide open for them" (461, 64). In short, from the macroscopic level—the outline of the sermon—to the microscopic—the choice of pronouns—"A Mystery! Saints Sorrowing and Jesus Glad!" illustrates the many ways in which Spurgeon's pulpit oratory is informed by the conventions of the oral tradition.

In terms of orality-literacy studies, John Henry Newman's "Tears of Christ at the Grave of Lazarus" bears little resemblance to Spurgeon's "A Mystery! Saints Sorrowing and Jesus Glad!" The differences between the two sermons are, I propose, largely a function of the circumstances under which they were composed. While Spurgeon preached extemporaneously, preparing "the sermon so far as thoughts go, and leaving the words to be found during delivery,"[11] Newman wrote complete manuscripts of his discourses, preparing in advance both his thoughts and the words in which they were to be expressed. Techniques such as the tripartite structure of introduction, exposition, and conclusion and the division of the exposition into four numbered parts are present in Newman's discourse, but they are simply "oral residue," vestiges of "preliterate" practices that, unlike Spurgeon's oral rhetoric, are "not especially contrived and seldom conscious at all."[12] From the opening sentence on, it is evident that the rhetorical paradigms of "Tears of Christ" are derived from literate rather than oral expression.

Walter Ong has suggested that "writing restructures consciousness" in part by enabling humans to think with a degree of "analytic precision" unknown in an oral culture.[13] A concern for such precision is evident throughout Newman's sermon. He begins not by telling a story, but by posing a question—"*why* did our Lord weep at the grave of Lazarus?" ("Tears of Christ," 128; Newman's emphasis). The introduction is an examination of the difficulties that he confronts in attempting to answer it.

The first difficulty, in Newman's view, lies in the nature of the text. The "very surface" of John's gospel contains "seeming inconsistencies"—why, for instance, would Christ, who "knew He had the power to raise" Lazarus, still "act the part of those who sorrow for the dead?" (128, 129). The second difficulty lies in the nature of the reader; because humans are finite and the trinity is infinite, "the thoughts of our Saviour's mind are far beyond our comprehension" (128). These difficulties are not insurmountable, but solutions will come only after prolonged study. As Newman notes, in order to "put one's-self, even in part, into the position of [Christ's] mind, and to state under what feelings and motives He said this or that," it is necessary to "feed upon [his words], and live in them, as if by little and little growing into their meaning" (130). Feeding upon Christ's words, moreover, does not consist of dealing in "vague statements about His love, His willingness to receive the sinner, His imparting repentance and spiritual aid, and the like" (131). Instead, it requires "contemplat[ing] Christ as manifested in the gospels," viewing "Him in His particular and actual works, set before us in Scripture" (131). The question Newman poses can, in short, be answered only by recourse to the technologies of literacy, for the study of Christ's "particular and actual works" is possible only because those works have been preserved in print.

The dominance of literacy over orality continues into the expository portion of Newman's sermon. Unlike Spurgeon, Newman does not emphasize the structure of his exposition. Instead of announcing the "heads" in advance, he simply says, "I will say a few words . . . by way of comment on our Saviour's weeping at Lazarus' grave; or rather, I will suggest what each of you may, please God, improve for himself" (131). Nor does he call special attention to these divisions as he moves through the exposition. Although he does provide some cues—the sections are numbered in the printed text, and he uses such standard transitional language as "First of all" and "But next" (132, 33)—he does not use repetition or special typefaces to emphasize his points as Spurgeon does. Finally, the form of the exposition itself is residually rather than explicitly oral. While Spurgeon's exposition, in accordance with established orally based practices, is divided into numerous heads, subpoints and sub-subpoints, Newman's consists only of four major divisions:

1. First of all, as the context informs us, He wept from very sympathy with the grief of others.
2. But next, we may suppose . . . that His pity, thus spontaneously excited, was led forward to dwell on the various circumstances in man's condition which excite pity.
3. Here I have suggested another thought which admits of being dwelt upon. Christ was come to do a deed of mercy, and it was a secret in His own breast.
4. Alas! there were other thoughts still to call forth His tears. This marvellous benefit to the forlorn sisters, how was it to be attained? at His own cost. . . . Christ was bringing life to the dead by His own death. (132–36)

The way in which this exposition progresses is especially significant. Spurgeon's exposition, like other forms of oral expression, is built on a succession of "thematic recurrences."[14] His principal assertion is that faith is strengthened by adversity, a theme he restates in each of the three main heads of his exposition. "Jesus Christ was glad that the trial had come," Spurgeon says, "*for the strengthening of the faith of the apostles;* secondly, *for strengthening the faith of the family;* and thirdly, *for giving faith to others*" ("A Mystery!," 455; Spurgeon's emphasis). Newman's exposition, in contrast, does not develop the same basic idea in three thematically related ways. Instead, he suggests four different answers to the question of why Jesus wept at Lazarus' grave, and each answer builds on what has come before. Christ wept, Newman says, first out of "sympathy with the grief of others" (132). Christ's pity was then "led forward to dwell on the various circumstances in man's condition which excite pity," circumstances such as "a mourning multitude" assembled before "a scene of death" (133, 134). Newman's meditations upon this *victory of death* (133) lead him to a third thought: Jesus wept not only because he felt pity, but also because he knew he had the power to remove that which had caused his pity; he "had a spell which could overcome death, and He was about to use it" (136). This idea, in turn, brings Newman to his final head, the observation that Jesus wept because he knew that the use of his "spell" carried a price, that he was "bringing life to the dead by His own death" (136).

At two places in the exposition, we find "oral residue" in Newman's "repetition of the just-said."[15] He begins by taking a full page to develop his claim that Jesus "wept from very sympathy with the grief of others," and before moving on to his second point, he restates his main ideas in a single paragraph:

> Jesus wept, therefore, not merely from the deep thoughts of His understanding, but from spontaneous tenderness; from the gentleness and mercy, the encompassing loving-kindness and exuberant fostering of affection of the Son of God for His own work, the race of man. Their tears touched Him at once, as their miseries had brought Him down from heaven. His ear was open to them, and the sound of weeping went at once to His heart. (132, 133)

Newman presents a similar synopsis at the end of his second point. His discussion of Christ's meditations "on the various circumstances in man's condition which excite pity" is also rather detailed, taking nearly two pages to develop, and he again helps his congregants to follow his analysis by providing a brief digest at the end: "Here, then, I say, were abundant sources for His grief . . . in the contrast between Adam . . . innocent and immortal . . . and man as the devil had made him, full of the poison of sin and the breath of the grave; and again, in the timid complaint of His sorrowing friends that that change had been permitted" (134–35).

Such repetition is not, however, a prominent rhetorical feature in "Tears of Christ at the Grave of Lazarus." He employs it at the end of only two of his four divisions; while he does point out that he is restating observations he has made before, he does not provide the copious reinforcements of his assertions that we find in Spurgeon's sermon. In short, Newman's exposition is based not on "thematic recurrences," but on progressive linear analysis, a mode of thought and expression which did not become possible until the development of writing and of print.[16]

The literate nature of Newman's exposition is also evident in the distance it maintains between the preacher and his congregation. Newman begins his exposition much as Spurgeon did, with a brief reference to his text followed by a more extended reference to his audience. He suggests that Jesus "wept from very sympathy with the grief of others" and supports his claim by quoting John 11:33: "When Jesus saw Mary weeping, and the Jews also weeping which came with her, He groaned in the spirit, and was troubled" ("Tears," 132). A few sentences later, it becomes evident that Newman is defining "others" not only as the characters mentioned in John's gospel, but as everyone who hears him preach:

> when He took flesh and appeared on earth, he showed us the Godhead in a new manifestation. He invested Himself with a new set of attributes, those of our flesh, taking into Him a human soul and body, in order that thoughts, feelings, affections might be His, which could respond to ours and certify to us His tender mercy. When, then, our Saviour weeps from sympathy at Mary's tears, let us not say it is the love of a man overcome by natural feeling. It is the love of God, the bowels of compassion of the Almighty and Eternal, condescending to show it as we are capable of receiving it, in the form of human nature. (132, 133)

This approach, however, is not the norm. In the rest of the exposition, Newman draws explanations for Jesus' tears exclusively from the text. It is only in his closing application that he examines the ways in which the story of Lazarus' death and resurrection is significant to the spiritual condition of his hearers. The governing rhetorical strategy in Newman's exposition is, therefore, precisely the opposite of Spurgeon's: while Spurgeon merely touches on the events in John's narrative and makes his congregation the subject of his sermon, Newman makes only a few references to his audience and uses the text itself as the focal point of his discourse.

Finally, Newman's choice of pronouns is significantly different from Spurgeon's. While "A Mystery!" is replete with second-person forms of address, the word "you" appears only three times in "Tears of Christ": once in a question Newman poses to the congregation, and twice in reference to the applications he proposes in the discourse. For Newman, the pronoun of choice is the first-person plural, which appears fifty-five times in the eleven pages of his sermon. Rather than giving direct instructions, as Spurgeon does when he says, "if you cannot yet claim the result of long experience, thank God for what grace you have" ("A Mystery!," 457), Newman issues indirect, less personal exhortations, such as his admonition that "till we learn to . . . view [Christ] in His particular and actual works, set before us in Scripture, surely we have not derived from the Gospels that very benefit which they are intended to convey" (131). This use of the first person indicates that Newman is aware that he is addressing an audience, but it is not as explicit an acknowledgment of its presence as Spurgeon's second-person address. His choice of pronouns is, therefore, yet another instance of "oral residue"; while echoes of the oral tradition are present, they are overshadowed by the practices of literate expression. As a written discourse delivered orally before a congregation, "Tears of Christ at the Grave of Lazarus" illustrates Newman's status as a practitioner of "secondary orality," a phrase which Walter Ong has used to describe an oral performance grounded in "the use of writing and print."[17]

The shift from orality to literacy we see in Newman's sermon is even more pronounced in MacDonald's sermon in *The Seaboard Parish*. Spurgeon and Newman, as we have seen, took different approaches to the preparation of their sermons, but they both delivered their sermons in front of a congregation before preserving them in print. MacDonald, in contrast, bypassed the oral component of preaching altogether, writing and publishing sermons that were never spoken aloud in a church. Once again, the circumstances of composition are reflected in the structure and content of the sermon. Just as Spurgeon's narrative introduction is the earliest indication of oral dominance in "A Mystery!" and Newman's analytical opening sets a largely literate tone for "Tears of Christ," evidence of "primary literacy," the phrase I have proposed to describe MacDonald's preaching, first appears in the one-paragraph introduction to the sermon:

> When Jesus Christ, the Son of God, and therefore our elder brother, was going about on the earth . . . there was one family he loved especially—a family of two sisters and a brother; for, although he loves everybody as much as they can be loved, there are some who can be loved more than others. Only God is always trying to make us such that we can be loved more and more. There are several stories . . . about that family and Jesus. And we have to do with one of them now. (578)

This introduction is significantly shorter than both Spurgeon's (nearly three pages long) and Newman's (which occupies nearly four pages of his twelve-page discourse). More important, it does not fulfill the criteria traditionally assigned to the exordium of an

extemporaneous sermon: that it be specifically related to the subject of the discourse, and that it "prepare [the audience's] minds
for the following explication of the text from its context."[18] Both
of these elements are present in Spurgeon's and Newman's introductions. Spurgeon ends his exordium with comments upon
Jesus' words in John 11:15—"I am glad for your sakes that I was
not there"—and he ends this part of the sermon by outlining the
heads under which his exposition will be organized. Newman's
introduction is similarly specific, focusing on John's observation
that "Jesus wept" at Lazarus' tomb; he informs his audience that
his exposition will consist of "a few words" on the significance of
Christ's tears (131). MacDonald's introduction, in contrast, does
not specifically address the passage in John 11 that will be the
subject of his sermon. In fact, he does not make it clear that the
death and resurrection of Lazarus is his subject at all. He simply
notes that "There are several stories" in the New Testament about
Jesus' relationship with Lazarus and his family, and his foreshad-
owing of the exposition consists only of the rather vague declaration that "we have to do with one of them now" (578). In short, the
introduction to MacDonald's sermon does not carry the rhetorical
significance ascribed to either the introductions to "A Mystery!"
and "Tears of Christ" or to the exordium of the traditional six-part
classical oration.

The primary literacy of "The Sermon" is even more evident in
the exposition than in the introduction. As we have seen, one of
the fundamental differences between oral and written expression
lies in the frequency with which mnemonic devices are employed.
This rhetorical strategy is evident throughout Spurgeon's heavily
oral exposition; the use of *copia,* multiple heads, and other mnemonic techniques appear in virtually every paragraph. Some repetition is present in Newman's residually oral exposition, but it is
confined to summary paragraphs at the end of only two of the four
major divisions of his discourse.

MacDonald's exposition, in contrast, lacks even the "residue" of
orality. Unlike Spurgeon and Newman, who focus on only a few
verses of John 11, MacDonald takes the entire narrative as his
subject. He begins with verse 3, in which Mary and Martha send
a message to Jesus informing him of Lazarus' illness, and ends
with verse 43, in which Jesus calls Lazarus forth from the grave.
MacDonald provides continuous commentary as he moves
through these forty verses, discoursing on such varied subjects as
the ways in which the "old painters and poets represented Faith" in
their works; the notion that the metaphorical equation of death

with sleep may have been "altogether a new and Christian idea"; and the speculation that "it might be interesting . . . to compare" Mary and Martha's actions in this chapter with their conduct in Luke 10, the account of another visit Jesus paid to Lazarus' household (581, 584, 585). MacDonald, moreover, never dwells on a single idea as Spurgeon does, nor does he pause to reflect upon and summarize where he has been as Newman does. Instead, he moves quickly from one observation to the next, and his exposition is not so much a sermon, an orally based discourse focused on a single main idea,[19] as it is an explication or a commentary, modes of analysis that are primarily linear, and therefore literate, in nature.

Finally, primary literacy in MacDonald's discourse is evident even in the pronouns that MacDonald employs throughout the sermon. Like Newman, MacDonald takes John's gospel, not his own audience, as his subject; when he addresses his audience, he does so in the first-person plural. At the beginning of the discourse, for example, MacDonald discusses the message that Mary and Martha sent to Jesus—"Lord, behold, he whom thou lovest is sick"—and he writes,

> You know when any one is ill we always want the person whom he loves most to come to him. . . . And we may not in the least suppose the person we want knows any secret that can cure his pain; yet love is the first thing we think of. And here we are more right than we know; for, at the long last, love will cure everything; which truth, indeed, this story will set forth to us. (579)

MacDonald, however, addresses his audience much less often than either Spurgeon or Newman; this passage and the final application are virtually the only places in which this language appears.[20] In the nine pages between these two paragraphs, the pronoun that appears most frequently is the first-person singular. The first extended use of "I" appears in MacDonald's analysis of Jesus' decision to go to Bethany. The disciples protest, fearing that Jesus will be stoned if he returns to Lazarus' hometown, and Jesus replies, "Are there not twelve hours in the day? If anyone walks in the day, he does not stumble, because he sees the light of the world. But if any one walks in the night, he stumbles, because the light is not in him" (John 11:9, 10 KJV). In response to Jesus' statement, MacDonald writes,

> The answer which [Jesus] gave them I am not sure whether I can thoroughly understand, but I think, in fact, I know it must bear on

the same region of life—the will of God. I think what he means by walking in the day, is simply doing the will of God. . . . I think he means that now he saw plainly what the Father wanted him to do. . . . Something not inharmonious with this, I think, he must have intended; but I do not see the whole thought clearly enough to be sure that I am right. (582–83)

MacDonald uses "I" a total of twenty times; this preference speaks directly to the question of his awareness of and interaction with his audience. We see in this sermon little of Newman's indirect references to his audience and none of Spurgeon's direct second-person addresses. Instead, the use of "I" to the exclusion of other rhetorical approaches suggests that MacDonald is preaching with little awareness of or consideration for his audience; it suggests that he sees himself as addressing no one but himself in the sermon.

MacDonald's elimination of the hearer from the preaching process exemplifies the shift from orality to literacy identified at the beginning of this chapter. Spurgeon's preaching adheres most closely to the practices of the oral tradition—he spoke extemporaneously, composing his sermon while in the presence of his congregation—and his choice of the second-person pronoun reflects the classical orator's direct involvement with his audience. Although he composed his discourses in isolation, Newman believed that an awareness of one's audience must be "included in the very idea of preaching,"[21] and his frequent use of "we" indicates a residual awareness of his audience consistent with the residual orality we find throughout his preaching. By using "I" instead of "we" or "you," MacDonald indicates that his preaching is a literacy-based, "solipsistic operation" rather than an orally-based communal enterprise.[22] He encapsulates, in other words, the distance that inevitably separates a writer from his readers. By so doing, he illustrates one of the fundamental distinctions between oral and written communication: while an orator addresses a specific audience at a specific time, "the writer's audience is always a fiction."[23]

Conclusion

A STUDY OF ORALITY-LITERACY THEORY AND THE VICTORIAN SER-
mon suggests several new avenues of scholarly inquiry. In 1982,
Alastair Fowler declared that it "is time to enlarge the critical rep-
ertory" of literary studies.[1] Reintroducing the sermon to the Victorian prose canon is one way to accomplish this goal. First, such a
reintroduction enables us to broaden the scope of scholarship on
such figures as John Henry Newman and George MacDonald; it
also adds new artists to the canon by identifying other ministers
whose works lend themselves to literary study.

A study of the sermon can help not only "to recover a sense of
the variety of literary forms,"[2] but also to provide another context
for the examination of orality-literacy relations in British literature. In their introduction to *Redrawing the Boundaries*, a collection of essays that examines the history of literary studies and
attempts to predict its future, Stephen Greenblatt and Giles Gunn
list the distinction of "print cultures from oral" as one of the "many
demarcation lines" that define the parameters of the profession.[3]
However, the study of this distinction, and of the modes of discourse that emerge when it is blurred, is "largely unfinished business."[4] The sermon, for example, has not been the focus of much
work in orality-literacy studies: preaching is the subject of only
eleven of the approximately seven hundred recent dissertations,
books, and articles that examine orality-literacy relations in specific works or genres. None of these eleven, moreover, focuses on
Victorian preaching—a mode of discourse in which, as I have
attempted to demonstrate here, "the oral and written traditions
intersect in significant ways."[5] The Victorian sermons that have
survived comprise a vast body of works which we can investigate
in the light of our emerging understanding of the differences between spoken and written expression and the tensions which can
result when the oral and literary traditions overlap or intersect.

Not only can such a study provide a new venue for the application of existing paradigms, but it can also expand the critical tools
available to orality-literacy theorists. I have, for example, suggested that the sermon's status as both oration and essay allows

130

us to reexamine the currency of the term "oral literature." I have also proposed the addition of new terms such as "primary literacy" and "secondary literacy" to the critical lexicon of orality-literacy studies.

A study of orality-literacy contrasts in Victorian literature need not—indeed, I propose, should not—be confined only to the sermon. We find a thriving oral tradition and an increasingly important print culture throughout Victorian Britain: in 1854, J. G. Wenham noted that "lectures on all subjects seem to be the rage," and, according to Richard Altick, the widespread "appetite for print" was "a major social phenomenon" in Victorian society.[6]

Orality-literacy contrasts in both the sacred and the secular worlds support Walter Ong's observation that "A new medium of verbal communication not only does not wipe out the old, but actually reinforces the older medium or media."[7] The sermon, as we have seen, participated in both the oral and written traditions. Discourses, which in many cases had been written out in part or in full, were first disseminated orally and were then preserved in print, in many cases almost immediately after they were preached. Printed sermons then helped to support the oral tradition; preachers frequently purchased or plagiarized the discourses of others, and many men and women who had read the sermons of a popular preacher such as Newman or Spurgeon made a point of incorporating a visit to his church into their business or leisure travels.

The symbiotic relationship between spoken and written word we find in pulpit discourse appears in Victorian secular literature as well. In both cases, "writing served largely to recycle knowledge back into the oral world."[8] In *The English Common Reader,* Richard Altick provides several examples of the ways in which Victorian oral tradition was grounded in the printed word. He recounts, for example, the story of an "old charwoman who never missed" a monthly "subscription tea" at which her "landlord read the newest number of *Dombey and Son* to his assembled guests"; he tells us that "In some milliners' and tailors' shops it was customary for one worker to read aloud to the others, who made up out of their own pockets the money he or she thereby lost"; and finally he notes that laborers frequently "clubbed together to buy [a newspaper] and read it aloud in the alehouses."[9] There is some evidence, moreover, that such "indirect contact with the printed word" encouraged reading and thereby helped to reinforce the print culture: in 1849, the Public Libraries Committee "asserted that the greatest single benefit of the lectures" presented at the mechanics' institutes "was that they stimulated the use of the institute libraries."[10]

Both the primary evidence and scholarly works such as Altick's study demonstrate, in short, that Victorian Britain, both inside and outside the church, was a "residually oral" culture, one characterized by the juxtaposition of the oral and written traditions.[11] I propose, moreover, that this residual orality is one of the most significant aspects of Victorian discourse. Orality-literacy studies can, therefore, profitably be added to the scholarly "cluster" of "class, race, and gender"—issues that have "come to the center of much of the dominant criticism of Victorian literature in recent years" and which George Levine has identified as the core issues in the profession's shift from literary studies to the "new establishment of cultural criticism."[12]

I began this study by citing the claim that "To tell the story of Victorian Britain and leave religion out" is "an example of blatant disregard of evidence."[13] As the survey of recent scholarship that I outlined in the introduction shows, the story of Victorian religion is being told well. I now propose that a study of the prominence of orality-literacy contrasts in sacred and secular discourse can help us to tell not only this story, but also the story of Victorian literature and rhetoric, even more completely.

Notes

Introduction

1. Walter Arnstein et al., "Recent Studies in Victorian Religion," *Victorian Studies* 33 (1989): 149.

2. Ibid.

3. Representative titles from 1952 to 1992 include Leonard E. Elliott-Binns, *The Development of English Theology in the Later Nineteenth Century* (London: Longman's, 1952); Josef Altholz, *The Churches in the Nineteenth Century* (Indianapolis: Bobbs-Merrill, 1967); Owen Chadwick, *The Victorian Church* (London: A & C Black, 1971); Gerald Parsons, ed., *Religion in Victorian Britain* (Manchester: Manchester University Press, 1988); and Peter Hinchcliff, *God and History: Aspects of British Theology 1875–1914* (Oxford: Oxford University Press, 1992).

4. Each year, works on religion account for approximately 10 percent of the publications indexed in Section III of the bibliography, which also covers scholarship in economics, education, politics, science, and the social environment. The figures for 1989 through 1994 are: 1989, ninety-nine books and articles, or 8.3 percent of the total; 1990, 123 (9.2 percent); 1991, 130 (10.3 percent); 1992, 111 (8.2 percent); 1993, 169 (11.8 percent); and 1994, 152 (10.4 percent).

5. Of the 305 items indexed under "Sermons" in the Modern Language Association bibliographies for 1963–June 1996, 90 deal with preaching in the Old English period; 83 with Middle English; 36 with the sixteenth century; 110 with the seventeenth; and 41 with the eighteenth. Only 25—or fewer than ten percent—are studies of the sermon in the nineteenth century. Seven of these focus on Coleridge, Wordsworth, and Austen, and two—G. Glen Wickens' "'Sermons in Stones': The Return to Nature in *Tess of the D'Urbervilles*" (*English Studies in Canada* 14 [1988]: 184–203) and Anthony Gully Lacy's "Sermons in Stone: Ruskin and Geology" (in *John Ruskin and the Victorian Eye* [New York: Abrams, 1993])—are only indirectly related to preaching as a rhetorical art. This leaves us with only sixteen studies of preaching—an article on Thomas Arnold's sermons and Matthew Arnold's "Rugby Chapel," an article on Gerard Manley Hopkins and a concordance to his sermons, an essay on Ruskin's sermons on the Pentateuch, and twelve books, articles, and dissertations on John Henry Newman—for the entire Victorian age.

6. Studies of medieval preaching include Thomas L. Amos, Eugene A. Green, and Beverly Maine Kienzle, ed., *De Ore Domini: Preacher and the Word in the Middle Ages* (Kalamazoo, Michigan: Medieval Institute Publications, 1989); Gerald Owst, *Literature and Pulpit in Medieval England* (Oxford: Basil Blackwell, 1961); and Gerald Owst, *Preaching in Medieval England* (New York: Russell & Russell, 1965). Four noteworthy books on the Renaissance pulpit are J. W.

Blench, *Preaching in England in the Late Fifteenth and Sixteenth Centuries* (New York: Barnes and Noble, 1964); Horton Davies, *Like Angels from a Cloud: The English Metaphysical Preachers, 1588–1645* (San Marino, California: Huntington Library, 1986); Millar MacLure, *The Paul's Cross Sermons, 1534–1642* (Toronto: University of Toronto Press, 1958); and W. Fraser Mitchell, *English Pulpit Oratory from Andrewes to Tillotson* (New York: Russell & Russell, 1962). Finally, the eighteenth century sermon is discussed in James Downey, *The Eighteenth Century Pulpit* (Oxford: Clarendon, 1966); and Rolf Lessenich, *Elements of Pulpit Oratory in Eighteenth-Century England (1660–1800)* (Koln, Germany: Bohlau-Verlag, 1972).

7. Despite the implications of its title, Graham Walker and Tom Gallagher's *Sermons and Battle Hymns: Protestant Popular Culture in Modern Scotland* (Edinburgh: Edinburgh University Press, 1990) is only marginally concerned with the pulpit. Nineteenth-century preaching is mentioned on fewer than 10 of the 261 pages in this collection, which is intended to be "a starting point for further research into the whole field of religious traditions and popular culture in Scotland," 2.

8. I. D. McCalman, "Popular Irreligion in Early Victorian England: Infidel Preachers and Radical Theatricality in 1830s London." In *Religion and Irreligion in Victorian Society: Essays in Honor of R. K. Webb*, ed. R. W. Davis and R. J. Helmstadter, 51–67. London: Routledge, 1992.

9. Webber, *A History of Preaching in Britain and America* (Milwaukee: Northwestern Publishing House, 1952), 1:9.

10. Dargan, *A History of Preaching* (Grand Rapids, Mich.: Baker Book House, 1974), 471, 578.

11. Webber, *History of Preaching,* 1:9.

12. Ibid.

13. Mackerness, *The Heeded Voice: Studies in the Literary Status of the Anglican Sermon, 1830–1900* (Cambridge: W. Heffer & Sons, 1959), 17.

14. Herbert, "The Art of Preaching," *National Review* 2 (1883): 26.

15. John Rechtien, "The Ramist Style of John Udall: Audience and Pictorial Logic in Puritan Sermon and Controversy," *Oral Tradition* 2 (1987): 188–213; Julia Dagenais, "Frontier Preaching as Formulaic Poetry," *Mid-America-Folklore* 19 (1991): 118–26; Bruce A. Rosenberg, "The Message of the American Folk Sermon," *Oral Tradition* 1 (1986): 695–727.

16. Rosenberg, "The Complexity of Oral Tradition," *Oral Tradition* 2 (1987): 75.

17. Ong, *Orality and Literacy* (New York: Methuen, 1982), 10–15.

18. Ibid., 11.

19. The ATLA Religion Database, for example, lists 30 studies of Spurgeon published between 1975 and May 1996. In contrast, literary reference sources list only nine—four in the MLA bibliographies for 1963 through June 1996, and five in the *Victorian Studies* bibliographies for 1989 through 1994.

20. Reis, *George MacDonald* (New York: Twayne, 1972), 27.

21. John Ruskin to George MacDonald, 18 December 1868, quoted in Greville MacDonald, *George MacDonald and His Wife* (New York: Dial Press, 1924), 337.

Chapter 1. Victorian Homiletic Theory

1. Aristotle defined rhetoric as "the faculty of observing in any given case the available means of persuasion" (*Rhetoric,* trans. W. Rhys Roberts, in *The*

Works of Aristotle: Volume II, ed. Robert Maynard Hutchins [Chicago: Encyclopaedia Britannica, 1952], I.2). In *De Inventione*, Cicero held that "the function of eloquence seems to be to speak in a manner suited to persuade an audience, the end is to persuade by speech" (in *De Inventione: De Optimo Genere Oratorum: Topica*, trans. and ed. H. M. Hubbell [Cambridge, Mass.: Harvard University Press, 1949], I.v.6). Similarly, Tillotson asserted that "The duty of a preacher is not so much to upbraid men for being bad, as to encourage them to be better" (William Gresley, *Ecclesiastes Anglicanus: Being a Treatise on Preaching, as Adapted to a Church of England Congregation: In a Series of Letters to a Young Clergyman* [New York: D. Appleton, 1844], 50); Ward defined oratory as "the art of speaking well upon any subject, in order to persuade" (*A System of Oratory* [Hildesheim, Germany: Georg Olms Verlag, 1969], 1:19); Blair stated that "the end of popular speaking is persuasion" ("Lectures on Rhetoric and Belles Lettres," in *The Rhetoric of Blair, Campbell, and Whately*, ed. James L. Golden and Edward P. J. Corbett [New York: Holt, Rinehart & Winston, 1968], 105); and Whately wrote that "the province of Rhetoric, in the widest acceptation that would be reckoned admissible, comprehends all 'Composition in Prose;' in the narrowest sense, it would be limited to 'Persuasive Speaking'" (*Elements of Rhetoric: Comprising an Analysis of the Laws of Moral Evidence and of Persuasion, with Rules for Argumentative Composition and Elocution*, ed. Douglas Ehninger [Carbondale: Southern Illinois University Press, 1963], 4).

2. Gresley stated that "The end of preaching is . . . like that of all other speaking—*persuasion*" (*Ecclesiastes Anglicanus*, 28); Rigg wrote that "The one great object of sacred as of secular oratory is persuasion" ("The Pulpit and Its Influence," review of *Sermons, Doctrinal and Practical*, by William Archer Butler, *Eclectic Magazine* 40 [1857]: 380).

3. Burns, "Modern Preaching," *North British Review* 38 (1863): 441; Wenham, "Sermons and Preachers," review of *The Grounds of Faith. A Series of Four Lectures*, by H. E. Manning, *Dublin Review* 36 (1854): 8; Thomson, "On the Emotions in Preaching," in *Homiletical and Pastoral Lectures*, ed. C. J. Ellicott (New York: A. C. Armstrong & Son, 1880), 81.

4. Rogers, "The British Pulpit," review of *Sermons to a Country Congregation*, by Augustus William Hare, *Edinburgh Review* 72 (1840): 70.

5. Thomson, "On the Emotions in Preaching," 92; Rogers, "The British Pulpit," 71; Harvey Goodwin, "What Constitutes a Plain Sermon?," in *Homiletical and Pastoral Lectures*, ed. C. J. Ellicott (New York: A. C. Armstrong & Son, 1880), 126.

6. Johns, "The Manufacture of Sermons," *Contemporary Review* 8 (1868): 264. Johns goes on to identify several inappropriate subjects for sermons; his list includes "Course of Lectures on Romanism—Transubstantiation, Auricular Confession, Purgatory, and the blasphemies of the Mass"; "The Iniquities of Jews, Ancient and Modern; the stubbornness and unbelief of Israel of old; the horrible unbelief of their faithless descendants"; and "Burnet on the Thirty-nine Articles" (265).

7. Newman, *The Idea of a University*, ed. I. T. Ker (Oxford: Clarendon Press, 1976), 337; "The Modern British Pulpit," *London Quarterly Review* 2 (1854): 366.

8. William Davies, "The English Pulpit," review of *The Penny Pulpit: a Collection of accurately-reported Sermons by the most eminent Ministers of various Denominations, Living Age* 120 (1874): 77, 79. The word "practical," in fact, appears throughout Victorian treatises on the art of preaching. C. H. Grundy,

for example, admonished preachers to "Aim at a practical discourse" ("Dull Sermons," *Macmillans* 34 [1876]: 266); William Davies insisted that the pulpit "confine itself . . . to the exposition of sound and earnest practical Christian truth" ("The English Pulpit," 84); B. G. Johns argued that sermons should consist of "clear, concise, well-applied argument, of the plainest and most practical kind" ("The Manufacture of Sermons," 266); and Louisa Merivale wrote that sermons achieve their "greatest notability" when they aspire "to shape the intellectual and practical conclusions of men" ("The English Pulpit," *North British Review* 45 [1866]: 147).

9. Burns, "Modern Preaching," 448.

10. Thomson, "On the Emotions in Preaching," 92; Gresley, *Ecclesiastes Anglicanus,* 254.

11. Gresley, *Ecclesiastes Anglicanus,* 254–55.

12. Dale, *Nine Lectures on Preaching,* 7th ed. (London: Hodder and Stoughton, 1893), 147.

13. Burns, "Modern Preaching," 441; Grundy, "Dull Sermons," 267; Davies, "The English Pulpit," 72.

14. Aristotle, *Rhetoric,* I.2, II.1.

15. Gresley, *Ecclesiastes Anglicanus,* 29. Gresley's footnote to this sentence identifies "lib. ii cap. i sec. 5" of *Rhetoric* as the source of these criteria. A few pages later, Gresley invokes Aristotle again, admonishing preachers that their sermons "should be what Aristotle calls 'ethical,' that is, such as shall show forth your character and feelings" (36).

16. "Of Sermon-Making," *The Congregationalist* 7 (1878): 723; Dale, *Nine Lectures on Preaching,* 223.

17. Thomson, "On the Emotions in Preaching," 101.

18. Cicero, *De Inventione,* I.vii.9.

19. Ibid.

20. Ibid, I.xiv.19. Aristotle's *Rhetoric* also contains a discussion of the proper structure of the classical oration: he holds that "the only necessary parts of a speech are the Statement and the Argument" and that a speech "cannot in any case have more than Introduction, Statement, Argument, and Epilogue" (III.13). It is Cicero's model, however, that the English rhetoricians most frequently invoke. Wilbur Samuel Howell, in fact, has argued that Aristotle had very little influence on British rhetorical theory. In *Logic and Rhetoric in England* (New York: Russell and Russell, 1961), Howell writes that "traditional rhetoric," that "system of precepts" in force from 700 to 1573, "owed its authority to the teachings and prestige of Cicero" (65). In *Eighteenth-Century British Logic and Rhetoric* (Princeton: Princeton University Press, 1971), he asserts that eighteenth-century rhetoricians looked to Cicero as the sole classical authority. In fact, when they thought of "ancient rhetoric," they were "completely unable to think of anyone but Cicero" (75).

21. Howell, *Logic and Rhetoric in England,* 90. Cox's book was not the first discussion of Ciceronian rhetoric published in England. That distinction belongs to *De Rhetorica,* a Latin "abridgement" of *De Inventione* published by Alcuin in 794 (ibid., 73). After what J. W. H. Atkins called a "prolonged eclipse" of "the tradition of learning in England," interest in the classical rhetorical tradition was revived by Stephen Hawes' 1509 poem *Pastime of Pleasure,* a "didactic allegory" which applies Ciceronian rhetoric to the art of poetry, and William Caxton's *Mirrour of the World,* which consists largely of definitions of such terms as "invention, arrangement, and style" (ibid., 48, 74, 81, 87). Cox's *Rhethoryke* is,

however, the first English-language treatise to apply the Ciceronian system to the art of British public speaking.

22. Howell, *Logic and Rhetoric in England,* 92, 93; Leonard Cox, *The Arte or Crafte of Rhethoryke,* ed. Frederic Ives Carpenter (Chicago: University of Chicago Press, 1899), 50. I have modernized the spelling in this quotation for the sake of clarity. I have also modernized the spelling in the quotations from Ward, Hyperius, and Sherry that appear later in this chapter.

23. Howell, *Logic and Rhetoric in England,* 318. Peter Ramus was a French academician who objected to the "redundancy and indecisiveness" he saw in the logical and rhetorical practices of his day (ibid., 147). He criticized, for example, the practice of allowing both logicians and rhetoricians to investigate the best means of inventing and arranging arguments, and he especially disliked the practice of placing "the six parts of an oration under the heading of invention" while at the same time retaining arrangement as a separate rhetorical category (ibid., 147, 148). His solution was to break up the five-part system of Ciceronian rhetoric, assigning invention and arrangement to logic, leaving style and delivery under the auspices of rhetoric, and virtually eliminating memory from his "scheme for the liberal arts" (ibid., 148). Ramus's ideas were introduced into England in 1577 by Gabriel Harvey, a member of the rhetoric faculty at Cambridge and author of two Ramist treatises, *Ciceronianus* and *Rhetor.* A passage from the latter concisely expresses Ramus's views: Harvey writes that "invention, disposition, and memory" are "the property . . . not of rhetoric but of dialectic," and that "style and delivery" are the "two sole and as it were native parts" that "remain as proper and germane to" the art of rhetoric (*Rhetor* [London, 1577], sigs. e4v-f1r, quoted in Howell, *Logic and Rhetoric in England,* 248, 249).

24. Howell, *Eighteenth-Century British Logic,* 321–24.

25. Howell, *Logic and Rhetoric in England,* 364.

26. Howell, *Eighteenth-Century British Logic,* 125.

27. Ibid., 128, 129.

28. James L. Golden and Edward P. J. Corbett, ed., *The Rhetoric of Blair, Campbell, and Whately* (New York: Holt, Rinehart, and Winston, 1968), 7.

29. Ward, *A System of Oratory,* 1:29, 177, 178.

30. Golden and Corbett, *Rhetoric of Blair, Campbell, and Whately,* 25.

31. Blair, "Lectures on Rhetoric," 106.

32. Mitchell, *English Pulpit Oratory from Andrewes to Tillotson* (New York: Russell & Russell, 1962), 59, 60.

33. Like many of their predecessors, both Traversagni and Wilson focus on invention: Traversagni devotes nearly two-thirds of his *Rhetorica* to "considering how to devise material for each of the six parts of the oration," and discussions of this art fill most of the first two volumes of Wilson's four-volume work (Howell, *Logic and Rhetoric in England,* 80, 81, 102). While neither theorist writes extensively about preaching, both discuss homiletics at some point in their works: Traversagni's concluding remarks indicate that he regards "the precepts of rhetoric as a treasure to be adapted to sacred speaking," and Wilson makes "frequent references to preaching throughout his *Rhetorique,* thus indicating unmistakably the application of rhetorical principles to pulpit oratory" (ibid., 80, 107).

34. Hyperius, Andreas Gerardus, *The Practise of Preaching, Otherwise Called the Pathway to the Pulpit: Conteyning an Excellent Method How to Frame Divine Sermons* (London, 1577), fol. 9r-9v, quoted in Howell, *Logic and Rhetoric in England,* 112.

35. Ibid., fol. 9v, quoted in Howell, *Logic and Rhetoric in England,* 113.

36. Ibid., fol. 22r, quoted in Howell, *Logic and Rhetoric in England*, 113.

37. Howell, *Eighteenth-Century British Logic*, 578, 607, 610.

38. Mitchell, *English Pulpit Oratory*, 96.

39. Lessenich tells us that, whereas "in theory exordium and explication were distinct parts" of a sermon, "there existed many exceptions, cases in which the explication was contained in the exordium, or the exordium altogether omitted" (*Elements of Pulpit Oratory in Eighteenth-Century England (1660–1800)* [Koln, Germany: Bohlau-Verlag, 1972], 56, 57). A few pages later, he writes, "Like exordium and explication, proposition and partition constituted two different parts of a neoclassic sermon which were often fused" (76).

One of the earliest works to illustrate Lessenich's claims is *Ecclesiastes, or, A Discourse Concerning the Gift of Preaching As It falls Under the Rules of Art* (London, 1646), in which Wilkins writes that because "the principal Scope of a Divine Orator" is "to teach clearly, convince strongly, and persuade powerfully," the major components of a sermon were "these three: *Explication, Confirmation, Application*" (4, 20, quoted in Mitchell, *English Pulpit Oratory*, 109). In *The Use of Holy Scripture Gravely and Methodically Discoursed* (London, 1653), Chappell employs virtually the same terminology, dividing discourses into "*explication, confirmation*, and *vindications from objections*" (prefatory matter, quoted in Mitchell, *English Pulpit Oratory*, 111).

Leechman, who lectured on homiletics at Glasgow University, and Claude, a French rhetorician, advocated a three-part division as well. According to Leechman's biographer, James Wodrow, Leechman "divided the principal part, or matter of the discourse, into three branches": "the Explication of the subject," "The conviction of the judgment," and "The moving of the Passions or Affections" (Wodrow, "Some Account of the Author's Life," foreword to *Sermons*, by William Leechman [London, 1789], 51–52, quoted in Lessenich, *Elements of Pulpit Oratory*, 41). In 1688, Claude published a treatise entitled *Traite de la composition d'un sermon*, which was translated into English in 1796 and given the title *Essay on the Composition of a Sermon*. In the *Essay*, Claude explicitly advocates a shift from a Ciceronian to a neoclassical approach to sermon structure. He writes, "There are in general *five* parts of a sermon, the exordium, the connexion, the division, the discussion, and the application, but, as connexion and division are parts which ought to be extremely short, we can properly reckon only *three* parts; exordium, discussion, and application" ("Essay on the Composition of a Sermon," in *The Young Preacher's Manual*, ed. Ebenezer Porter [New York: Jonathan Leavitt, 1829], 137).

40. Lessenich, *Elements of Pulpit Oratory*, 40.

41. Ong, *Rhetoric, Romance, and Technology: Studies in the Interaction of Expression and Culture* (Ithaca: Cornell University Press, 1971), 25.

42. William Gresley devotes an entire chapter to a detailed discussion of sermon exordia. In Letter XXIV of *Ecclesiastes*, he argued that the exordium "deserves particular attention." His discussion includes an enumeration of six different types of exordia and a list of five specific characteristics that should be present in any introduction to a sermon (204–9). Other discussions, in contrast, are as brief as B. G. Johns' simple declaration that "every sermon should have a beginning, a middle, and an end" ("Manufacture of Sermons," 271). R. W. Dale states that "The Introduction should be as brief as possible" (*Nine Lectures on Preaching*, 145); Edward Manson gives just a paragraph of his fifteen-page "Art of Rhetoric" to the exordium ("The Art of Rhetoric," *Westminster Review* 148 [1897]: 640, 41); and Louisa Merivale quotes the Abbe Mullois' admonition to

"Omit all generalities from the exordium, all useless demonstrations from the body . . . all vague phrases from the peroration" ("English Pulpit," 182).

43. Rogers, "British Pulpit," 75; Gresley, *Ecclesiastes Anglicanus*, 246.

44. Johns, "Manufacture of Sermons," 266; E. T. Vaughan, "J. H. Newman as Preacher," review of *Parochial and Plain Sermons,* by John Henry Newman, *Contemporary Review* 10 (1869): 47.

45. James Davies, "Preachers and Preaching," *Contemporary Review* 9 (1868): 209.

46. Cicero, *De Inventione,* I.xxii.31. This is the "second form" of the Ciceronian partition; another type of partition "shows in what we agree with our opponents and what is left in dispute; as a result of this some definite problem is set for the auditor on which he ought to have his attention fixed"; ibid.

47. Gerald R. Owst, *Preaching in Medieval England* (New York: Russell and Russell, 1965), 304.

48. According to G. R. Owst, Wycliffe was "as careful as any other schoolman to maintain the scholastic divisions as well as the tropology intact in his preaching" (*Preaching in Medieval England,* 310). This practice is also advocated in a number of rhetorics of Wycliffe's time; they include Bernard's 1607 treatise *The Faithfull Shepheard,* which gives "minute directions for finding the 'intendment' of a text . . . and for its division" (Mitchell, *English Pulpit Oratory,* 110); Wilkins' *Ecclesiastes,* which asserts that hearers "may understand and retain a Sermon with greater ease and profit, when they are before-hand acquainted with the generall heads of matter that are discoursed of" (4, quoted in Lessenich, *Elements of Pulpit Oratory,* 79); and a 1671 treatise entitled *Directions Concerning the Matter and Style of Sermons,* in which Arderne writes, "When you have cleared and distributed the *Theme,* it will be expedient that you declare what course and method you will use, what you intend to perform before you conclude, and to number up all the particulars, on which you shall speak" (11–12, quoted in Lessenich, *Elements of Pulpit Oratory,* 79). Finally, in Lecture XXXI of *Lectures on Rhetoric and Belles Lettres* (1783), Blair argues that "the present method of dividing a sermon into heads, ought not to be laid aside" because "The heads of a sermon are great assistances to the memory and recollection of a hearer. They serve also to fix his attention. They enable him more easily to keep pace with the progress of the discourse; they give him pauses and resting places, where he can reflect on what has been said, and look forward to what is to follow" ("Lectures on Rhetoric," 113).

49. Gresley, *Ecclesiastes Anglicanus,* 192–93.

50. Spurgeon, *C. H. Spurgeon Autobiography* (Edinburgh: Banner of Truth Trust, 1962), 1 : 19.

51. Thorold, "The Preparation of a Sermon," in *Homiletical and Pastoral Lectures,* ed. C. J. Ellicott (New York: A. C. Armstrong & Son, 1880), 9; Dale, *Nine Lectures on Preaching,* 140. Harvey Goodwin, Lord Bishop of Carlisle, also employed the metaphor of a journey to convey his dislike of sermon divisions. Borrowing an analogy first advanced by William Paley, Goodwin writes, "a preacher who describes beforehand all that he is going to do, is like a guide who, in commencing a walk, explains to his party all the difficulties of the road. Let him only start and guide his party well, and the whole excursion will seem pleasant; whereas, if the journey be described too carefully in the first instance, the party, or at least some of them, may feel a sense of weariness creeping over them almost before the start is made" ("What Constitutes a Plain Sermon?" 108–9).

52. Rogers, "British Pulpit," 88; Davies, "English Pulpit," 71; S. Leslie Breakey, "A Few Words About Sermons," *Cornhill Magazine* 3 (1861): 549.

53. Rogers, "British Pulpit," 67.

54. Herbert, "Art of Preaching," 26.

55. "Preachers of the Day," *Living Age* 161 (1884): 294.

56. Marcus Tullus Cicero, *De Oratore,* in *Cicero on Oratory and Orators; with His Letters to Quintus and Brutus,* trans. and ed. J. S. Watson (London: Henry G. Bohn, 1862), III.xiv, xxv, xxxi.

57. Bede, *Liber de Schematibus et Tropis,* in *Rhetores Latini Minores,* ed. Karl Halm (Lipsiae: B. G. Teubneri, 1863), 607, quoted in Howell, *Logic and Rhetoric in England,* 117.

58. According to Wilbur Samuel Howell, Bede "enumerates twenty-nine schemes and forty-one tropes, but he succeeds in condensing these into seventeen of the former and thirteen of the latter" (*Logic and Rhetoric in England,* 116).

59. Like Cicero and Bede, Sherry believed that "true effectiveness in speech proceeds, not from its accurate correspondence to states of reality, but from its lack of resemblance to the idiom of ordinary life" (Howell, *Logic and Rhetoric in England,* 128). In his 1550 *Treatise of Schemes and Tropes,* he argued that "no eloquent writer may be perceived as he should be, without the knowledge of them: for asmuch as all together they belong to Elocution, which is the third and principal part of rhetoric" (sig. A6v, quoted in Howell, *Logic and Rhetoric in England,* 126).

Several sixteenth- and seventeenth-century rhetoricians shared Sherry's insistence on ornament in oratory. Peacham discussed a total of 199 stylistic devices in his *The Garden of Eloquence Conteyning the Figures of Grammer and Rhetorick* (1577), a work that brought "to full maturity the English stylistic theory of rhetoric" (Howell, *Logic and Rhetoric in England,* 133). Similarly, Puttenham's *The Art of English Poesie* (1589) contains "an elaborate analysis of the figures of grammar and rhetoric" (ibid., 327), and Prideaux published two treatises on "the art of speaking ornamentally" (*Hypomnemata* [Oxford, c. 1650], 104, quoted in Howell, *Logic and Rhetoric in England,* 333). *Hypomnemata,* which appeared around 1650, is divided into three chapters, "one dealing with the tropes, one with the figures, and one with the schemes," and his 1659 *Sacred Eloquence* likewise dealt with "Tropes, Figures, Schemes, Patheticks, Characters, Antitheses, and Parallels" (Howell, *Logic and Rhetoric in England,* 333, 334).

Attention to ornament appears in important eighteenth-century treatises as well. In *A System of Oratory* (1759), John Ward argued that "the force of oratory appears in nothing more, than a *copiousness of expression*" (1:24). Accordingly, he devoted one lecture in his *System* to an introduction to the use of tropes, three lectures to the specific tropes of metaphor, metonymy, synecdoche, and irony, and a total of five lectures to the use of figures in public speaking. In *Lectures Concerning Oratory* (1758), Lawson maintained that "Clearness, Propriety, and Harmony, are not sufficient to answer the Ends of Oratory, which require beside these, that Discourse should be lively and animated: To this Purpose the Use of Figures is necessary" (*Lectures Concerning Oratory,* ed. E. Neal Claussen and Karl R. Wallace [Carbondale: Southern Illinois University Press, 1972], 247). To help orators add "Ornament" to "Purity and Perspicuity" (210), Lawson devoted his thirteenth lecture to ornament and his fifteenth to figures; portions of his twelfth, eighteenth, and twenty-second lectures are also concerned with matters of style.

60. Beryl Smalley, *English Friars and Antiquity in the Early Fourteenth Century* (Oxford: Basil Blackwell, 1960), 42; Mitchell, *English Pulpit Oratory*, 63.

61. Mitchell, *English Pulpit Oratory*, 63; Owst, *Preaching in Medieval England*, 35, 262.

62. T. Harwood Pattison, *The History of Christian Preaching* (Philadelphia: American Baptist Publication Society, 1903), 171.

63. Spingarn, *Critical Essays of the Seventeenth Century*, vol. 1 (Oxford, 1908), xxxix–xl, quoted in Mitchell, *English Pulpit Oratory*, 6; Mitchell, *English Pulpit Oratory* 149, 150.

64. Mitchell, *English Pulpit Oratory*, 119. According to Mitchell, "classical allusions are constant" in Adams' sermons, and "classical quotations so numerous that it is difficult to open his works at random without lighting on some reference to the stories of Aesop or the *Metamorphoses,* or finding a quotation from Juvenal, Horace, or Martial, or, most frequently of all, Seneca" (*English Pulpit Oratory,* 214). He offers much the same assessment of Hall's preaching, writing that "There is much learning, often of an out-of-the-way character" in his allusions to and quotations from a variety of authorities, including the Rabbinical teachers, the Church Fathers, and the classical satirists (225). Finally, Mitchell notes that Culverwell's sermons "abound in learned quotations," and "there is a tendency to illustrations rather fanciful than poetical" (287,88).

65. Ibid., 289.

66. Ibid., 136.

67. Joseph Glanvill, *An Essay Concerning Preaching* (1678), 10, quoted in Howell, *Logic and Rhetoric in England*, 394. Eachard, a minister in Suffolk, criticized preachers who overused Greek, Latin, and Hebrew in their sermons (Mitchell, *English Pulpit Oratory,* 359). In Book II of *Ecclesiastes* (1646), Wilkins uses a culinary metaphor to object to elaborate sermon rhetoric. He writes, "To stuff a Sermon with citations of Authors, and the witty sayings of others, is to make a feast of vinegar and pepper; which are healthful and delightful being used moderately as *sauces,* but must needs be very improper and offensive to be fed upon as diet" (20, quoted in Mitchell, *English Pulpit Oratory* 107). Baxter, a prominent Puritan who exerted considerable influence on Charles Haddon Spurgeon, also argued that preachers should not display their learning by filling their sermons with patristic quotations and other passages of Latin or Greek (Mitchell, *English Pulpit Oratory,* 359). Finally, South objected to the "luscious style," the "elaborate metaphors and poetical language" used by many of his contemporaries, arguing that sermons should be "plain, natural, and familiar" instead (ibid., 315).

68. Mitchell, *English Pulpit Oratory*, 62, 115, 123, 261.

69. Lessenich, *Elements of Pulpit Oratory*, 15.

70. Ibid., 9.

71. Lessenich, *Elements of Pulpit Oratory*, 9; Fordyce, *The Folly, Infamy, and Misery of Unlawful Pleasure* (Edinburgh, 1760), 63–64, quoted in Lessenich, *Elements of Pulpit Oratory*, 34); Secker, "A Charge Delivered to the Clergy of the Diocese of Canterbury, in the Year 1766," in *The Works of Thomas Secker, LL.D.*, vol. 5 (London: Rivington, 1811), 478; J. Barecroft, *Ars Concionandi*, 4th ed. (London, 1715), 118, quoted in Lessenich, *Elements of Pulpit Oratory*, 36.

72. Lessenich, *Elements of Pulpit Oratory*, 9, 34.

73. Barecroft, *Ars Concionandi*, 119, quoted in Lessenich, *Elements of Pulpit Oratory*, 30; Rollin, *The Method of Teaching and Studying the Belles Lettres* (London, 1734), 2:317, quoted in Lessenich, *Elements of Pulpit Oratory*, 27;

Leechman, *Sermons* (London, 1789), 1:159, quoted in Lessenich, *Elements of Pulpit Oratory,* 28.

74. Lessenich, *Elements of Pulpit Oratory,* 10, 13.

75. Bede, *Liber de Schematibus et Tropis,* 607, quoted in Howell, *Logic and Rhetoric in England,* 117.

76. Breakey, "A Few Words About Sermons," 545.

77. Johns, "The Manufacture of Sermons," 280; "The Modern British Pulpit," 368.

78. Wenham, "Sermons and Preachers," 16.

79. Gresley, *Ecclesiastes Anglicanus,* 55, 56; Dale, *Nine Lectures on Preaching,* 221, 222.

80. "The Abolition of Sermons," *Saturday Review* 56 (1883): 500.

81. "Sermons," *Church Quarterly Review* 25 (1887): 115.

82. Davies, "Preachers and Preaching," 210; Wenham, "Sermons and Preachers," 5; Rogers, "The British Pulpit," 69, 78.

83. Rogers, "The British Pulpit," 69.

84. Frederic Harrison, "On Style in English Prose," *Living Age* 218 (1898): 234. Harrison was no admirer of "elaborate disquisitions on Style which some of the most consummate masters have amused themselves in compiling" (231). He argued that because the "maxims" in these books were as "barren of any solid food as the shell of a cocoa-nut," prose writers should not waste time in fruitless formal instruction, but should instead devote themselves to "skilful tuition and assiduous practice" (231, 232).

The author of an essay entitled "The Philosophy of Style" agreed with Harrison's declaration that "Style cannot be taught" ("On Style in English Prose," 232). He believed that formal education in writing would be wasted on those of lesser ability because "no amount of instruction will remedy the defect" of "deficient verbal memory, or but little perception of order, or a lack of constructive ingenuity" ("The Philosophy of Style," *Living Age* 35 [1852]: 401). Talented writers, moreover, had no need of such teaching because "practice and natural aptitude" were far more important than "acquaintance" with the "laws" of composition. In this critic's view, a "clear head, a quick imagination, and a sensitive ear will go far towards making all rhetorical precepts needless" (401).

85. "Philosophy of Style," 401.

86. Harrison, "On Style in English Prose," 233.

87. "Some Tendencies of Prose Style," *Edinburgh Review* 190 (1899): 364.

88. "Philosophy of Style," 401, 402.

89. G. Otto Trevelyan, *The Life and Letters of Lord Macaulay* (New York, 1877), 2:99–100, quoted in William A. Madden, "Macaulay's Style," in *The Art of Victorian Prose,* ed. George Levine and William A. Madden (New York: Oxford University Press, 1968), 129; Rogers, "The British Pulpit," 85, 86; William Hanna, "Recent Sermons—Scotch, English, and Irish," *North British Review* 24 (1856): 481.

90. Davies, "Preachers and Preaching," 210.

91. Matthew Arnold, "Preface to Poems, 1853," in *Prose of the Victorian Period,* ed. William E. Buckler (Boston: Houghton Mifflin, 1958), 417; Matthew Arnold, "The Literary Influence of Academies," in *Prose of the Victorian Period,* ed. William E. Buckler (Boston: Houghton Mifflin, 1958), 449–50.

92. Pater, "Style," in *Prose of the Victorian Period,* ed. William E. Buckler (Boston: Houghton Mifflin, 1958), 560.

93. "Some Modern Sermons," *Church Quarterly Review* 34 (1892): 471; "Preachers of the Day," 297; Pater, "Style," 557, 559.

94. Review of *Sermons, Bearing on Subjects of the Day*, by John Henry Newman. *Christian Remembrancer* 7 (1844): 104.

CHAPTER 2. METHODS OF DELIVERY

1. Richard Reis, *George MacDonald*, 69. According to W. Fraser Mitchell, the use of written sermons began during the Reformation, when a preacher needed a "record of what [he] had said, should he be questioned for heresy" (*English Pulpit Oratory*, 17). Although preaching from manuscripts was banned for a time—in 1674, the Duke of Monmouth "censured 'in the king's name' the use of MS. in the pulpit" (ibid., 23)—the practice was generally "the rule in the English Establishment" in the "generations" prior to the Victorian period (J. H. Rigg, "On Preaching," *London Quarterly Review* 28 [1867]: 390). In the nineteenth century, Henry Parry Liddon, Henry Melvill, and John Henry Newman were among the eminent Anglicans who read their sermons in the pulpit (S. Parkes Cadman, "Famous English Preachers," *Chautauquan* 19 [1894]: 184; Webber, *History of Preaching* 1:734).

Although reading from manuscript was largely confined to the Church of England, extemporaneous preaching was practiced by both Anglicans and Dissenters. In accordance with the ban on reading issued by Charles II, Anglican clergymen of the late seventeenth century preached extemporaneously (Mitchell, *English Pulpit Oratory*, 25; Pattison, *The History of Christian Preaching*, 206). Outside the Established Church, the practice was especially common in Methodist preaching. Horton Davies has written that "The Methodists were renowned for their sermons delivered without the benefit of manuscript" (*Worship and Theology in England*, vol. 4 [Princeton: Princeton University Press, 1962], 254); in 1866, Louisa Merivale credited the Wesleyans with the "substitution of extempore for written addresses," a development she regarded as a "very important innovation" in British preaching ("The English Pulpit," 167). Some of the most eminent extempore preachers of the Victorian age were William Connor Magee, Bishop of Peterborough; Christopher Newman Hall, an eminent Congregationalist; and Charles Haddon Spurgeon, the best-known Baptist pulpiteer of the nineteenth century (Dargan, *History of Preaching*, 501, 548).

Mitchell tells us that Puritan preachers "favoured the carefully written sermon, delivered *memoriter*," and he notes further that preaching from memory was normative in the Scottish preaching of the seventeenth and eighteenth centuries (*English Pulpit Oratory*, 16, 26). The Victorian minister who was perhaps best able to achieve this middle ground was Thomas Guthrie, minister of St. John's church in Edinburgh. He memorized his sermons, but his delivery "showed as much freedom and abandon as if the words had leaped impromptu to his lips" (Pattison, *History of Christian Preaching*, 326).

2. Rigg, "On Preaching," 386–87.

3. Spurgeon, *Lectures to My Students* (Grand Rapids, Mich.: Zondervan, 1975), 142; Mulock, "Sermons," *Cornhill* 9 (1864): 35.

4. Rigg, "On Preaching," 401.

5. Burns, "Modern Preaching," 451. B. G. Johns, for example, believed that "Every man must decide on that style for which he feels and knows himself to be best suited, and which is best suited for his subject and for his people" ("The

Manufacture of Sermons," 280). Two unidentified theorists writing in the latter part of the century echoed the arguments of Burns and Johns: the author of an essay published in the *London Quarterly Review* in 1872 held that "every man ought to aim at discovering that which suits him best" ("Extempore Preaching," *London Quarterly Review* 37 [1872]: 450), and the author of an 1887 article in the *Church Quarterly Review* asked, "is it not best to leave it to the preacher to find out what he can do well and what he cannot?" ("Sermons," 117). Victorian arguments for flexibility in sermon preparation were summed up simply by the author of an 1878 article in *The Congregationalist:* "As many men, so many methods" ("Of Sermon-Making," 721).

6. Rigg, "On Preaching," 386.

7. Heurtley, "The Preparation of Sermons for Village Congregations," in *Homiletical and Pastoral Lectures,* ed. C. J. Ellicott (New York: A. C. Armstrong & Son, 1880), 135; Garbett, "The Preacher's Gifts," in *Homiletical and Pastoral Lectures,* ed. C. J. Ellicott (New York: A. C. Armstrong & Son, 1880), 179.

8. Burns, "Modern Preaching," 452.

9. Rigg, "On Preaching," 387.

10. Goodwin, "What Constitutes a Plain Sermon?" 117.

11. R. W. Dale, *Nine Lectures on Preaching,* 164.

12. Rigg, "On Preaching," 387.

13. Johns, "Manufacture of Sermons," 280; Newman, *Idea of a University,* 342; "Modern Preaching," *Fraser's Magazine* 79 (1869): 265.

14. Gresley, *Ecclesiastes Anglicanus,* 287, 295, 298.

15. Ibid., 287.

16. Ibid., 201, 202.

17. Evans, "A Discourse Upon Sermons," *Macmillans* 57 (1887): 61; Canon Robinson, "Sermons and Preaching," *Macmillans* 7 (1863): 416.

18. "Modern Preaching," 265; Rigg, "On Preaching," 399; Newman, *Idea of a University,* 343.

19. Evans, "Discourse Upon Sermons," 62.

20. "Extempore Preaching," 458.

21. Dale, *Nine Lectures on Preaching,* 165.

22. Newman, *Idea of a University,* 342.

23. Rigg, "On Preaching," 401.

24. Herbert, "Art of Preaching," 30.

25. Burns, "Modern Preaching," 451; Rigg, "On Preaching," 388.

26. Robinson, "Sermons and Preaching," 416.

27. Johns, "Manufacture of Sermons," 279.

28. Davies, "English Pulpit," 70.

29. Robinson, "Sermons and Preaching," 416.

30. Dale, *Nine Lectures on Preaching,* 165.

31. John Saul Howson, "Homely Hints on Preaching," in *Homiletical and Pastoral Lectures,* ed. C. J. Ellicott (New York: A. C. Armstrong & Son, 1880), 50; "Charles Spurgeon and the Pulpit," review of *The Park Street Pulpit, Containing Sermons Preached and Revised by the Rev. C. H. Spurgeon,* by Charles Haddon Spurgeon, *Eclectic Magazine* 42 (1857): 226; Rogers, "The British Pulpit," 93.

32. Evans, "A Discourse Upon Sermons," 62; Davies, "English Pulpit," 71.

33. Johns, "Manufacture of Sermons," 280; "Extempore Preaching," 449; Burns, "Modern Preaching," 452.

34. "An Essay on Extemporary Preaching," *Methodist Magazine* 38 (1815): 580.

35. Johns, "Manufacture of Sermons," 280.
36. Gresley, *Ecclesiastes Anglicanus,* 196.
37. Ibid., 295, 297.
38. Herbert, "Art of Preaching," 28.
39. Heurtley, "Preparation of Sermons," 156.
40. Herbert, "Art of Preaching," 27.
41. "Sermons," 117.
42. Goodwin, "What Constitutes a Plain Sermon?" 124.
43. Ibid.
44. Evans, "Discourse Upon Sermons," 62; Herbert, "Art of Preaching," 27.
45. Spurgeon, *Lectures to My Students,* 132, 140; "Extempore Preaching," 457, 58.
46. "Extempore Preaching," 456–57; Rogers, "British Pulpit," 92; Spurgeon, *Lectures to My Students,* 153.
47. "Extempore Preaching," 455.
48. Spurgeon, *Lectures to My Students,* 141.
49. Newman, *Idea of a University,* 341.
50. Dale, *Nine Lectures on Preaching,* 156.
51. Rigg, "On Preaching," 398.

Chapter 3. Preaching and Sermon Publishing

1. Eric Mackerness, *The Heeded Voice,* xi; Lewis Drummond, *Spurgeon: Prince of Preachers* (Grand Rapids, Mich.: Kregel Publications, 1992), 25; Horton Davies, *Worship and Theology in England,* 283.
2. Arnstein et al., "Recent Studies," 149; Desmond Bowen, *The Idea of the Victorian Church: A Study of the Church of England, 1833–1889* (Montreal: McGill University Press, 1968), 139.
3. Cruse, *The Victorians and Their Reading* (Boston: Houghton Mifflin Company, 1935), 108; Dargan, *History of Preaching,* 471.
4. Clark, *The Making of Victorian England* (New York: Athenaeum, 1962), 20, quoted in Arnstein et al., "Recent Studies," 150.
5. Wenham, "Sermons and Preachers," 1.
6. Harry Jones, "The Parish Priest," *Fraser's Magazine* 71 (1865): 526; Mackerness, *The Heeded Voice,* xi.
7. Mackerness, *Heeded Voice,* xi.
8. Horton Davies, *Worship and Theology in England,* 217; J. Baldwin Brown, "Is the Pulpit Losing its Power?" *Living Age* 133 (1877): 309.
9. Brown, "Is the Pulpit Losing its Power?" 309.
10. "A Plebiscite about Preachers," *The Spectator* 57 (October 4, 1884): 1296.
11. Webber, *History of Preaching,* 2:386, 387, 508; Lewis O. Brastow, *Representative Modern Preachers* (New York: Hodder & Stoughton, 1904), 361.
12. Webber, *History of Preaching,* 2: 290, 395, 405, 411, 472.
13. Webber, *History of Preaching,* 1:500, 506; "Preachers of the Day," 295.
14. Dargan, *History of Preaching,* 525; Webber, *History of Preaching,* 1:566.
15. "Preachers of the Day," 294.
16. Pattison, *History of Christian Preaching,* 308; Webber, *History of Preaching,* 1:733.
17. Dargan, *History of Preaching,* 525, 528; Webber, *History of Preaching,* 1:644.

18. Davies, *Worship and Theology in England*, 284.

19. Josef L. Altholz, *The Religious Press in Britain, 1760–1900* (New York: Greenwood Press, 1989), 135; "Extempore Preaching," 455.

20. Merivale, "English Pulpit," 145; Mackerness, *Heeded Voice*, xv.

21. Reis, *George MacDonald*, 126.

22. Reliable information on the publication and sale of Victorian sermons is scarce. Analyses of publishing in pre-Victorian Britain have shown that "sermons dominated religious publishing from the Restoration to the middle of the eighteenth century" (Thomas R. Preston, "Biblical Criticism, Literature, and the Eighteenth-Century Reader," in *Books and Their Readers in Eighteenth-Century England*, ed. Isabel Rivers [Leicester: Leicester University Press, 1982], 98), but no comparable studies have yet been done of the nineteenth-century book trade. First, scholars disagree about what percentage of the total book market was occupied by religious writings. Richard D. Altick, for example, estimates that religious books comprised 37 percent of total publishing in 1880, a figure that is much higher than Patrick Scott's 17.1 percent for 1879 and Simon Eliot's 15.6 percent for the 1870s and 9.5 percent for the 1890s (Altick, *The English Common Reader: A Social History of the Mass Reading Public, 1800–1900* [Chicago: University of Chicago Press, 1957], 108; Scott, "The Business of Belief: The Emergence of 'Religious' Publishing," in *Sanctity and Secularity: The Church and the World*, ed. Derek Baker [Oxford: Basil Blackwell, 1973], 224; Eliot, electronic mail to the author, 8 March 1994).
Statements specifically addressing the sermon trade reveal a similar lack of consensus. Some scholars have argued that the sermon enjoyed bestseller status. According to Amy Cruse, sermons occupied "the place that is now held by novels" (*Victorians and Their Reading*, 116); Horton Davies argues that "sermons were the most popular form of reading" in the middle of the nineteenth century (*Worship and Theology in England*, 286); and Walter Houghton simply states that "Sermons outsold novels" (*The Victorian Frame of Mind, 1830–1870* [New Haven: Yale University Press, 1957], 21n). All of these claims were made without supporting documentation; they have been recently called into question by Patrick Scott, who maintains that "the cheapening of periodicals in the eighteen-sixties, after the end of paper duty, meant the end of sermon publishing in volume form" ("Business of Belief," 217), and Simon Eliot, who writes, "although there were no doubt occasions when a specific sermon did outsell a specific novel, this was a relatively rare event and became rarer as the century progressed" (electronic mail to the author, 8 March 1994). Such discrepancies lend credence to Patrick Leary's claim that it is "high time that someone took a close look at the business of Victorian sermon-publishing" (electronic mail to the author, 8 March 1994).

23. "Modern Sermons," review of *Sermons, Explanatory and Practical, on the Thirty-Nine Articles of the Church of England, in a Series of Discourses Delivered at the Parish Church of St. Alphage, Greenwich*, by T. Waite, *Monthly Review* 112 (1827): 225.

24. Burns, "Modern Preaching," 425, 432.

25. William Cleaver Wilkinson, *Modern Masters of Pulpit Discourse* (New York: Funk & Wagnall's, 1905), 128; S. Parkes Cadman, "Famous English Preachers," 189.

26. Brastow, *Representative Modern Preachers*, 310.

27. H. W. Wilberforce, "F. Newman's Oxford Parochial Sermons," review of *Parochial and Plain Sermons*, by John Henry Newman, *Dublin Review* ns 12 (1869): 309.

28. Spurgeon, *Autobiography*, 1:393–94.

29. Drummond, *Spurgeon*, 25, 324. The sale of Spurgeon's sermons was not limited to the weekly circulation of individually published texts; weekly sermons were collected and republished in annual volumes, thirty-seven of which appeared during Spurgeon's lifetime (Spurgeon, *Autobiography*, 1:394).

30. Spurgeon, *Autobiography*, 2:350.

31. Rogers, "British Pulpit," 68, 89.

32. David Masson, "The Pulpit in the Nineteenth Century," *Fraser's Magazine* 30 (1844): 290; Hanna, "Recent Sermons," 490; "A Preacher on Preaching," review of *Lectures on Preaching*, by W. Boyd Carpenter, *Saturday Review* 80 (1895): 245.

33. James Davies, "Preachers and Preaching," 203; Hanna, "Recent Sermons," 489.

34. "Modern Preaching," 255.

35. Robinson, "Sermons and Preaching," 415.

36. Johns, "The Traffic in Sermons," *Nineteenth Century* 31 (1892): 198.

37. "Sermons and Sermonizers," *Fraser's Magazine* 55 (1857): 88.

38. Rogers, "British Pulpit," 68.

39. Davies, "English Pulpit," 82.

40. Johns, "Traffic in Sermons," 198.

41. Herbert, "Art of Preaching," 25; "Modern Preaching," 260–61.

42. Howard Littlewood, "The Sermon Trade," *St. Paul's* 3 (1869): 594.

43. Johns, "Traffic in Sermons," 199; Littlewood, "Sermon Trade," 594. These fees represented a significant expense for many ministers. Patrick Scott has estimated that Victorian clergymen earned between £100 and £800 per year, with most salaries "in the £200 to £300 range" (Online posting, VICTORIA: 19th-Century British Culture and Society, 11 Dec. 1997). A fee of £5 4s for a year's supply of sermons represented, then, approximately a full week's wages for the "average" pulpiteer.

44. "Sermons and Sermonizers," 88, 90.

45. Johns, "Traffic in Sermons," 199, 203.

46. Rogers, "British Pulpit," 92.

47. "Abolition of Sermons," 500; "Modern British Pulpit," 350.

48. "Sermons and Their Hearers," *Eclectic Magazine* ns 44 (1886): 259; Merivale, "English Pulpit," 183.

49. Margaret Oliphant, "Sermons," *Blackwood's* 92 (1862): 203.

50. "Sermons and Sermonizers," 92.

51. Ernest W. Bacon, *Spurgeon: Heir of the Puritans* (London: George Allen & Unwin, 1967), 105; Robinson, "Sermons and Preaching," 411.

52. Davies, "English Pulpit," 84.

53. Hanna, "Recent Sermons," 487–89.

54. Herbert, "Art of Preaching," 28; Merivale, "English Pulpit," 180.

55. Johns, "Manufacture of Sermons," 279.

56. Robinson, "Sermons and Preaching," 413.

57. Burns, "Modern Preaching," 425, 426.

58. "Modern Preaching," 258, 267.

59. Oliphant, "Sermons," 210.

60. "The Pulpit," *Tait's Edinburgh Magazine* ns 26 (1859): 413.

61. Rigg, "Pulpit and Its Influence," 378.

62. Dowden, review of *The Decay of Modern Preaching*, by J. P. Mahaffy, *The Academy* 21 (1882): 226.

63. Masson, "Pulpit in the Nineteenth Century," 289.

64. Davies, "English Pulpit," 67.

65. Herbert, "Art of Preaching," 25; "Abolition of Sermons," 500.

66. Only two of the nineteen reviews consulted were negative. I discuss these articles—an 1857 review of Spurgeon's *New Park Street Pulpit* in *Fraser's* magazine and Nicholas Wiseman's review of Newman's *Sermons Bearing on Subjects of the Day* in the *Dublin Review*—in the following chapters.

67. "Modern Sermons," 228.

68. Rogers, "British Pulpit," 86; Review of *Sermons, Bearing on Subjects of the Day,* 104.

69. Hervey, "Spurgeon as a Preacher," *Christian Review* 22 (1857): 300, 301, 305.

70. Church, "Newman's Parochial Sermons," review of *Parochial and Plain Sermons,* by John Henry Newman, *Living Age* 102 (1869): 151.

71. Hanna, "Recent Sermons," 481, 492, 497.

72. "Mr. George MacDonald's New Sermons," review of *Unspoken Sermons,* by George MacDonald, *The Spectator* 58 (1885): 852–53.

73. "Some Modern Sermons," 470, 471, 473.

74. Breakey, "A Few Words About Sermons," 551.

75. Bacon, *Spurgeon,* 75.

76. F. R. Webber, for example, records that "a visitor to the ancient city of York was told to do three things: see the Five Sisters windows in the north transept of the great minster church, make a circuit of the city on the top of the old city walls, and then go to Salem Chapel and hear a sermon by 'Parsons of York'" (*History of Preaching,* 1:483). C. H. Spurgeon and John Henry Newman enjoyed similar celebrity status; their popularity is discussed in upcoming chapters.

77. Webber, *History of Preaching,* 1:499.

78. Dargan, *History of Preaching,* 522; Davies, *Worship and Theology in England,* 313. Lewis Brastow has argued that these sermons place Robertson in the first rank of Victorian preachers. In his 1904 assessment of Robertson, Brastow wrote, "It is since his death that his place as a preacher has been established, and it is hardly too much to say that among the educated classes . . . his name has become more widely cherished, and his work more widely influential, than that of any other English preacher of his century" (*Representative Modern Preachers,* 50).

79. Evans, "Discourse Upon Sermons," 63.

80. By 1988, Tannen had abandoned this term, arguing that "the power of the terms *oral* and *literate* is far greater than the power of the nouns to which they may be attached: *tradition, continuum,* or *strategies*" ("The Commingling of Orality and Literacy in Giving a Paper at a Scholarly Conference," *American Speech* 63 [1988]: 40; Tannen's emphasis). The notion of a continuum, with orality and literacy at the extremes and varying conflations of the traditions in the middle, remains, I believe, a useful paradigm for the study I am undertaking here.

CHAPTER 4. CHARLES HADDON SPURGEON

1. Quotations from Spurgeon's works are cited in the text according to the following key:

Autobiography: C. H. Spurgeon *Autobiography,* 2 vols. (Edinburgh: Banner of Truth Trust, 1962).

Lectures: *Lectures to My Students* (Grand Rapids, Michigan: Zondervan, 1975).

Sermons: *Sermons of Rev. C. H. Spurgeon,* 19 vols. (New York: Funk and Wagnalls, n.d.).

2. Lewis Drummond, *Spurgeon: Prince of Preachers,* Grand Rapids, Mich.: Kregel Publications, 1992. 161. He had actually begun preaching several years earlier. Spurgeon gave his "first formal public speech" in a missionary meeting on September 10, 1849 and preached his first sermon—an impromptu discourse in a thatched cottage in Teversham—in August of that year (ibid., 57; *Autobiography,* 1:183). In October 1851, the Lay Preacher's Association assigned him to preach at the Waterbeach chapel, and what began as a two-week temporary position grew into Spurgeon's first full-time pastorate (Drummond, *Spurgeon,* 161).

3. Drummond, *Spurgeon,* 163, 186, 197, 199.

4. *Autobiography,* 1:263; Drummond, *Spurgeon,* 201.

5. Drummond, *Spurgeon,* 210, 211.

6. As Spurgeon put it, "To return to New Park Street Chapel, greatly enlarged as it was during the time of our first sojourn at Exeter Hall, resembled the attempt to put the sea into a tea-pot. We were more inconvenienced than ever. To turn many hundreds away from the doors, was the general if not the universal necessity, and those who gained admission were but little better off, for the packing was dense in the extreme, and the heat something terrible even to remember" (*Autobiography,* 1:427).

7. Drummond, *Spurgeon,* 222, 237.

8. *Autobiography,* 1:472; Drummond, *Spurgeon,* 237, 336.

9. Drummond, *Spurgeon,* 238.

10. Drummond, *Spurgeon,* 238, 248; *Autobiography,* 1:527.

11. Drummond, *Spurgeon,* 93.

12. *C. H. Spurgeon's Autobiography: Compiled from His Diary, Letters, and Records, by His Wife and His Private Secretary* (London: Passmore and Alabaster, 1897–1900), 1:350, quoted in Drummond, *Spurgeon,* 201.

13. Archives of the Metropolitan Tabernacle, London, quoted in Drummond, *Spurgeon,* 380.

14. Peabody, "Spurgeon," *North American Review* 86 (1858): 275. Spurgeon's popularity was even exploited for financial gain. Some merchants advertised lithographs "In best finished gold frames, 19 x 23 inches—25 shillings," others printed his picture "on their yearly calendars," and still others used Spurgeon as an unauthorized endorsement for their products (Drummond, *Spurgeon,* 454, 501). One observer lamented the prevalence of Spurgeon-worship when he wrote, "Everybody with plenty of leisure and taste for gush is now writing the life of Mr. Spurgeon. Are good clergymen so scarce? Why, there are more lives of Spurgeon about than lives of Jesus Christ" (ibid., 600).

15. Bacon, *Spurgeon,* 78; *Autobiography,* 2:318.

16. "Extempore Preaching," 461; Drummond, *Spurgeon,* 330.

17. Bacon, *Spurgeon,* 77; *Autobiography,* 2:335.

18. "Preachers and Preaching," *Tait's Edinburgh Magazine* ns 23 (1856): 693.

19. Drummond, *Spurgeon,* 760, 762.

20. "The Tabernacle Church's 'In Memoriam' Resolution" (in the archives of the Metropolitan Tabernacle, London), quoted in Drummond, *Spurgeon*, 763–64.

21. Drummond, *Spurgeon*, 752.

22. *C. H. Spurgeon's Autobiography: Compiled from His Diary, Letters, and Records*, 4:376, quoted in Drummond, *Spurgeon*, 755.

23. Godfrey Holden Pike, *The Life and Work of Charles Haddon Spurgeon*, vol. 6 (London: Cassell and Company, n.d.), 337, quoted in Drummond, *Spurgeon*, 766.

24. Cadman, "Famous English Preachers," 187.

25. Rosenberg, *Can These Bones Live?* (Urbana, Illinois: University of Illinois Press, 1988), 11, 29, 45.

26. "Charles Spurgeon and the Pulpit," 224. Spurgeon did, however, pursue a lifelong program of self-education. He read widely and rapidly, "making it a point to read half a dozen of the meatiest books per week." By his death at age fifty-seven, he had accumulated a library of more than twelve thousand volumes (Bacon, *Spurgeon*, 108, 109). Most of these books—approximately seven thousand—were Puritan religious treatises, but he was also well acquainted with the Latin authors, with "works on natural history and the sciences," and with literary works, including the writings of Carlyle, Macaulay, and Ruskin (Bacon, *Spurgeon*, 108; *Autobiography*, 2:335–36).

27. Carl F. H. Henry, foreword to *Spurgeon: Prince of Preachers*, by Lewis Drummond (Grand Rapids, Michigan: Kregel Publications, 1992); Drummond, *Spurgeon*, 197; *Autobiography*, 1:157.

28. Rosenberg, *Can These Bones Live?* 40.

29. "Sermons and Sermonizers," 86.

30. Drummond, *Spurgeon*, 410.

31. Rosenberg, *Can These Bones Live?* 39.

32. Rigg, "On Preaching," 387.

33. John De Kewer Williams, "My Memories and Estimate of My Friend Spurgeon," quoted in Drummond, *Spurgeon*, 568.

34. Drummond, *Spurgeon*, 756.

35. Williams, "My Memories," quoted in Drummond, *Spurgeon*, 568; Drummond, *Spurgeon*, 296.

36. "Mr. Spurgeon at Fifty," *The Critic and Good Literature* 5 (1884): 21.

37. Ong, *Orality and Literacy*, 67.

38. "Sermons and Sermonizers," 87.

39. George Campbell, *Lectures on Systematic Theology and Pulpit Eloquence*, ed. Henry J. Ripley (Boston: Lincoln and Edmands, 1832), 159.

40. Blair, "Lectures on Rhetoric," 113.

41. Gresley, *Ecclesiastes Anglicanus*, 247.

42. Ibid.

43. Ong, *Orality and Literacy*, 34; Deborah Tannen, "Oral and Literate Strategies In Spoken and Written Narratives," *Language* 58 (1982): 7.

44. In Wallace Chafe's studies, for example, "first person references" account for approximately sixty-one of every thousand words in spoken discourse, but fewer than five of every thousand in written English ("Integration and Involvement in Speaking, Writing, and Oral Literature," in *Spoken and Written Language: Exploring Orality and Literacy*, ed. Deborah Tannen [Norwood, New Jersey: Ablex, 1982], 46).

45. Ong, *Orality and Literacy*, 42; Drummond, *Spurgeon*, 157.

46. Albert B. Lord, "Characteristics of Orality," *Oral Tradition* 2 (1987): 55.

47. Scholars who have made this observation include Walter Ong, who has described oral language as "Redundant or 'copious'" (*Orality and Literacy*, 39); Deborah Tannen, who writes that orality is marked by "frequent repetition and paraphrase" ("The Commingling of Orality and Literacy," 36); and Bruce Rosenberg, who has called "repetition—of some sort" the "most marked trait of oralature" ("The Complexity of Oral Tradition," 82).

48. Burns, "Modern Preaching," 435; *Autobiography*, 1:332; "Charles Spurgeon and the Pulpit," 226.

49. Hervey, "Spurgeon as a Preacher," 307.

50. Ong, *Orality and Literacy*, 42; Hervey, "Spurgeon as a Preacher," 302.

51. *Autobiography*, 2:360; Hervey, "Spurgeon as a Preacher," 302.

52. "Mr. Spurgeon at Fifty," 21; "Charles Spurgeon and the Pulpit," 225.

53. Merivale, "English Pulpit," 179.

54. "Preachers of the Day," 303; Eva Hope, *Spurgeon: The People's Preacher* (London: The Walter Scott Publishing Company, n.d.), 42–43, quoted in Drummond, *Spurgeon*, 236.

55. *C. H. Spurgeon's Autobiography*, 1:354, quoted in Drummond, *Spurgeon* 202.

56. Hope, *Spurgeon*, 49–50, quoted in Drummond, *Spurgeon*, 236.

57. *C. H. Spurgeon's Autobiography*, 1:348, quoted in Drummond, *Spurgeon* 197.

58. Drummond, *Spurgeon*, 249.

59. Drummond, *Spurgeon*, 589; *Autobiography*, 1:317.

60. Charles Ray, *The Life of Charles Haddon Spurgeon* (London: Passmore and Alabaster, 1903), 192, quoted in Drummond, *Spurgeon*, 280–81.

61. "Mr. Spurgeon at Fifty," 21.

62. "Charles Spurgeon and the Pulpit," 225.

63. Williams, "My Memories," quoted in Drummond, *Spurgeon*, 568.

64. Drummond, *Spurgeon*, 177.

65. *C. H. Spurgeon's Autobiography*, 1:272, quoted in Drummond, *Spurgeon* 177.

66. William Young Fullerton, *C. H. Spurgeon: A Biography* (London: Williams and Norgate, 1920), 125, quoted in Drummond, *Spurgeon*, 254.

67. Drummond, *Spurgeon*, 283.

68. Ibid., 284.

69. "Modern Preaching," 258; Merivale, "English Pulpit," 179.

70. Drummond, *Spurgeon*, 241.

71. Ibid., 513.

72. "Sermons and Sermonizers," 84–87.

73. Ibid., 85.

74. Ibid., 86.

75. Ibid., 85.

76. Ong, *Orality and Literacy*, 42.

77. "Sermons and Sermonizers," 85.

78. Ong, *Orality and Literacy*, 45.

79. "Sermons and Sermonizers," 86, 93, 94.

80. Ibid., 86, 87.

81. Ibid., 86.

82. Ong, *Orality and Literacy* 39–41.

83. Rosenberg, *Can These Bones Live?* 131.
84. Ong, *Orality and Literacy* 136, 37.
85. Drummond, *Spurgeon,* 162.

CHAPTER 5. JOHN HENRY NEWMAN

1. Bruce Rosenberg identifies a link between formal education and the use of manuscripts when he notes that "Prepared sermons that are read in their entirety . . . are almost invariably the mark of seminary-trained preachers" (*Can These Bones Live?* 45). Conversely, J. H. Rigg suggested that the reading of sermons was appropriate when the preacher was addressing an educated congregation such as Newman's, one "trained closely to follow a sustained argument or discussion" ("On Preaching," 387).

2. Quotations from Newman's works are cited in the text according to the following key:

Belief: *Sermons, Chiefly on the Theory of Religious Belief, Preached Before the University of Oxford,* 2nd ed. (London: Francis and John Rivington, 1844).

Idea: *The Idea of a University,* ed. I. T. Ker (Oxford: The Clarendon Press, 1976).

PPS: *Parochial and Plain Sermons,* 8 vols (London: Rivington, 1868).

3. Eric Griffiths, "Newman: The Foolishness of Preaching," in *Newman after a Hundred Years,* ed. Ian Ker and Alan G. Hill (Oxford: Clarendon Press, 1990), 67; Mackerness, *Heeded Voice,* 4.

4. John Henry Newman, *The Letters and Diaries of John Henry Newman,* ed. Gerard Tracey (New York: Oxford University Press, 1984), 6 : 193, quoted in Ian Ker, *John Henry Newman: A Biography* (Oxford: Oxford University Press, 1988), 150.

5. In "University Preaching," Newman writes, "We may of course work ourselves up into a pretence, nay, into a paroxysm, of earnestness; as we may chafe our cold hands till they are warm. But when we cease chafing, we lose the warmth again; on the contrary, let the sun come out and strike us with his beams, and we need no artificial chafing to be warm. The hot words, then, and energetic gestures of a preacher, taken by themselves, are just as much signs of earnestness as rubbing the hands or flapping the arms together are signs of warmth" (*Idea,* 331).

6. *Idea,* 329; J. V. Tracey, "John Henry Newman as a Preacher," *American Catholic Quarterly Review* 16 (1891): 226.

7. Tracey, "John Henry Newman as a Preacher," 226.

8. Ibid.

9. While at Oxford, Newman "made an 'elaborate analysis' of Aristotle's *Rhetoric*" and contributed an article on Cicero to Coleridge's *Encyclopedia Metropolitana* (Walter Jost, *Rhetorical Thought in John Henry Newman* [Columbia: University of South Carolina Press, 1989], 8, 9). Which figure exercised the greater influence on his thought is not entirely clear; Mariella Gable argues that he is more Aristotle's disciple than Cicero's ("Newman's Anglican Sermons," *Catholic World* 148 [1939]: 434), whereas Newman himself once acknowledged Cicero as "the only master of style [he] ever had" (Ker, *John Henry Newman* 630). This issue is not at stake here; what is significant is that, in his *Parochia*

and Plain Sermons, Newman does not "subsume" the principles of classical rhetoric, as Jost suggests (*Rhetorical Thought in John Henry Newman,* 209), as much as he sets them aside in favor of a more literate method of sacred speaking.

10. The most familiar expressions of this distinction appear in *Orality and Literacy,* in which Walter Ong notes that oral language tends to be "*Additive rather than subordinative,*" "*Aggregative rather than analytic,*" and "*Redundant or 'copious'*" (37–39; Ong's emphasis). Other scholars who have made similar claims include Eric Havelock, whose "General Theory of Primary Orality" includes the concepts of "thematic" and "ideological echo" (*The Muse Learns to Write: Reflections on Orality and Literacy from Antiquity to the Present* [New Haven: Yale University Press, 1926], 73); Deborah Tannen, who notes that oral expression is marked by "frequent repetition and paraphrase" ("The Commingling of Orality and Literacy," 36); and Bruce Rosenberg, who asserts that "the most marked trait of oralature is repetition" ("Complexity of Oral Tradition," 82).

11. Spurgeon, *Autobiography,* 1:19.

12. Spurgeon, *Sermons of Rev. C. H. Spurgeon,* 1:123, 204, 378.

13. This terminology belongs to Rosalind Horowitz and S. Jay Samuels, who include "reference to a previous part of a text" and "connectives such as *however, moreover*" in their list of devices that can be used to "show intra-and intersentential relations" in written language ("Comprehending Oral and Written Language: Critical Contrasts for Literacy and Schooling," in *Comprehending Oral and Written Language,* ed. Rosalind Horowitz and S. Jay Samuels [San Diego: Academic Press, 1987], 8).

14. John Henry Newman, *Letters and Correspondence of John Henry Newman During His Life in the English Church,* ed. Anne Mozley (London: Longmans, Green, 1891), 2:202, quoted in Mackerness, *Heeded Voice,* 5.

15. I have been able to locate only one negative review of Newman's Anglican sermons. In 1843, Nicholas Wiseman published a review of *Sermons Bearing on Subjects of the Day* in the *Dublin Review.* At the time the review appeared, Wiseman was an established figure in the Roman Catholic Church, and his article is written from a distinctly anti-Anglican perspective. Early in the review, Wiseman writes, "The reason . . . for which we lay before our readers these sermons rather than others is, that they save us the trouble of doing in our own words, what we have repeatedly done already—exposing the confusion, the inconsistency, the crumbling, sinking, failing condition of the English Church" (Nicholas Wiseman, "Newman's Sermons," review of *Sermons bearing on Subjects of the Day,* by John Henry Newman, *Dublin Review* 15 [1843]: 547).

16. Breakey, "A Few Words About Sermons," 549.

17. Dargan, *History of Preaching,* 517–18.

18. Church, "Newman's Parochial Sermons," 152; review of *Sermons, Bearing on Subjects of the Day,* 105, 106.

19. Vaughan, "J. H. Newman as Preacher," 43.

20. Prothero, "Newman in the English Church," *Edinburgh Review* 173 (1891): 556.

21. Church, "Newman's Parochial Sermons," 151.

22. Wildman, "Newman in the Pulpit: The Power of Simplicity," *Studies in the Literary Imagination* 8 (1975): 73.

23. Mackerness, *Heeded Voice,* 6–8.

24. Review of *Sermons, Bearing on Subjects of the Day,* 103; Wilberforce, "F. Newman's Oxford Parochial Sermons," 330.

25. Church, "Newman's Parochial Sermons," 151–53. Newman's Catholic sermons were often recognized as important works of literature as well. Arthur Wollaston Hutton argued that Newman's Catholic sermons "display a fervour of eloquence, a liveliness of manner . . . that would be looked for in vain in the classical Oxford volumes" (*Cardinal Manning* [London: Methuen, 1892], 222, quoted in Mackerness, *Heeded Voice,* 11–12). J. V. Tracey wrote that *Discourses Addressed to Mixed Congregations* "contain the most eloquent and elaborate specimens of his eloquence as a preacher" ("John Henry Newman as a Preacher," 235). Similarly, W. G. Ward's review of the collection called his readers' attention to Newman's "powers of description," "free and natural style," and "powers of mind" which would have made him "a novelist of the very highest class" if he had chosen to write fiction instead of sermons ("Newman's Discourses," review of *Discourses Addressed to Mixed Congregations,* by John Henry Newman, *Dublin Review* 28 [1850]: 186, 203).

26. Jost, *Rhetorical Thought in John Henry Newman,* 5.

27. Ibid., 3.

28. Nicholas Lash, "Literature and Theory: Did Newman Have a 'Theory' of Development?," in *Newman and Gladstone: Centennial Essays,* ed. James D. Bastable (Dublin: Veritas Publications, 1978), 162, quoted in Jost, *Rhetorical Thought in John Henry Newman,* 5.

29. Review of *Sermons Bearing on Subjects of the Day,* 105.

30. Vaughan, "J. H. Newman as Preacher," 39, 44.

31. Church, "Newman's Parochial Sermons," 154.

32. R. D. Middleton, "The Vicar of St. Mary's," in *John Henry Newman, Centenary Essays,* ed. Henry Tristram (London: Burns, Oates, and Washbourne, 1945), 129.

33. We do not know precisely the demographics of Newman's congregation. The parish of St. Mary's encompassed both the university and part of the city of Oxford, but references to Newman's influence outside the academic community are scarce. Only two articles, both written in the twentieth century, address this issue, and they are somewhat contradictory. Edward DeSantis tells us that Newman preached to a "mixed congregation of university scholars, shopkeepers and scrub-women" ("Newman's Concept of the Church in the World as in His *Parochial and Plain Sermons,*" *American Benedictine Review* 21 [1970]: 269). L. Bouyer, on the other hand, has maintained that as Newman's popularity within the university grew, attendance among the other classes declined, and "shopkeepers, college and domestic servants, and the like"—the people for whom Newman's sermons were "first intended"—eventually formed "only a small section of the congregation" ("Great Preachers—XIII. John Henry Newman," *Theology* 55 [1952]: 87–88).

The rapidity with which Newman's congregation came to be dominated by university men is also unclear. R. D. Middleton suggests that students who had come to respect Newman during his days as a tutor at Oriel followed him to St. Mary's and therefore comprised the nucleus of his congregation from the start ("The Vicar of St. Mary's," 127). Bouyer, in contrast, tells us that while members of the university were not initially part of Newman's congregation, they began to attend his services "very soon" after he was installed as Vicar ("Great Preachers," 87); H. W. Wilberforce, a contemporary of Newman, wrote that the shift to a primarily academic following was far from immediate, that Newman's "parish services became gradually well attended by university men" ("F. Newman's Oxford Parochial Sermons," 323). Finally, there is some disagreement about the university administration's response to Newman's growing popularity. Wilberforce tells us that some of the colleges changed the Sunday dinner hour "on purpose to allow their men to attend S. Mary's without deserting the hall" (324). Amy Cruse and Mariella Gable have stated just the opposite, maintaining that the "authorities discouraged the undergraduates from attending" and even attempted to "frustrate the influence of Newman by placing the dinner hour at the time of the sermon" (Cruse, *The Victorians and Their Reading*, 10; Gable, "Newman's Anglican Sermons," 431).

34. DeLaura, "'O Unforgotten Voice': The Memory of Newman in the Nineteenth Century," *Renascence* 43 (1990): 82; Tracey, "John Henry Newman as a Preacher," 230. There is some evidence, in fact, that Newman had achieved the status of a tourist attraction. According to DeLaura, attendance at one of the services was seen as a "mandatory part" of the "serious" visitor's itinerary, and Eric Griffiths has noted that people coming to Oxford on business often decided "to remain over the Sunday in order that they might hear him preach" (DeLaura, "'O Unforgotten Voice'," 82; Middleton, "Vicar of St. Mary's," 135).

35. Cruse, *Victorians and Their Reading*, 10; Griffiths, "Newman: The Foolishness of Preaching," 63; Middleton, "Vicar of St. Mary's," 130.

36. Mackerness, *Heeded Voice*, 1.

37. Vaughan, "J. H. Newman as Preacher," 41.

38. DeLaura, "'O Unforgotten Voice'," 82; Griffiths, "Newman: The Foolishness of Preaching," 63; Mackerness, *The Heeded Voice*, 2. Blunt met Newman in 1876 or 1877. In his diary, he credits Newman with healing him of a toothache: "at the instant of touching his hand when he received me, my pains vanished, nor did they return while I was staying in the house. Newman's was a wonderful hand, soft, nervous, emotional, electric; and I felt that a miracle had been wrought" (*My Diaries: Being a Personal Narrative of Events, 1888–1914* [London: M. Secker, 1932], 338, quoted in Mackerness, *Heeded Voice*, 2).

39. DeLaura, "'O Unforgotten Voice'," 85.

40. Ibid., 83, 89.

41. Arnold, *Discourses in America* (London: Macmillan, 1885), 139–40.

42. Froude, *Short Studies on Great Subjects,* vol. 4 (London: Longmans, Green, 1886), 286.

43. DeLaura, "'O Unforgotten Voice'," 89, 94.

44. Shairp, "Balliol Scholars," *Macmillan's Magazine* 27 (1873): 376, quoted in DeLaura, "'O Unforgotten Voice'," 95.

45. Shairp, *Studies in Poetry and Philosophy* (Edinburgh: Edmonston and Douglas, 1868), 255, quoted in Middleton, "Vicar of St. Mary's," 137.

46. Froude, *Short Studies on Great Subjects,* 283.

47. Lake, *Memorials of William Charles Lake, Dean of Durham* (London: E. Arnold, 1901), 41–42, quoted in Middleton, "Vicar of St. Mary's," 132.

48. Charles Kingsley, "The Irrationale of Speech," *Fraser's Magazine* 20 (1859): 13, quoted in DeLaura, "'O Unforgotten Voice'," 91.

49. "Of Sermon-Making," 723.

50. Review of *Sermons, Bearing on Subjects of the Day*, 104; Church, "Newman's Parochial Sermons," 151.

Chapter 6. George MacDonald

1. G. B. Tennyson, foreword to *An Expression of Character: The Letters of George MacDonald*, ed. Glenn Edward Sadler (Grand Rapids, Michigan: William B. Eerdmans, 1994).

2. The author of an anonymously published review in *The Spectator* maintained that the "Scottish stories" were "almost perfect," that not even Sir Walter Scott could "deal with average middle-class Scottish life with the inward fidelity of George MacDonald" ("A Great Scottish Teacher," *The Spectator* 86 [1901]: 382). The comparison of MacDonald and Wordsworth was made in 1871 by Henry Holbrach, who believed that MacDonald's poem "Light" inevitably "reminds you of Wordsworth's Ode" and that Wordsworth "would have been proud" of MacDonald's "perfect" poem "The Child-Mother" ("George MacDonald," review of *Works of Fancy and Imagination,* by George MacDonald, *Contemporary Review* 19 [1871]: 44, 47). The other comparisons are those of W. D. Geddes, who compared MacDonald's sonnets to those of Shakespeare, Milton, Coleridge, and Keats, and even went so far as to rank MacDonald's poetic talents with those of Tennyson, the current Poet Laureate ("George MacDonald as a Poet," *Blackwoods Magazine* 149 [1891]: 363, 369). This latter comparison is particularly appropriate, for there is some evidence that MacDonald was among the candidates for Poet Laureate after Tennyson's death in 1892 (Reis, *George MacDonald,* 26).

3. On the whole, modern scholars do not share Victorian critics' high regard for MacDonald's poetry and realistic novels. Richard Reis, for example, has asserted that MacDonald's poems are often "slack and wordy" and that even "Within and Without," MacDonald's best-known poem, shows no "vigor of expression" (*George MacDonald,* 23, 26). William Raeper has offered a similar assessment. He believes that, while MacDonald may have written a handful of "substantial" poems, most of his verse is merely "mawkish, sentimental, and ridiculous" (*George MacDonald* [Herts, England: Lion Publishing, 1987], 121, 123). Reis and Raeper find the same faults in MacDonald's realistic novels as well: Raeper criticizes MacDonald for his "clumsy and very uneven" plots and his syrupy and affected language (195, 315), and Reis has stated that MacDonald's "permanent 'rank'" as a realistic novelist "must remain secondary, for there is no way to excuse his artistic faults—sentimentality, verbosity, preachiness, sheer lack of craft" (143).

When they turn to MacDonald's fantasy novels, however, the critics are much more positive in their assessments. C. S. Lewis, who has been credited with reviving MacDonald's reputation in the twentieth century, stated that MacDonald "does fantasy better than anyone else" (*George MacDonald: An Anthology* [New York: Macmillan, 1947], 14), and Raeper and Reis have readily agreed; in their view, MacDonald was at his best as a writer of fairy tales and as a "novelist of the unconscious," and they believe that it is these books that commend MacDonald to literary scholars today (Raeper, *George MacDonald,* 213, 309; Reis, *George MacDonald,* Preface).

4. Reis, *George MacDonald,* 27.

5. His tenure in the pulpit was therefore much shorter than either Spurgeon's—whose London ministry spanned nearly four decades—or Newman's—who served as vicar of St. Mary's for fifteen years. Moreover, the congregations to which MacDonald preached were much smaller than Newman's and Spurgeon's. Whereas, Spurgeon spoke to thousands in the Metropolitan Tabernacle and Newman addressed several hundred people in St. Mary's, MacDonald's largest congregation consisted of only 117 people (George MacDonald to George MacDonald, Sr., 15 April 1851, *An Expression of Character: The Letters of George MacDonald,* ed. Glenn Edward Sadler [Grand Rapids, Michigan: William B. Eerdmans, 1994], 50). Finally, Spurgeon and Newman preached to many

outside their churches through their published sermons—and set precedents in the field of Victorian publishing in the process—but I have found no evidence that MacDonald published the sermons he preached during his Arundel ministry.

6. Greville MacDonald, *George MacDonald and His Wife*, 118, 138. David S. Robb has written that MacDonald "hesitated for some time before committing himself to the ministry" ("George MacDonald at Blackfriars Chapel," *North Wind* 5 [1986]: 17). Robb may be correct in this assertion, but MacDonald himself describes his experience not as a conscious hesitation, but rather as an unconscious, gradual realization of a call to the ministry. In a questionnaire completed as part of his application to Highbury, MacDonald wrote, "I can hardly say how long I have wished to be a minister—perhaps nearly two years. The desire awoke so gradually in my mind that I cannot tell when it began" (MacDonald's answers to "Queries to Candidates," 8 August 1848, *An Expression of Character*, 23). MacDonald's letters provide some evidence of this gradual awakening. In March 1846, while he was employed as a tutor in London, he wrote, "I do not trouble myself much, about my future prospects. I certainly should like something else too, but I hope I am willing to remain here as long as God wishes. If he shows me plainly that he wishes me to give myself entirely to him & his service, I am ready to do so . . . but I have formed no resolution at all on the matter" (MacDonald to George MacDonald, Sr., 13 March 1846, *An Expression of Character*, 15). A year later, he wrote that, although he would not want "any employment besides in which I could take a real interest—lest it should make me forget God," he had not "finally made up my mind as to the ministry" (MacDonald to George MacDonald, Sr., 11 April 1847, *An Expression of Character*, 17). By 1848, MacDonald had made up his mind; and believing the ministry to be "the greatest and the best of employments," the only profession "worth following with heart and soul" (MacDonald's answers to "Queries to Candidates," 8 August 1848, *An Expression of Character*, 24), he applied to Highbury.

7. Greville MacDonald, *George MacDonald and His Wife*, 79.

8. Reis, *George MacDonald*, 23.

9. Ibid., 33, 36.

10. Greville MacDonald, *George MacDonald and His Wife*, 178.

11. MacDonald's address to his Arundel congregation, 5 July 1852, *An Expression of Character*, 53.

12. Ibid.

13. MacDonald, *An Expression of Character*, 54.

14. Greville MacDonald, *George MacDonald and His Wife*, 183.

15. In 1860, MacDonald wrote an article on Shelley for the *Encyclopedia Britannica*. He was also a frequent contributor to the *Christian Spectator*, and from 1869 to 1872 served as the editor of *Good Words for the Young* (Greville MacDonald, *George MacDonald and His Wife*, 212, 361; George MacDonald, *An Expression of Character*, 177n). His other works include *Exotics: A Translation of the Spiritual Songs of Novalis, the Hymn Book of Luther, and Other Poems from the German and Italian* (London: Strahan, 1876); *A Threefold Cord: Poems by Three Friends* (London: Unwin Brothers, 1883); and *A Cabinet of Gems Cut and Polished by Sir Philip Sydney, Now for the More Radiance Presented without Their Setting by George MacDonald* (London: Elliot Stock, 1892); and *The Tragedie of Hamlet, Prince of Denmark: A Study of the Text of the Folio of 1623* (London: Longmans, 1885).

In 1869, MacDonald undertook a lecture tour of Scotland; and three years later, he traveled to America, where he regularly spoke to capacity crowds and met such prominent writers as Emerson, Longfellow, and Harriet Beecher Stowe (Greville MacDonald, *George MacDonald and His Wife*, 389, 421; Louisa Mac-Donald to Mary Josephine MacDonald, 3 October 1872, *An Expression of Character*, 201; Louisa MacDonald to Lilia Scott MacDonald, 5 October 1872, *An Expression of Character*, 203). His lectures in England were delivered in three very different venues. He began in February 1855 with "two courses of lectures—one for ladies in the morning, the others for anybody in the evening—both at my house" (MacDonald to George MacDonald, Sr., 8 February 1855, *An Expression of Character*, 83). A few years later, he moved his lectures from his living room to a formal academic setting, serving as a lecturer at Edinburgh's Philosophical Institute during the summer of 1859; as a professor of English literature at Bedford College for Ladies in London from 1859 to 1865; and as a lecturer at King's College beginning in 1865 (Greville MacDonald, *George MacDonald and His Wife*, 307, 366). Finally, MacDonald addressed popular as well as academic audiences; from 1858 to 1891, he spent many evenings delivering public addresses on such literary figures as Milton, Shakespeare, Wordsworth, and Tennyson (MacDonald to John Thorpe, 15 July 1868, *An Expression of Character*, 164).

16. MacDonald to George MacDonald, Sr., 17 October 1853, *An Expression of Character*, 67.

17. In a letter to his father, 20 May 1853, MacDonald wrote, "The few young who are here and not [adversely] influenced by their parents, the simple, honest and poor, are much attached to me—at least most of them—and that means but a very few" (*An Expression of Character*, 60).

18. Ibid.

19. MacDonald to George MacDonald, Sr., 67.

20. MacDonald, *An Expression of Character*, 73n. In a letter written October 17, 1853, he told his father that, "for various reasons" he "would rather not" be introduced to any of the vacant churches in Manchester (*An Expression of Character*, 67). He did not elaborate on his reasons, but his position is consistent with the disdain for denominationalism we find in some of his other correspondence. Later that year, he told his father, "I have no love for *any* sect of Christians as such—as little for independents as any" (16 November 1853, *An Expression of Character*, 68). Two years later, he wrote that he had "more and more cause to rejoice that I am not connected with any so-called church under the sun" (MacDonald to Louisa MacDonald, 15 July 1855, *An Expression of Character*, 94). Even after he joined the Church of England, which he believed allowed "the individual a greater freedom in faith than any other Christian organization," MacDonald retained his conviction that sectarianism was a chief source of schism within the Christian community; a letter he wrote in August 1865 noted that he "care[d] neither for that nor any other denomination as dividing or separating" (Greville MacDonald, *George MacDonald and His Wife*, 401; MacDonald to the secretary of a Congregational church in North London, August 1865, *An Expression of Character*, 151).

21. MacDonald to George MacDonald, Sr., 16 November 1853, *An Expression of Character*, 70.

22. MacDonald to George MacDonald, Sr., 26 June 1854, *An Expression of Character*, 80.

23. MacDonald to George MacDonald, Sr., August 1855, *An Expression of Character*, 100.

24. J. Joseph Flynn and David Edwards, preface to *George MacDonald in the Pulpit: The 'Spoken' Sermons of George MacDonald*, comp. J. Joseph Flynn and David Edwards (Whitethorn, California: Johannesen Printing and Publishing, 1996).

25. E. W., "Half-An-Hour with George MacDonald," in *George MacDonald in the Pulpit*,133.

26. Quotations from MacDonald's works are cited in the text according to the following key:

Annals: Annals of a Quiet Neighbourhood (1867; reprint, Eureka, Cal.: Sunrise Books, 1991).

Parish: The Seaboard Parish: A Sequel to "Annals of a Quiet Neighbourhood" (London: George Routledge and Sons, n.d.).

Pulpit: George MacDonald in the Pulpit, comp. J. Joseph Flynn and David Edwards (Whitethorn, Cal.: Johannesen Printing and Publishing, 1996).

US: Unspoken Sermons, 3 vols. (1867, 1885, 1889; reprint, Eureka, Cal.: Sunrise Books, 1988, 1989, 1995).

27. MacDonald to George MacDonald, Sr., 51.

28. A sentence early in "The Child in the Midst" reads: "It is not for the sake of setting forth this lesson that I write about these words of our Lord, but for the sake of a truth, a revelation about God, in which his great argument reaches its height." Similarly, he begins a paragraph of "The Temptation in the Wilderness" by declaring that he is "ashamed to yield here to the necessity of writing what is but as milk for babes, when I would gladly utter, if I might, only that which would be as bread for men and women" (*US*, 1:2, 142).

29. Erving Goffman, for example, writes that an "unresponsive" audience can "freeze [a speaker] to his script," but that a "'good' or 'warm'" one "is likely to induce the speaker to extend each response-provoking phrase or phrasing: he will continue along for a moment extemporaneously where gestured feedback . . . suggests he has touched home" (*Forms of Talk* [Philadelphia: University of Pennsylvania Press, 1981], 180). Similarly, Bruce Rosenberg has observed that congregational involvement is an essential element of spiritual preaching, that the success or failure of a sermon can often be attributed to the extent of the audience's response to the preacher (*Can These Bones Live?*, 150). Such interaction is not possible when one is writing rather than speaking; as Walter Ong puts it, the "poetic of oral cultures is participatory," but writing "normally calls for some kind of withdrawal" from one's audience (*Interfaces of the Word: Studies in the Evolution of Consciousness and Culture* [Ithaca: Cornell University Press, 1977], 57, 276).

30. Dennis P. Seniff, "Orality and Textuality in Medieval Castilian Prose," *Oral Tradition* 2 (1987): 153; Chafe, "Integration and Involvement," 45–47.

31. Wallace Chafe, for example, has maintained that, generally speaking, "first person reference" is common in spoken communication but "much less frequent in formal written language" ("Integration and Involvement," 46).

32. Johns, "Manufacture of Sermons," 266.

33. Johns, "The Manufacture of Sermons," 264; James Davies, "Preachers and Preaching," 209.

34. Ronald MacDonald, "George MacDonald: A Personal Note," in *From a Northern Window: Papers Critical, Historical, and Imaginative*, ed. Ian

Maclaren (London: J. Nisbet & Co., 1911), 66–67, quoted in Reis, *George Mac-Donald*, 47.

35. Greville MacDonald, *George MacDonald and His Wife*, 375.

36. Ibid.

37. I realize that, in making this proposition, I am assuming that Harry Walton accurately reflects MacDonald's own views on preaching. While such an assumption is not always valid, David S. Robb has argued that "it is often fairly safe to take what a narrator says to the reader of a MacDonald novel as indeed representing what MacDonald, in his own person, wants the reader to think" ("George MacDonald at Blackfriars Chapel," 4). Robb makes this argument in a study of MacDonald's rejection of Calvinism—he suggests that the narrator in *Weighed and Wanting* reflects MacDonald's views when he says he could not believe in a God who did not offer salvation "to all men" (4)—and I believe his claim holds true for Harry Walton's words as well.

38. Ong, *Interfaces of the Word*, 278.

39. Rosenberg, *Can These Bones Live?*, 45.

40. MacDonald to George MacDonald, Sr., 16 October 1850, *An Expression of Character*, 37.

41. MacDonald, *An Expression of Character*, 32n.

42. Greville MacDonald, *George MacDonald and His Wife*, 118–19.

43. MacDonald to George MacDonald, Sr., 23 February 1850, *An Expression of Character*, 32.

44. MacDonald to George MacDonald, Sr., 3 June 1853, *An Expression of Character*, 61.

45. Ong, *Orality and Literacy*, 6.

46. MacDonald to George MacDonald, Sr., 15 November 1850, *An Expression of Character*, 40.

47. Ong, *Orality and Literacy*, 104, 105.

48. Rosenberg, *Can These Bones Live?*, 29.

49. Greville MacDonald, *George MacDonald and His Wife*, 150; MacDonald to George MacDonald Sr., 29 October 1850, *An Expression of Character*, 38.

50. MacDonald to George MacDonald, Sr., 25 July 1849, *An Expression of Character*, 30.

51. MacDonald to George MacDonald, Sr., 16 October 1850, *An Expression of Character*, 37.

52. Ibid.; MacDonald to George MacDonald, Sr., 4 October 1850, *An Expression of Character*, 35.

53. Evans, "Discourse Upon Sermons," 62.

54. According to Bruce Rosenberg, folk, or "spiritual," preachers do little by way of formal preparation. They may "'work up' their sermons . . . by reviewing in their minds the basic outlines," but they insist that the sermon itself is, and must be, a product of spontaneous divine inspiration. Thus, many spiritual preachers share the Reverend Rubin Lacy's belief that they need not study in advance, that they "simply had to step up to the pulpit and [be] 'fed' directly from God" (*Can These Bones Live?*, 39, 40).

55. Tracey, "John Henry Newman as a Preacher," 226.

56. Notice in "The Chicago Pulpit," April 1873, in *George MacDonald in the Pulpit*, 25; Mr. Dexter, "George MacDonald in the Pulpit," in *George MacDonald in the Pulpit*, 7; J. Joseph Flynn and David Edwards, preface to *George MacDonald in the Pulpit*.

57. "Great Scottish Teacher," 383.

58. Brooks, *Lectures on Preaching* (London: Macmillan, 1904), 16, quoted in MacDonald, *An Expression of Character*, 220n.

59. "Great Scottish Teacher," 383.

60. "Mr. George MacDonald's New Sermons," 852.

61. Ibid., 852, 853.

62. John Ruskin to George MacDonald, 18 December 1868, quoted in Greville MacDonald, *George MacDonald and His Wife*, 337.

63. "Mr. George MacDonald's New Sermons," 852.

64. "George MacDonald as a Teacher of Religion," *London Quarterly Review* 31 (1869): 423.

65. Ibid., 418.

66. Review of *Robert Falconer*, by George MacDonald, *Fortnightly Review* 4 (1868): 115–16, quoted in Rolland Hein, *George MacDonald: Victorian Mythmaker* (Nashville, Tenn.: Star Song Publishing Group, 1993), 184.

67. Review of *Paul Faber, Surgeon*, by George MacDonald, *Athenaeum* 21 December 1878; 801, quoted in Hein, *George MacDonald*, 310.

68. Lewis, *George MacDonald: An Anthology*, 14, 17.

69. Raeper, *George MacDonald*, 195; Reis, *George MacDonald*, 74, 106.

70. Spurgeon, *Lectures*, 153.

71. Flynn and Edwards, preface to *George MacDonald in the Pulpit*.

72. Ong, *Orality and Literacy*, 6.

CHAPTER 7. A RHETORICAL COMPARISON OF SPURGEON, NEWMAN, AND MACDONALD

1. W. J. Copeland, preface to *Parochial and Plain Sermons*, by John Henry Newman, vol. 1 (London: Rivington, 1868).

2. Ong, *Interfaces of the Word*, 278.

3. The sermons discussed in this chapter will be cited in the text according to the following key:

"A Mystery!": Charles Haddon Spurgeon, "A Mystery! Saints Sorrowing and Jesus Glad!," in *Spurgeon's Expository Encyclopedia*, vol. 3 (Grand Rapids, Mich.: Baker Book House, 1951).

"Tears": John Henry Newman, "Tears of Christ at the Grave of Lazarus," in *Parochial and Plain Sermons*, vol. 3 (London: Rivington, 1868).

"The Sermon": George MacDonald, "The Sermon," chap. 8 in *The Seaboard Parish* (London: George Routledge and Sons, n.d.).

4. Howell, *Logic and Rhetoric in England*, 72.

5. Ong, *Interfaces of the Word*, 244.

6. Ong, *Orality and Literacy*, 31–36.

7. Blair, "Lectures on Rhetoric," 113.

8. Ong, *Orality and Literacy*, 40, 41.

9. Ibid., 42.

10. Ibid.

11. Spurgeon, *Lectures To My Students*, 153.

12. Ong, *Rhetoric, Romance, and Technology*, 25, 26.

13. Ong, *Orality and Literacy*, 78, 104.

14. Ibid., 144.

15. Ong, *Rhetoric, Romance and Technology*, 25; Ong, *Orality and Literacy*, 40.

16. Ong, *Orality and Literacy*, 141–151.

17. Ibid., 136.

18. Lessenich, *Elements of Pulpit Oratory*, 51.

19. The insistence on unity of thought in pulpit oratory appears throughout homiletic articles published in Victorian periodicals. A representative statement is H. Rogers' assertion that a good sermon is one in which the preacher "never wanders from the subject, that each remark tells upon the matter in hand, that all his illustrations are brought to bear upon the point, and that he is never found making any step in any direction which does not advance his main object, and lead towards the conclusion to which he is striving to bring his hearers" ("The British Pulpit," 75, 76).

20. Other uses, such as "But let us read the verses" and "Here we have a glimpse of the faith of Thomas the doubter" (582, 584) appear fewer than half-a-dozen times and are largely incidental to the question of audience awareness in MacDonald's sermon.

21. Newman, *Idea of a University*, 336.

22. Ong, *Orality and Literacy*, 101.

23. Ong, *Interfaces of the Word*, 74.

Conclusion

1. Fowler, *Kinds of Literature* (Cambridge, Mass.: Harvard University Press, 1982), v.

2. Ibid.

3. Greenblatt and Gunn, introduction to *Redrawing the Boundaries* (New York: MLA, 1992).

4. Ong, *Orality and Literacy*, 156.

5. Walter J. Ong, letter to the author, 7 February 1994.

6. Wenham, "Sermons and Preachers," 2; Altick, *English Common Reader*, 7.

7. Ong, *Interfaces of the Word*, 82.

8. Ong, *Orality and Literacy*, 119.

9. Altick, *English Common Reader*, 2, 249–50, 324.

10. Ibid., 204, 330.

11. Walter J. Ong, *The Presence of the Word: Some Prolegomena for Cultural and Religious History* (New Haven: Yale University Press, 1967), 22.

12. Levine, "Victorian Studies," in *Redrawing the Boundaries*, ed. Stephen Greenblatt and Giles Gunn (New York: MLA, 1992), 144.

13. Arnstein et al., "Recent Studies," 149.

Bibliography

"The Abolition of Sermons." *Saturday Review* 56 (1883): 499–500.

Altholz, Josef L. *The Religious Press in Britain, 1760–1900.* New York: Greenwood Press, 1989.

Altick, Richard D. *The English Common Reader: A Social History of the Mass Reading Public, 1800–1900.* Chicago: University of Chicago Press, 1957.

Arderne, James. *Directions Concerning the Matter and Style of Sermons,* 11–12. London, 1671. Quoted in Rolf P. Lessenich, *Elements of Pulpit Oratory in Eighteenth-Century England (1660–1800)* (Koln, Germany: Bohlau-Verlag, 1972): 79.

Aristotle. *Rhetoric.* Trans. W. Rhys Roberts. In *The Works of Aristotle,* vol. 2, ed. Robert Maynard Hutchins, 593–675. Chicago: Encyclopaedia Britannica, 1952.

Arnold, Matthew. *Discourses in America.* London: Macmillan, 1885.

―――. "The Literary Influence of Academies." In *Prose of the Victorian Period,* ed. William E. Buckler, 441–57. Boston: Houghton Mifflin, 1958.

―――. "Preface to *Poems,* 1853." In *Prose of the Victorian Period,* ed. William E. Buckler, 409–420. Boston: Houghton Mifflin, 1958.

Arnstein, Walter, et al. "Recent Studies in Victorian Religion." *Victorian Studies* 33 (1989): 149–75.

Bacon, Ernest W. *Spurgeon: Heir of the Puritans.* London: George Allen & Unwin, 1967.

Barecroft, J. *Ars Concionandi,* 118, 199. 4th ed. London, 1715. Quoted in Rolf P. Lessenich, *Elements of Pulpit Oratory in Eighteenth-Century England (1660–1800)* (Koln, Germany: Bohlau-Verlag, 1972), 30, 36.

Bede, The Venerable. *Liber de Schematibus et Tropis.* In *Rhetores Latini Minores,* ed. Karl Halm (Lipsiae: B. G. Teubneri, 1863), 607. Quoted in Wilbur Samuel Howell, *Logic and Rhetoric in England, 1500–1700* (New York: Russell & Russell, 1961), 117.

Blair, Hugh. "Lectures on Rhetoric and Belles Lettres." In *The Rhetoric of Blair, Campbell, and Whately,* ed. James L. Golden and Edward P. J. Corbett, 28–137. New York: Holt, Rinehart & Winston, 1968.

Blunt, Wilfrid Scawen. *My Diaries: Being a Personal Narrative of Events, 1888–1914,* 338. London: M. Secker, 1932. Quoted in Eric David Mackerness, *The Heeded Voice: Studies in the Literary Status of the Anglican Sermon, 1830–1900* (Cambridge: W. Heffer & Sons, 1959), 2.

Bouyer, L. "Great Preachers―XIII. John Henry Newman." *Theology* 55 (1952): 87–91.

Bowen, Desmond. *The Idea of the Victorian Church: A Study of the Church of England, 1833–1889*. Montreal: McGill University Press, 1968.

Brastow, Lewis O. *Representative Modern Preachers*. New York: Hodder & Stoughton, 1904.

Breakey, S. Leslie. "A Few Words About Sermons." *Cornhill Magazine* 3 (1861): 544–52.

Brooks, Phillips. *Lectures on Preaching*, 16. London: Macmillan, 1904. Quoted in *An Expression of Character: The Letters of George MacDonald*, ed. Glenn Edward Sadler (Grand Rapids, Mich.: William B. Eerdmans, 1994), 220n.

Brown, J. Baldwin. "Is the Pulpit Losing its Power?" *Living Age* 133 (1877): 304–13.

Burns, Islay. "Modern Preaching." *North British Review* 38 (1863): 423–53.

Cadman, S. Parkes. "Famous English Preachers." *Chautauquan* 19 (1894): 184–91.

Campbell, George. *Lectures on Systematic Theology and Pulpit Eloquence*. Ed. Henry J. Ripley. Boston: Lincoln and Edmands, 1832.

Chafe, Wallace L. "Integration and Involvement in Speaking, Writing, and Oral Literature." In *Spoken and Written Language: Exploring Orality and Literacy*, ed. Deborah Tannen, 35–53. Norwood, N.J.: Ablex, 1982.

Chappell, William. *The Use of Holy Scripture Gravely and Methodically Discoursed*, prefatory matter. London, 1653. Quoted in W. Fraser Mitchell, *English Pulpit Oratory from Andrewes to Tillotson* (New York: Russell & Russell, 1962), 111.

"Charles Spurgeon and the Pulpit." Review of *The Park Street Pulpit, Containing Sermons Preached and Revised by the Rev. C. H. Spurgeon*, by Charles Haddon Spurgeon. *Eclectic Magazine* 42 (1857): 224–28.

Church, R. W. "Newman's Parochial Sermons." Review of *Parochial and Plain Sermons*, by John Henry Newman. *Living Age* 102 (1869): 151–57.

Cicero, Marcus Tullius. *De Inventione*. In *De Inventione: De Optimo Genere Oratorum: Topica*, trans. and ed. H.M. Hubbell, 2–346. Cambridge, Mass.: Harvard University Press, 1949.

———. *De Oratore*. In *Cicero on Oratory and Orators; with His Letters to Quintus and Brutus*, trans. and ed. J. S. Watson, 142–401. London: Henry G. Bohn, 1862.

Clark, George Kitson. *The Making of Victorian England*, 20. New York: Athenaeum, 1962. Quoted in Walter Arnstein et al., "Recent Studies in Victorian Religion," *Victorian Studies* 33 (1989): 150.

Claude, Jean. "Essay on the Composition of a Sermon." In *The Young Preacher's Manual*, ed. Ebenezer Porter, 135–230. New York: Jonathan Leavitt, 1829.

Copeland, W. J. Preface to *Parochial and Plain Sermons*, by John Henry Newman. Vol. 1. London: Rivington, 1868.

Cox, Leonard. *The Arte or Crafte of Rhethoryke*. Ed. Frederic Ives Carpenter. Chicago: University of Chicago Press, 1899.

Cruse, Amy. *The Victorians and Their Reading*. Boston: Houghton Mifflin Company, 1935.

Dale, R. W. *Nine Lectures on Preaching*. 7th ed. London: Hodder & Stoughton, 1893.

Dargan, Edwin Charles. *A History of Preaching.* Vol. 2. Grand Rapids, Mich.: Baker Book House, 1974.

Davies, Horton. *Worship and Theology in England.* Vol. 4. Princeton: Princeton University Press, 1962.

Davies, James. "Preachers and Preaching." *Contemporary Review* 9 (1868): 203–20.

Davies, William. "The English Pulpit." Review of *The Penny Pulpit: a Collection of accurately-reported Sermons by the most eminent Ministers of various Denominations. Living Age* 120 (1874): 67–86. First published in *Quarterly Review* 135 (1873): 297–331.

DeLaura, David J. "'O Unforgotten Voice': The Memory of Newman in the Nineteenth Century." *Renascence* 43 (1990): 81–104.

DeSantis, Edward. "Newman's Concept of the Church in the World as in His *Parochial and Plain Sermons.*" *American Benedictine Review* 21 (1970): 268–92.

Dexter, Mr. "George MacDonald in the Pulpit." In *George MacDonald in the Pulpit: The 'Spoken' Sermons of George MacDonald,* comp. J. Joseph Flynn and David Edwards, 1–8. Whitethorn, Cal.: Johannesen Printing and Publishing, 1996.

Dowden, John. Review of *The Decay of Modern Preaching,* by J. P. Mahaffy. *The Academy* 21 (1882): 225–26.

Drummond, Lewis. *Spurgeon: Prince of Preachers.* Grand Rapids, Mich.: Kregel Publications, 1992.

Eliot, Simon. Electronic-mail message to the author, 8 March 1994.

"An Essay on Extemporary Preaching." *Methodist Magazine* 38 (1815): 577–85.

Evans, A. Eubule. "A Discourse Upon Sermons." *Macmillans* 57 (1887): 58–63.

E. W. "Half-An-Hour with George MacDonald." In *George MacDonald in the Pulpit: The 'Spoken' Sermons of George MacDonald,* comp. J. Joseph Flynn and David Edwards, 131–40. Whitethorn, Cal.: Johannesen Printing and Publishing, 1996.

"Extempore Preaching." *London Quarterly Review* 37 (1872): 448–72.

Flynn, J. Joseph, and David Edwards. Preface to *George MacDonald in the Pulpit: The 'Spoken' Sermons of George MacDonald.* Comp. J. Joseph Flynn and David Edwards. Whitethorn, Cal.: Johannesen Printing and Publishing, 1996.

Fordyce, James. *The Folly, Infamy, and Misery of Unlawful Pleasure,* 63–64. Edinburgh, 1760. Quoted in Rolf P. Lessenich, *Elements of Pulpit Oratory in Eighteenth-Century England (1660–1800)* (Koln, Germany: Bohlau-Verlag, 1972), 34.

Fowler, Alastair. *Kinds of Literature.* Cambridge, Mass.: Harvard University Press, 1982.

Froude, James Anthony. *Short Studies on Great Subjects.* Vol. 4. London: Longmans, Green, 1886.

Fullerton, William Young. *C. H. Spurgeon: A Biography,* 125. London: Williams and Norgate, 1920. Quoted in Lewis Drummond, *Spurgeon: Prince of Preachers* (Grand Rapids, Mich.: Kregel Publications, 1992), 254.

Gable, Mariella. "Newman's Anglican Sermons." *Catholic World* 148 (1939): 431–37.

Garbett, Edward. "The Preacher's Gifts." In *Homiletical and Pastoral Lectures,* ed. C. J. Ellicott, 161–185. New York: A. C. Armstrong & Son, 1880.

Geddes, W. D. "George MacDonald as a Poet." *Blackwoods Magazine* 149 (1891): 361–70.

"George MacDonald as a Teacher of Religion." *London Quarterly Review* 31 (1869): 402–26.

Glanvill, Joseph. *An Essay Concerning Preaching,* 10. 1678. Quoted in Wilbur Samuel Howell, *Logic and Rhetoric in England, 1500–1700* (New York: Russell & Russell, 1961), 394.

Goffman, Erving. *Forms of Talk.* Philadelphia: University of Pennsylvania Press, 1981.

Golden, James L., and Edward P. J. Corbett, eds. *The Rhetoric of Blair, Campbell, and Whately.* New York: Holt, Rinehart & Winston, 1968.

Goodwin, Harvey. "What Constitutes a Plain Sermon?" In *Homiletical and Pastoral Lectures,* ed. C. J. Ellicott, 105–131. New York: A. C. Armstrong & Son, 1880.

"A Great Scottish Teacher." *The Spectator* 86 (1901): 382–83.

Greenblatt, Stephen, and Giles Gunn. Introduction to *Redrawing the Boundaries.* New York: MLA, 1992.

Gresley, W. *Ecclesiastes Anglicanus: Being a Treatise on Preaching, as Adapted to a Church of England Congregation: In a Series of Letters to a Young Clergyman.* New York: D. Appleton, 1844.

Griffiths, Eric. "Newman: The Foolishness of Preaching." In *Newman after a Hundred Years,* ed. Ian Ker and Alan G. Hill, 63–91. Oxford: Clarendon Press, 1990.

Grundy, C. H. "Dull Sermons." *Macmillans* 34 (1876): 264–67.

Hanna, William. "Recent Sermons—Scotch, English, and Irish." *North British Review* 24 (1856): 479–504.

Harrison, Frederic. "On Style in English Prose." *Living Age* 218 (1898): 230–38. First published in *Nineteenth Century* 42 (1868): 432–42.

Harvey, Gabriel. *Rhetor,* sigs. e4v-f1r. London, 1577. Quoted in Wilbur Samuel Howell, *Logic and Rhetoric in England, 1500–1700* (New York: Russell & Russell, 1961).

Havelock, Eric. *The Muse Learns to Write: Reflections on Orality and Literacy from Antiquity to the Present.* New Haven: Yale University Press, 1926.

Henry, Carl F. H. Foreword to *Spurgeon: Prince of Preachers,* by Lewis Drummond. Grand Rapids, Mich.: Kregel Publications, 1992.

Herbert, H. H. M. "The Art of Preaching." *National Review* 2 (1883): 23–34.

Hervey, G. N. "Spurgeon as a Preacher." *Christian Review* 22 (1857): 296–316.

Heurtley, Charles Abel. "The Preparation of Sermons for Village Congregations." In *Homiletical and Pastoral Lectures,* ed. C. J. Ellicott, 135–157. New York: A. C. Armstrong & Son, 1880.

Holbrach, Henry. "George MacDonald." Review of *Works of Fancy and Imagination,* by George MacDonald. *Contemporary Review* 19 (1871): 37–54.

Hope, Eva. *Spurgeon: The People's Preacher.* London: Walter Scott Publishing Company, n.d., 42–43, 49–50. Quoted in Lewis Drummond, *Spurgeon: Prince of Preachers* (Grand Rapids, Mich.: Kregel Publications, 1992), 236.

Horowitz, Rosalind, and S. Jay Samuels. "Comprehending Oral and Written Language: Critical Contrasts for Literacy and Schooling." In *Comprehending Oral and Written Language,* ed. Rosalind Horowitz and S. Jay Samuels, 1–54. San Diego: Academic Press, 1987.

Houghton, Walter E. *The Victorian Frame of Mind, 1830–1870.* New Haven: Yale University Press, 1957.

Howell, Wilbur Samuel. *Eighteenth-Century British Logic and Rhetoric.* Princeton: Princeton University Press, 1971.

————. *Logic and Rhetoric in England, 1500–1700.* New York: Russell & Russell, 1961.

Howson, John Saul. "Homely Hints on Preaching." In *Homiletical and Pastoral Lectures,* ed. C. J. Ellicott, 49–77. New York: A. C. Armstrong & Son, 1880.

Hutton, Arthur Wollaston. *Cardinal Manning,* 222. London: Methuen, 1892. Quoted in Eric David Mackerness, *The Heeded Voice: Studies in the Literary Status of the Anglican Sermon, 1830–1900* (Cambridge: W. Heffer & Sons, 1959), 11–12.

Hyperius, Andreas Gerardus. *The Practise of Preaching, Otherwise Called the Pathway to the Pulpit: Conteyning an Excellent Method How to Frame Divine Sermons,* fol. 9r-9v, 22r. London, 1577. Quoted in Wilbur Samuel Howell, *Logic and Rhetoric in England, 1500–1700* (New York: Russell & Russell, 1961), 112, 113.

Johns, B. G. "The Manufacture of Sermons." *Contemporary Review* 8 (1868): 262–81.

————. "The Traffic in Sermons." *Nineteenth Century* 31 (1892): 197–207.

Jones, Harry. "The Parish Priest." *Fraser's Magazine* 71 (1865): 526–36.

Jost, Walter. *Rhetorical Thought in John Henry Newman.* Columbia: University of South Carolina Press, 1989.

Ker, Ian. *John Henry Newman: A Biography.* Oxford: Oxford University Press, 1988.

Kingsley, Charles. "The Irrationale of Speech." *Fraser's Magazine* 20 (1859): 13. Quoted in David J. DeLaura, "'O Unforgotten Voice': The Memory of Newman in the Nineteenth Century," *Renascence* 43 (1990): 91.

Lake, William Charles. *Memorials of William Charles Lake, Dean of Durham,* 41–42. London: E. Arnold, 1901. Quoted in R. D. Middleton, "The Vicar of St. Mary's," in *John Henry Newman, Centenary Essays,* ed. Henry Tristram (London: Burns, Oates, and Washbourne, 1945), 132.

Lash, Nicholas. "Literature and Theory: Did Newman Have a 'Theory' of Development?" In *Newman and Gladstone: Centennial Essays.* Ed. James D. Bastable. 162. Dublin: Veritas Publications, 1978. Quoted in Walter Jost, *Rhetorical Thought in John Henry Newman* (Columbia: University of South Carolina Press, 1989), 5.

Lawson, John. *Lectures Concerning Oratory.* Ed. E. Neal Claussen and Karl R. Wallace. Carbondale: Southern Illinois University Press, 1972.

Leary, Patrick. Electronic-mail message to the author, 8 March 1994.

Leechman, William. *Sermons,* 1:159. London, 1789. Quoted in Rolf P. Lessenich, *Elements of Pulpit Oratory in Eighteenth-Century England (1660–1800)* (Koln, Germany: Bohlau-Verlag, 1972), 28.

Lessenich, Rolf P. *Elements of Pulpit Oratory in Eighteenth-Century England (1660–1800).* Koln, Germany: Bohlau-Verlag, 1972.

Levine, George. "Victorian Studies." In *Redrawing the Boundaries,* ed. Stephen Greenblatt and Giles Gunn, 130–153. New York: MLA, 1992.

Lewis, C. S. *George MacDonald: An Anthology.* New York: Macmillan, 1947.

Littlewood, Howard. "The Sermon Trade." *St. Paul's* 3 (1869): 594–98.

Lord, Albert B. "Characteristics of Orality." *Oral Tradition* 2 (1987): 54–72.

MacDonald, George. *Annals of a Quiet Neighbourhood.* 1867. Reprint, Eureka, Cal.: Sunrise Books, 1992.

———. *An Expression of Character: The Letters of George MacDonald.* Ed. Glenn Edward Sadler. Grand Rapids, Mich.: William B. Eerdmans, 1994.

———. *George MacDonald in the Pulpit: The 'Spoken' Sermons of George MacDonald.* Comp. J. Joseph Flynn and David Edwards. Whitethorn, Cal.: Johannesen Printing and Publishing, 1996.

———. *The Seaboard Parish.* London: George Routledge and Sons, n.d.

———. *Unspoken Sermons.* 3 vols. 1867–1889. Reprint, Eureka, Cal.: Sunrise Books, 1988–1995.

MacDonald, Greville. *George MacDonald and His Wife.* New York: Dial Press, 1924.

MacDonald, Ronald. "George MacDonald: A Personal Note." In *From a Northern Window: Papers Critical, Historical, and Imaginative.* Ed. Ian Maclaren, 66–67. London: J. Nisbet & Co., 1911. Quoted in Richard Reis, *George MacDonald* (New York: Twayne, 1972), 47.

Mackerness, Eric David. *The Heeded Voice: Studies in the Literary Status of the Anglican Sermon, 1830–1900.* Cambridge: W. Heffer & Sons, 1959.

Manson, Edward. "The Art of Rhetoric." *Westminster Review* 148 (1897): 630–44.

Masson, David. "The Pulpit in the Nineteenth Century." *Fraser's Magazine* 30 (1844): 287–94.

Merivale, Louisa A. "The English Pulpit." *North British Review* 45 (1866): 145–88.

Middleton, R. D. "The Vicar of St. Mary's." In *John Henry Newman, Centenary Essays,* ed. Henry Tristram, 127–38. London: Burns, Oates, and Washbourne, 1945.

Mitchell, W. Fraser. *English Pulpit Oratory from Andrewes to Tillotson.* New York: Russell & Russell, 1962.

"The Modern British Pulpit." *London Quarterly Review* 2 (1854): 349–74.

"Modern Preaching." *Fraser's Magazine* 79 (1869): 254–68.

"Modern Sermons." Review of *Sermons, Explanatory and Practical, on the Thirty-Nine Articles of the Church of England, in a Series of Discourses Delivered at the Parish Church of St. Alphage, Greenwich,* by T. Waite. *Monthly Review* 112 (1827): 225–30.

"Mr. George MacDonald's New Sermons." Review of *Unspoken Sermons,* by George MacDonald. *The Spectator* 58 (1885): 852–53.

"Mr. Spurgeon at Fifty." *The Critic and Good Literature* 5 (1884): 21.

Mulock, Dinah. "Sermons." *Cornhill* 9 (1864): 33–40.

Newman, John Henry. *The Idea of a University.* Ed. I. T. Ker. Oxford: The Clarendon Press, 1976.

——. *Letters and Correspondence of John Henry Newman During His Life in the English Church,* 2:202. Ed. Anne Mozley. London: Longmans, Green, 1891. Quoted in Eric David Mackerness, *The Heeded Voice: Studies in the Literary Status of the Anglican Sermon, 1830–1900* (Cambridge: W. Heffer & Sons, 1959), 5.

——. *The Letters and Diaries of John Henry Newman,* 6:193. Ed. Gerard Tracey. New York: Oxford University Press, 1984. Quoted in Ian Ker, *John Henry Newman: A Biography* (Oxford: Oxford University Press, 1988), 150.

——. *Parochial and Plain Sermons.* 8 vols. London: Rivington, 1868.

——. *Sermons, Chiefly on the Theory of Religious Belief, Preached Before the University of Oxford.* 2nd ed. London: Francis & John Rivington, 1844.

Notice in "The Chicago Pulpit." In *George MacDonald in the Pulpit: The 'Spoken' Sermons of George MacDonald,* comp. J. Joseph Flynn and David Edwards, 24–25. Whitethorn, Cal.: Johannesen Printing and Publishing, 1996.

"Of Sermon-Making." *The Congregationalist* 7 (1878): 720–23.

Oliphant, Margaret. "Sermons." *Blackwood's* 92 (1862): 202–20.

Ong, Walter J. *Interfaces of the Word: Studies in the Evolution of Consciousness and Culture.* Ithaca: Cornell University Press, 1977.

——. Letter to the author, 7 February 1994.

——. *Orality and Literacy.* New York: Methuen, 1982.

——. *The Presence of the Word: Some Prolegomena for Cultural and Religious History.* New Haven: Yale University Press, 1967.

——. *Rhetoric, Romance, and Technology: Studies in the Interaction of Expression and Culture.* Ithaca: Cornell University Press, 1971.

Owst, Gerald R. *Preaching in Medieval England.* New York: Russell & Russell, 1965.

Pater, Walter. "Style." In *Prose of the Victorian Period,* ed. William E. Buckler, 553–70. Boston: Houghton Mifflin, 1958.

Pattison, T. Harwood. *The History of Christian Preaching.* Philadelphia: American Baptist Publication Society, 1903.

Review of *Paul Faber, Surgeon,* by George MacDonald. *Athenaeum* 21 December 1878. Quoted in Rolland Hein, *George MacDonald: Victorian Mythmaker* (Nashville, Tenn.: Star Song Publishing Group, 1993), 310.

Peabody, A. P. "Spurgeon." *North American Review* 86 (1858): 275–79.

"The Philosophy of Style." *Living Age* 35 (1852): 401–10.

Pike, Godfrey Holden, *The Life and Work of Charles Haddon Spurgeon,* 6:337. London: Cassell and Company, n.d. Quoted in Lewis Drummond, *Spurgeon: Prince of Preachers* (Grand Rapids, Mich.: Kregel Publications, 1992), 766.

"A Plebiscite about Preachers." *The Spectator* 57 (1884): 1296–97.

"A Preacher on Preaching." Review of *Lectures on Preaching,* by W. Boyd Carpenter. *Saturday Review* 80 (1895): 245.

"Preachers and Preaching." *Tait's Edinburgh Magazine* ns 23 (1856): 689–93.

"Preachers of the Day." *Living Age* 161 (1884): 294–304.

Preston, Thomas R. "Biblical Criticism, Literature, and the Eighteenth-Century Reader." In *Books and Their Readers in Eighteenth-Century England,* ed. Isabel Rivers, 97–126. Leicester: Leicester University Press, 1982.

Prideaux, John. *Hypomnemata,* 104. Oxford, c.1650. Quoted in Wilbur Samuel Howell, *Logic and Rhetoric in England, 1500–1700* (New York: Russell & Russell, 1961), 333.

Prothero, Roland. "Newman in the English Church." *Edinburgh Review* 173 (1891): 526–62.

"The Pulpit." *Tait's Edinburgh Magazine* ns 26 (1859): 412–19.

Raeper, William. *George MacDonald.* Herts, England: Lion Publishing, 1987.

Ray, Charles. *The Life of Charles Haddon Spurgeon,* 192. London: Passmore and Alabaster, 1903. Quoted in Lewis Drummond, *Spurgeon: Prince of Preachers* (Grand Rapids, Mich.: Kregel Publications, 1992), 280–81.

Reis, Richard. *George MacDonald.* New York: Twayne, 1972.

Rigg, J. H. "On Preaching." *London Quarterly Review* 28 (1867): 365–403.

————. "The Pulpit and Its Influence." Review of *Sermons, Doctrinal and Practical,* by William Archer Butler. *Eclectic Magazine* 40 (1857): 377–88. First published as "The Pulpit: Professor Butler's Sermons." *London Quarterly* 7 (1857): 461–77.

Robb, David S. "George MacDonald at Blackfriars Chapel." *North Wind* 5 (1986): 3–20.

Review of *Robert Falconer,* by George MacDonald, 115–16. *Fortnightly Review* 4 (July 1868). Quoted in Rolland Hein, *George MacDonald: Victorian Mythmaker* (Nashville, Tenn.: Star Song Publishing Group, 1993), 184.

Robinson, Canon. "Sermons and Preaching." *Macmillans* 7 (1863): 409–16.

Rogers, H. "The British Pulpit." Review of *Sermons to a Country Congregation,* by Augustus William Hare, *Edinburgh Review* 72 (1840): 66–98.

Rollin, Charles. *The Method of Teaching and Studying the Belles Lettres,* 2:317. London, 1734. Quoted in Rolf P. Lessenich, *Elements of Pulpit Oratory in Eighteenth-Century England (1660–1800)* (Koln, Germany: Bohlau-Verlag, 1972), 27.

Rosenberg, Bruce A. *Can These Bones Live?* Urbana: University of Illinois Press, 1988.

————. "The Complexity of Oral Tradition." *Oral Tradition* 2 (1987): 73–90.

Ruskin, John. Letter to George MacDonald, 18 December 1868. In Greville MacDonald, *George MacDonald and His Wife,* 337. New York: Dial Press, 1924.

Scott, Patrick. "The Business of Belief: The Emergence of 'Religious' Publishing." In *Sanctity and Secularity: The Church and the World,* ed. Derek Baker, 213–23. Oxford: Basil Blackwell, 1973.

————. Online posting. VICTORIA: 19th-Century British Culture and Society. 11 Dec. 1997.

Secker, Thomas. "A Charge Delivered to the Clergy of the Diocese of Canterbury, in the Year 1766." *The Works of Thomas Secker, LL.D.* Vol. 5. London: Rivington, 1811.

Seniff, Dennis P. "Orality and Textuality in Medieval Castilian Prose." *Oral Tradition* 2 (1987): 73–90.

"Sermons." *Church Quarterly Review* 25 (1887): 107–18.

"Sermons and Their Hearers." *Eclectic Magazine* ns 44 (1886): 258–60.

"Sermons and Sermonizers." *Fraser's Magazine* 55 (1857): 84–94.

Review of *Sermons, Bearing on Subjects of the Day,* by John Henry Newman. *Christian Remembrancer* 7 (1844): 102–13.

Shairp, John Campbell. "Balliol Scholars." *Macmillan's Magazine* 27 (1873): 376. Quoted in David J. DeLaura, "'O Unforgotten Voice': The Memory of Newman in the Nineteenth Century," *Renascence* 43 (1990): 95.

———. *Studies in Poetry and Philosophy,* 255. Edinburgh: Edmonston and Douglas, 1868. Quoted in R. D. Middleton, "The Vicar of St. Mary's," in *John Henry Newman, Centenary Essays,* ed. Henry Tristram (London: Burns, Oates, and Washbourne, 1945), 137.

Sherry, Richard. *Treatise of Schemes and Tropes,* sig. A6v. 1550. Quoted in Wilbur Samuel Howell, *Logic and Rhetoric in England, 1500–1700* (New York: Russell & Russell, 1961), 126.

Smalley, Beryl. *English Friars and Antiquity in the Early Fourteenth Century.* Oxford: Basil Blackwell, 1960.

"Some Modern Sermons." *Church Quarterly Review* 34 (1892): 470–79.

"Some Tendencies of Prose Style." *Edinburgh Review* 190 (1899): 356–76.

Spingarn, J. E. *Critical Essays of the Seventeenth Century,* 1:xxxix–xl. Oxford, 1908. Quoted in W. Fraser Mitchell, *English Pulpit Oratory from Andrewes to Tillotson* (New York: Russell & Russell, 1962), 6.

Spurgeon, Charles Haddon. *C. H. Spurgeon Autobiography.* 2 vols. Edinburgh: Banner of Truth Trust, 1962.

———. *C. H. Spurgeon's Autobiography: Compiled from His Diary, Letters, and Records, by His Wife and His Private Secretary.* 4 vols. London: Passmore and Alabaster, 1897–1900. Quoted in Lewis Drummond, *Spurgeon: Prince of Preachers* (Grand Rapids, Mich.: Kregel Publications, 1992).

———. *Lectures to My Students.* Grand Rapids, Mich.: Zondervan, 1975.

———. *Sermons of Rev. C.H. Spurgeon.* 19 vols. New York: Funk & Wagnalls, n.d.

———. *Spurgeon's Expository Encyclopedia.* Vol. 3. Grand Rapids, Mich.: Baker Book House, 1951.

"The Tabernacle Church's 'In Memoriam' Resolution." In the archives of the Metropolitan Tabernacle, London. Quoted in Lewis Drummond, *Spurgeon: Prince of Preachers* (Grand Rapids, Mich.: Kregel Publications, 1992), 763–64.

Tannen, Deborah. "The Commingling of Orality and Literacy in Giving a Paper at a Scholarly Conference." *American Speech* 63 (1988): 34–43.

———. "Oral and Literate Strategies in Spoken and Written Narratives." *Language* 58 (1982): 1–21.

Tennyson, G. B. Foreword to *An Expression of Character: The Letters of George MacDonald,* ed. Glenn Edward Sadler. Grand Rapids, Mich.: William B. Eerdmans, 1994.

Thomson, William. "On the Emotions in Preaching." In *Homiletical and Pastoral Lectures,* ed. C. J. Ellicott, 81–102. New York: A. C. Armstrong & Son, 1880.

Thorold, Anthony W. "The Preparation of a Sermon." In *Homiletical and Pastoral Lectures,* ed. C. J. Ellicott, 1–23. New York: A. C. Armstrong & Son, 1880.

Tracey, J. V. "John Henry Newman as a Preacher." *The American Catholic Quarterly Review* 16 (1891): 225–39.

Trevelyan, G. Otto. *The Life and Letters of Lord Macaulay* 2 : 99–100. New York, 1877. Quoted in William A. Madden, "Macaulay's Style," in *The Art of Victorian Prose*, ed. George Levine and William A. Madden (New York: Oxford University Press, 1968), 129.

Vaughan, E. T. "J. H. Newman as Preacher." Review of *Parochial and Plain Sermons*, by John Henry Newman. *Contemporary Review* 10 (1869): 37–52.

Walker, Graham, and Tom Gallagher. Introduction to *Sermons and Battle Hymns: Protestant Popular Culture in Modern Scotland*, ed. Graham Walker and Tom Gallagher. Edinburgh: Edinburgh University Press, 1990.

Ward, John. *A System of Oratory*. 2 vols. Hildesheim, Germany: Georg Olms Verlag, 1969.

Ward, W. G. "Newman's Discourses." Review of *Discourses Addressed to Mixed Congregations*, by John Henry Newman. *Dublin Review* 28 (1850): 181–209.

Webber, F. R. *A History of Preaching in Britain and America*. 3 vols. Milwaukee: Northwestern Publishing House, 1952.

Wenham, J. G. "Sermons and Preachers." Review of *The Grounds of Faith. A Series of Four Lectures*, by H. E. Manning. *Dublin Review* 36 (1854): 1–19.

Whately, Richard. *Elements of Rhetoric: Comprising an Analysis of the Laws of Moral Evidence and of Persuasion, with Rules for Argumentative Composition and Elocution*. Ed. Douglas Ehninger. Carbondale: Southern Illinois University Press, 1963.

Wilberforce, H. W. "F. Newman's Oxford Parochial Sermons." Review of *Parochial and Plain Sermons*, by John Henry Newman. *Dublin Review* ns 12 (1869): 309–30.

Wildman, John Hazard. "Newman in the Pulpit: The Power of Simplicity." *Studies in the Literary Imagination* 8 (1975): 63–75.

Wilkins, John. *Ecclesiastes, or, A Discourse Concerning the Gift of Preaching As It falls Under the Rules of Art*, 4. London, 1646. Quoted in Rolf P. Lessenich, *Elements of Pulpit Oratory in Eighteenth-Century England (1660–1800)* (Koln, Germany: Bohlau-Verlag, 1972), 79.

———. *Ecclesiastes, or, A Discourse Concerning the Gift of Preaching As It falls Under the Rules of Art*, 4, 20. London, 1646. Quoted in W. Fraser Mitchell, *English Pulpit Oratory from Andrewes to Tillotson* (New York: Russell & Russell, 1962), 107, 109.

Wilkinson, William Cleaver. *Modern Masters of Pulpit Discourse*. New York: Funk & Wagnall's, 1905.

Williams, John De Kewer. "My Memories and Estimate of My Friend Spurgeon." Quoted in Lewis Drummond, *Spurgeon: Prince of Preachers* (Grand Rapids, Mich.: Kregel Publications, 1992), 568.

Wiseman, Nicholas. "Newman's Sermons." Review of *Sermons bearing on Subjects of the Day*, by John Henry Newman. *Dublin Review* 15 (1843): 547–57.

Wodrow, James. "Some Account of the Author's Life," foreword to *Sermons*, by William Leechman, 51–52. London, 1789. Quoted in Rolf P. Lessenich, *Elements of Pulpit Oratory in Eighteenth-Century England (1660–1800)* (Koln, Germany: Bohlau-Verlag, 1972), 41.

Index